Homicide

Homicide: Towards a Deeper Understanding offers an in-depth analysis into the phenomenon of homicide, examining different types of homicide and how these types have changed over time.

Based on original analysis on Scottish data, this book draws upon an international body of research to contextualise the findings in a global setting, filling an important gap in the homicide literature pertaining to the relationship between trends in homicide and violence. Examining homicide from gendered as well as Gothic perspectives, this book also relates homicide to novel, critical theory. The book covers a thorough description of different types of homicide, including sexual homicide and provides an explorative approach to the identification of homicide subtypes. The book also explores how these findings relate to current homicide theory, and proposes a new theoretical framework to gain a deeper understanding of this crime. The main argument of the book is that if homicide and its relationship to wider violence is to be fully understood, theoretically as well as empirically, this crime needs to be disaggregated in a way that reflects the underlying data. Overall, this book therefore fills an important gap in criminological literature, providing an in-depth understanding of one of the most serious violent crimes.

Sara Skott is Associate Professor in Criminology at Mid Sweden University. Her research concerns different types and aspects of violence, including exploring violence through Gothic and gendered lenses. Her research also concerns the characteristics and offending pathways of sexual homicide, and the social construction of violence, shaped by different power orders. Some of her recent work has appeared in *Critical Criminology, Games and Culture, International Journal of Offender Therapy and Comparative Criminology*, and in the *Journal of Interpersonal Violence*.

Routledge Studies in Criminal Behaviour

Psychological Violence in the Workplace
New perspectives and shifting frameworks
Emily Schindeler, Janet Ransley, and Danielle Reynald

Domestic Homicide
Patterns and Dynamics
Marieke Liem and Frans Koenraadt

Intergenerational Continuity of Criminal and Antisocial Behaviour
An International Overview of Studies
Edited by Veroni I. Eichelsheim and Steve G. A. van de Weijer

Evidence-Based Offender Profiling
Edited by Bryanna H. Fox, David P. Farrington, Andreas Kapardis, and Olivia C. Hambly

Empathy versus Offending, Aggression and Bullying
Advancing Knowledge Using the Basic Empathy Scale
Darrick Jolliffe and David P. Farrington

The Life Course of Serious and Violent Youth Grown Up
A Twenty-year Longitudinal Study
Evan C. McCuish, Patrick Lussier, and Raymond Corrado

Killer Data
Modern Perspectives on Serial Murder
Enzo Yaksic

Homicide
Towards a Deeper Understanding
Sara Skott

For more information about this series, please visit: www.routledge.com/
Routledge-Studies-in-Criminal-Behaviour/book-series/RSCB

Homicide
Towards a Deeper Understanding

Sara Skott

LONDON AND NEW YORK

First published 2023
by Routledge
4 Park Square, Milton Park, Abingdon, Oxon OX14 4RN

and by Routledge
605 Third Avenue, New York, NY 10158

Routledge is an imprint of the Taylor & Francis Group, an informa business

© 2023 Sara Skott Söderholm

The right of Sara Skott Söderholm to be identified as author of this work has been asserted in accordance with sections 77 and 78 of the Copyright, Designs and Patents Act 1988.

All rights reserved. No part of this book may be reprinted or reproduced or utilised in any form or by any electronic, mechanical, or other means, now known or hereafter invented, including photocopying and recording, or in any information storage or retrieval system, without permission in writing from the publishers.

Trademark notice: Product or corporate names may be trademarks or registered trademarks, and are used only for identification and explanation without intent to infringe.

British Library Cataloguing-in-Publication Data
A catalogue record for this book is available from the British Library

Library of Congress Cataloging-in-Publication Data
Names: Skott, Sara, author.
Title: Homicide : towards a deeper understanding / Sara Skott.
Description: Milton Park, Abingdon, Oxon ; New York, NY : Routledge, 2022. |
Series: Routledge studies in criminal behaviour |
Includes bibliographical references and index.
Identifiers: LCCN 2022004623 (print) | LCCN 2022004624 (ebook) |
ISBN 9780367615086 (hardback) | ISBN 9780367615109 (paperback) |
ISBN 9781003105282 (ebook)
Subjects: LCSH: Homicide.
Classification: LCC HV6515 .S57 2022 (print) |
LCC HV6515 (ebook) | DDC 364.152/3–dc23/eng/20220302
LC record available at https://lccn.loc.gov/2022004623
LC ebook record available at https://lccn.loc.gov/2022004624

ISBN: 978-0-367-61508-6 (hbk)
ISBN: 978-0-367-61510-9 (pbk)
ISBN: 978-1-003-10528-2 (ebk)

DOI: 10.4324/9781003105282

Typeset in Times New Roman
by Newgen Publishing UK

To Clara and Linus,
You give me hope in the darkness that I will see the light

Contents

List of figures	x
List of tables	xii
Acknowledgements	xiv

1 Introduction 1
Why study homicide? 1
The aim and objectives of the book 3
Structure of the book 5

PART I
Understanding homicide 7

2 What is homicide? 9
Introduction 9
Legal definitions of homicide 9
Homicide defined in research 13
The SHD – Scottish Homicide Database 14
The homicide dataset 16
Conclusions 23

3 Homicide in Scotland: placing murder in context 25
Introduction 25
Revisiting the 'murder capital of the world': exploring the
 homicide legacy of Scotland 26
Trends in homicide over time 29
Policies and interventions of violence in Scotland 36
Conclusions 40

4 Theories of homicide 42
Introduction 42
Dominant theories to understand homicide 43
Gender and homicide 56

viii *Contents*

From murderer to monster: exploring serial homicide in
    popular culture 59
Conclusions 63

PART II
Different types of homicide   65

  5 Different types of homicide in Scotland   67
Introduction 67
Homicide committed by men 69
Homicide committed by women 74
Homicide committed against children 78
Homicide committed by children 81
Change in homicide types over time 85
Conclusions 86

  6 Disaggregating homicide: explorative subtypes   89
Introduction 89
Typologies of homicide in previous research 89
Towards an exploratory approach to disaggregation 93
Disaggregating homicide using MLCA 96
Subtypes of homicide 101
Change over time 115
Conclusions 118

  7 Sexual homicide   120
Introduction 120
Sexual homicide compared to nonsexual homicides 122
Sexual homicides committed by female offenders 126
Sexual homicides committed against children 132
A comparison between Scotland and Canada: subtypes of
    sexual homicide 137
Theories of sexual homicide 147
Conclusions 149

PART III
Theorising homicide   151

  8 The relationship between homicide and violence   153
Introduction 153
A gap in our knowledge: the lack of previous research 153
Subtypes of nonlethal violence 159
The relationship between homicide and violence over time 173
Conclusions 177

Contents ix

9 A theory of homicide: towards a deeper understanding   179
Introduction 179
Policy implications 179
Theoretical implications 184
Towards a new theoretical framework: Doing Violence *188*
Conclusions 196

10 Overview and conclusions   198
Introduction 198
The overall argument 200
What have we learned? 201
Limitations and directions for future research 203
Concluding remarks 204

References   207
Index   227

Figures

2.1	Flowchart of the legal framework for homicide in Scotland and England and Wales	11
3.1	Absolute change in police-recorded violent crime 1976–2019/2020	30
3.2	Relative change in police-recorded violent crime 1976–2019/2020	31
3.3	International homicide rates per 100 000 population, 1990–2018	34
3.4	Homicide rate per 100 000 population, UK comparison, 1990–2017	34
3.5	Male homicide victim rate per 100 000 population, 2000–2017	35
3.6	Female victim homicide rate per 100 000 population, 2000–2017	35
5.1	Number of types of homicides over time 2000–2015	85
5.2	Percentage change in homicide types over time 2000–2015	86
6.1	Class response probabilities of method of killing	103
6.2	Class response probabilities for weapon selection	104
6.3	Class response probabilities of relationship between offender and victim	104
6.4	Class response probabilities of motive	105
6.5	Class response probabilities of public or private location	105
6.6	Class response probabilities of outside or inside location	106
6.7	Class response probabilities of victim gender, ethnicity, and victim number	106
6.8	Class response probabilities for victim influence, employment status, and home address	107
6.9	Class response probabilities for victim age	109
6.10	Class response probabilities for binary offender variables	109
6.11	Class response probabilities for offender age	110
6.12	Absolute change in homicide types over time	116
6.13	Relative change of homicide types over time	117
7.1	Victim variables in sexual homicide types in Scotland	142
7.2	Incident variables for sexual homicide types in Scotland	142
7.3	Location variables for sexual homicide types in Scotland	143
7.4	Victim variables of sexual homicide types in Canada	144
7.5	Incident variables for sexual homicide types in Canada	144

Figures xi

7.6	Location variables for sexual homicide types in Canada	145
8.1	Class response probabilities of relationship between offender and victim	163
8.2	Class response probabilities of motive	164
8.3	Class response probabilities of location of the crime	165
8.4	Class response probabilities of binary offender variables	165
8.5	Class response probabilities of offender age	166
8.6	Class response probabilities of case-related variables	166
8.7	Class response probabilities of type of violence used	167
8.8	Class response probabilities of type of injury	167
8.9	Class response probabilities of type of weapon used	169
8.10	Class response probabilities for victim variables	169
8.11	Absolute change in violence types over time	171
8.12	Average (mean) probability of within type over time	171

Tables

2.1	Distribution of homicide cases in each legacy police force	17
2.2	Number of offenders and victims in homicide cases	17
2.3	Cross-tabulation of number of victims and offenders	18
2.4	Victim variables of the SHD dataset	19
2.5	Offender variables of the SHD dataset	20
2.6	Distribution of victim gender among male and female offenders	20
2.7	Incident variables of the SHD dataset	23
5.1	Victim variables of homicide committed by men	69
5.2	Offender variables of homicide committed by men	70
5.3	Incident variables of homicide committed by men	72
5.4	Victim variables of homicide committed by women	74
5.5	Offender variables of homicide committed by women	75
5.6	Incident variables of homicide committed by women	76
5.7	Victim variables of homicide committed against children	78
5.8	Offender variables of homicide committed against children	79
5.9	Incident variables of homicide committed against children	80
5.10	Victim variables of homicide committed by children	82
5.11	Offender variables of homicide committed by children	82
5.12	Incident variables of homicide committed by children	83
6.1	Homicide typologies based on victim, offender, and incident variables	91
6.2	Classifying variables in typologies in Table 6.1	93
6.3	Classifying variables used in the homicide dataset	99
6.4	Class selection statistics of two-level LCA Homicide model (2000–2015)	101
6.5	Identified subtypes of homicide	102
6.6	P-values of Mann Whitney U-tests of relative change in homicide types over time	118
7.1	Chi-square analyses between offender characteristics and the type of homicide	123
7.2	Chi-square analyses between victim characteristics and the type of homicide	124

7.3	Chi-square analyses between incident characteristics and the type of homicide	126
7.4	Fisher's exact tests between offender characteristics and type of homicide	128
7.5	Fisher's exact tests between victim characteristics and type of homicide	129
7.6	Fisher's exact tests between incident characteristics and the type of homicide	131
7.7	Significance tests between offender characteristics and type of homicide	133
7.8	Fisher's exact tests between victim characteristics and type of homicide	134
7.9	Fisher's exact tests between incident characteristics and the type of homicide	135
7.10	BIC and entropy for 2–5 class models of Scottish and Canadian subtypes	138
7.11	Chi-square analyses between victim and incident characteristics and the type of homicide	140
8.1	Classifying variables of the violence dataset	160
8.2	Class selection statistics of two-level LCA violence model	162
8.3	Identified subtypes of nonlethal violence	163
8.4	P-values of Mann Whitney U-tests of relative change in violence types over time	172
8.5	Subtypes of the homicide and violence typologies	173

Acknowledgements

There are several people I would like to thank for making this book possible. First, I would like to give very special thanks to Professor Susan McVie and Dr Paul Norris, my previous PhD supervisors, for invaluable guidance and inspiration throughout my PhD journey. My thesis, and therefore this book, would not have been possible without your amazing input and support. Sincere thanks also to AQMeN for funding parts of this research and for once upon a time providing an amazing opportunity for a hopeful girl from Sweden to complete a PhD at the University of Edinburgh. Thanks also to all the people at JAS during my internship with the Scottish Government, especially Ben Cavanagh and Neil Grant. Huge thanks also to the Homicide Governance and Review Team at Gartcosh, particularly Cats Sutherland, for vital help with the Scottish Homicide Database.

A very big thank you also to Eric Beauregard at Simon Fraser University, guiding me into the realm of sexually motivated homicide research. The studies we conducted on this topic, together with the brilliant Raj Darjee and Melissa Martineau, would not have been possible without his input and guidance. Thanks a million!

Thanks also to the people at Routledge and Taylor and Francis, especially Lydia de Cruz, who believed in this book and who helped me creating it.

I would also like to give special thanks to Katarina Giritli-Nygren and Sara Nyhlén at Mid Sweden University (monsterbrudarna). Not only have you both made my days working in Sundsvall infinitely more fun, but your guidance and input on my theoretical work has been invaluable. I look forward to future inspiring fizzy collaborations, pushing the boundaries for what can (and cannot!) be done.

Finally, I want to give huge thanks to my friends and family who have supported me throughout this journey. Iva – thanks for still lifting my spirits with spirits, albeit digitally. Tora and Kattis – thanks for always being there, no matter what. My family – Mamma, K-F, and Kalle – thanks for your endless support and encouragement. And last but certainly not least, thank you Linus – my rock, my heart, my love. Thank you for always believing in me even when I don't. Thanks for helping me put my chapters back together after Clara has ripped them to shreds. Thank you for being you.

1 Introduction

Why study homicide?

> Violence haunts commonplace geographies and the imaginations of everyday actors, through the lens of banal crime reporting and celebrated true crime novels.
>
> (Linneman, 2015: 514)

Few other crimes appear to fascinate the public as much as homicide. The sheer volume of crime podcasts, television shows, and documentaries dedicated to this crime can attest to this fact, not to mention the constant stream of news and media reports of different types of murder flooding our news outlets. There appears to be something deeply captivating, yet simultaneously horrifying, about the act of taking another human life that has kept us fascinated with grim tales of murder for centuries, if not longer. As the quote by Linneman (2015) mentioned above would indicate, violence truly seems to haunt our everyday lives. It is therefore safe to say that there is a widespread, general interest in homicide, which warrants a deeper examination of this crime.

However, while few crimes are more fascinating to our society than homicide, few crimes also cause us more harm. Homicide has profound social and structural impacts, including increased stress placed on emergency systems, trauma inflicted upon families and strain placed upon communities (Harries, 1989; Harvey, Williams, & Donnelly, 2012). Homicide furthermore has an unparalleled impact on the fear of crime in society (Perkins & Taylor, 1996; Warr, 2000), placing further stress on important social institutions. In addition, homicide also entails great economic costs for the communities in which it occurs (Harvey et al., 2012; Waters, Hyder, Rajkoti, Basu, & Butchart, 2005). Moreover, the study of whether homicide has increased or decreased in a country can tell us something about the general wellbeing of that country. Scholars have studied the changing trends of violent crime for centuries (Quetelet, 1842), using the shifts in violent crime as important social indicators. As such, studying homicide and the change in this crime over time does not only provide a deeper understanding of homicide, but this does also

DOI: 10.4324/9781003105282-1

2   *Introduction*

provide information about our society on a larger scale. Further studies about homicide are therefore very important if we are to gain a full understanding of this crime.

As this volume will argue, however, there are important gaps in the knowledge about homicide. This volume is intended to fill some of these gaps. While many countries have seen a marked decrease of lethal violence over the past decades, perhaps this decline has been most dramatic in Scotland, which transformed from 'one of the most violent countries in the Western World' (BBC News, 2005; The Guardian, 2005) to one of the countries with the lowest homicide rates in Europe (Eurostat, 2017). As this volume will demonstrate in subsequent chapters however, much still remains unknown about the nature of this decline. Are there different types of homicide in Scotland, and if so, have all these types of homicide decreased equally? Are there some types of homicide that have remained stable or even increased over time? How does the change in lethal violence correspond to the change in nonlethal violence? In fact, the knowledge about the relationship between homicide and nonlethal violence has been identified as lacking for over 30 years (Harries, 1989). This means that even though we know that both lethal and nonlethal violence have decreased in Scotland over time, as indeed these crimes have decreased in many other Western countries, we still do not know the nature of the relationship between these two crimes. Can similar types of homicide and violence be identified across lethal and nonlethal incidents? Does the overall decrease of lethal and nonlethal violence, in fact, obscure hidden countertrends of these crimes? Do types of homicide and violence decrease equally over time or do these crimes display different patterns over time? The answers to these questions may provide us with enough information to determine whether or not homicide and violence may be regarded as similar underlying behaviours only differentiated by outcome, or whether in fact these two crimes are too different to be regarded along a continuum of violence.

While the research presented in this volume is mostly based on Scottish data, the findings presented here will have theoretical and practical implications that are of great international relevance and have important impact for the field. Cross-national examination of homicide furthermore has validity issues in regards to differences of crime data, which may lead to problems (Aebi & Linde, 2010), some of which we will discuss in Chapter 2. While international comparisons are still very important, national explorations of homicide are equally important and may furthermore mitigate such validity issues. Scotland is suitable for such an analysis for two main reasons: first, the relationship between homicide and violence has never been examined in Scotland, making this country ideal for such examination. Second, as previously mentioned, Scotland has gained the unenviable reputation as one of the most violent countries in the developed world (BBC News, 2005; The Guardian, 2005). This reputation is, however, no longer true, as Scotland has seen a dramatic decrease of violent crime over the past years. This remarkable

Introduction 3

change in violence over time makes Scotland particularly suitable for this in-depth analysis of homicide.

Overall, this means that a deeper understanding of homicide and violence, how these two crimes relate to each other, and how they have changed over time, is lacking. This incomplete understanding of homicide and violence is problematic for a number of reasons. As mentioned, homicide as well as nonlethal violence place profound stress on the community and emergency systems (Harries, 1989). If homicide is considered from a harm reduction perspective, it therefore becomes very important to have a full understanding of the characteristics of homicide as well as how this crime has changed over time. If such knowledge is lacking, or incomplete, the impact of homicide on our society, as well as the people in it, also remains lacking. Furthermore, as policy interventions and preventative work require a comprehensive understanding of the characteristics and patterns of homicide and violence in order to be effective, it becomes very problematic when such knowledge is lacking. In order to ensure effective prevention of violence, we must first ensure that we understand all aspects of this crime. Similarly, any theoretical perspectives attempting to explain lethal and nonlethal violence should include a comprehensive understanding of the characteristics of these crimes, as well as what the relationship between these two crimes really looks like. While there are many different theoretical perspectives aiming to explain lethal and nonlethal violence, the gaps in our understanding of these crimes further underline the need to theorise homicide in order to gain a deeper understanding of this crime.

The aim and objectives of the book

As such, if we are to gain a deeper understanding of homicide, including the characteristics of this crime, how this crime has changed over time, its relationship to nonlethal violence, and the implications for policy and theory, we need to conduct a thorough, in-depth analysis of homicide. This book will therefore attempt to fill the knowledge gap about lethal violence by analysing these important questions in relation to homicide. This will include exploring the foundations of this crime in order to improve the understanding of homicide, exploring different types of homicide and finally, theorising homicide in order to provide a deeper understanding of lethal and nonlethal violence.

The main aim of this book is therefore to provide a deeper understanding of homicide, nationally as well as internationally. In order to fulfil this aim, the following objectives will be explored:

1. How can homicide be defined and how does this definition differ depending on jurisdiction?
2. What different types of homicide may be identified?
3. How have these types of homicide changed over time?

4   *Introduction*

4. What is the relationship between trends in types of homicide and trends in types of nonlethal violence?
5. What implications does this relationship have for policy and theory?
6. How can we theoretically understand homicide?

The first objective is designed to provide a foundation for the understanding of homicide by exploring the legal and social underpinnings of this crime. This will also help to clarify the concepts that this book engages with as well as help to contextualise homicide. The second objective is about exploring different types of homicide in Scotland by examining the characteristics of homicide and nonlethal violence. Characteristics refer to variables relating to the victim, offender and incident, while types are defined as the identified profiles of these characteristics of both homicide and violence, respectively. The third objective is designed to explore the changing pattern of trends in homicide by examining how the identified types of lethal violence have changed over time. Trends are defined as the change in homicide or violence over time, while the patterns of these trends are defined as the direction and magnitude of that change.

The fourth objective of this research is to explore the relationship between trends of homicide and nonlethal violence by comparing the identified types of these two crimes in order to establish whether there are any similarities between lethal and nonlethal types. Examining the similarities between homicide and nonlethal violence is important in order to establish the nature of the relationship between these two crimes. If similarities between types of lethal and nonlethal violence are found, this would suggest that homicide indeed can be regarded as the extreme end of a violence spectrum. This would mean that we can assess the lethality of violent acts, which in turn has important implications for preventative measures as well as for theoretical frameworks for understanding the relationship between these two crimes. Contrastingly, if similar types of lethal and nonlethal violence cannot be identified, this would instead suggest that there are important underlying differences between these two crimes. This, in turn, could imply that there is something qualitatively different about the act of homicide compared to nonlethal acts of violence, which would be an important area for further research.

The fourth objective furthermore entails the examination of whether lethal and nonlethal violence have changed similarly over time. Whether or not the trends in homicide and violence are following a similar pattern over time is highly relevant for understanding the decline evident in these two crimes in Scotland. If the trends in lethal and nonlethal violence are very different, this could indicate that factors affecting one trend do not seem to affect the other. Such results would have important implications for policy as homicide might require different prevention strategies compared to other types of nonlethal violence. Conversely, if homicide trends follow a similar pattern to types of nonlethal violence over time, the changing trends in homicide could be used to monitor the changing trends in violence. As will be explained

Introduction 5

in subsequent chapters, homicide is generally considered to be one of the most robust measurements of crime compared to other crimes, with a lower dark figure compared to for instance nonlethal violence (Brookman, 2005; Granath, 2011; Haen Marshall & Summers, 2012; Tonry, 2014). Because of this, we generally know more about homicide compared to other violent crimes. If homicide trends are used as a barometer for trends in nonlethal violence, we could therefore gain more information about the changing pattern in nonlethal violence. This would be very beneficial for the police by increasing the efficiency when directing resources to reduce lethal and nonlethal violence, as well as when preventing these crimes.

The fifth objective is to explore the implications of this research on policy as well as theory. As mentioned, the lacking knowledge of the precise relationship between homicide and nonlethal violence have important effects on prevention strategies for these crimes as well as our theoretical understanding of them. This volume therefore intends to shed some light on not only the relationship between homicide and nonlethal violence but on the effects and implications of this relationship as well. Finally, the sixth objective of this volume is to theoretically explore homicide from a critical perspective in order to increase our understanding of this crime. This will be done by presenting a new, theoretical framework that attempts to provide a deeper understanding of homicide and its effects. While this book also engages in the study of nonlethal violence, homicide is the primary focus. This means that while subtypes of violence will be examined, this will be done as a comparison to the identified homicide subtypes. The following section will provide an overview of the structure of this volume.

Structure of the book

As this book provides an in-depth analysis of homicide, the primary intended audience for this volume is scholars and postgraduate students in the fields of criminology, criminal justice, psychology, sociology, gender studies and public health. This book is also relevant and helpful to academics and professionals (for instance working in law enforcement, law and criminal justice) who have a specific interest in homicide and how homicide relates to wider violence. As such, this book is relevant for both scholars, researchers, and practitioners, as well as students.

The book is divided into three main parts, aiming to provide an interconnected and progressive understanding of homicide. The first part describes the foundations for understanding homicide. This part will explain how homicide is defined in different jurisdictions, fulfilling the first objective of the volume, while also providing some historical context to this crime in Scotland. This part of the volume will also explore the dominant theories attempting to explain homicide, examining biological, psychological, and sociological theoretical perspectives. Here, more critical perspectives on homicide will also be explored, examining the gendered dimensions of homicide as well as cultural and Gothic criminological theories in relation to this crime.

6 *Introduction*

The second part of the book explores different types of homicide, providing in-depth descriptions of various types of homicide that are also of international relevance. This includes homicides committed by male offenders, homicides committed by female offenders, homicides committed against children, and homicides committed by children. This section of the volume will also take a closer look at a very rare type of homicide that receives a lot of media attention, namely sexual homicide. While this part of the book explores homicide disaggregated in a traditional manner (by sex and age), this section will also take an explorative approach to disaggregating homicide, providing a description of homicide subtypes based on actual data rather than being determined *a priori*. This is the first step to fill an international knowledge gap relating to the relationship between trends in homicide and violence. As such, the second part of the book will provide answers to the second and third research objectives.

The third and final part of the book theorises homicide. First, this section explores the relationship between homicide and nonlethal violence by comparing subtypes of lethal and nonlethal violence over time. As this section of the volume will explain, homicide and nonlethal violence do follow a similar trend over time, even when the overall trends are different, if these crimes are disaggregated into subtypes. This part of the book furthermore explores the implications of the findings, examining the effects of these findings on policy as well as on existing theory, including theories of the crime drop. Homicide is then explored from a gendered perspective by the use of gender theory, exploring the relationship between masculinities and types of homicide. Finally, a new theoretical framework is presented in order to explain and understand homicide and how this crime have changed over time. This theoretical framework, called *Doing Violence*, is based on an intersectional understanding of violence, proposing that violence is shaped by structures of power and inequality. This final part of the book will consequently provide answers to the fourth, fifth, and sixth research objectives. The book then ends with a summary of the conclusions.

Overall, this book will provide a deeper, more comprehensive understanding of homicide and the effects of homicide on our society. In order to provide clarity and to guide the reader, case studies will also be employed throughout the book, providing anonymised, real-life examples of different types of homicide and how these may be understood. As with any book, this volume will not provide the answers to all the questions about homicide. The aim is, however, to provide any reader with a comprehensive, in-depth understanding of what homicide is, how this crime has changed over time and how we can theoretically contextualise lethal violence in our society. Hopefully, this book will inspire current or future researchers and practitioners to pursue increased knowledge of lethal violence, to critically explore this crime, and to find new, innovative ways of understanding and preventing homicide.

Part I

Understanding homicide

The first part of this volume will provide a background to understanding homicide. We will explore what homicide really is, and is not, how this crime may be defined legally, and how the definitions may differ internationally. We will also explore the main homicide dataset used for the empirical chapters that will constitute the second part of this volume (Chapters 5–7), in order to provide with elementary knowledge of the analysis to follow. Chapter 3 will then contextualise homicide in Scotland by exploring how homicide has changed over time in this country, as well as how this differ to international trends. The changes in policy and crime prevention initiatives in Scotland will also be explored in this chapter in order to provide a deeper understanding of the socio-political context in which the analysis was conducted. The fourth and final chapter of the first part of the volume will then examine different theories of homicide, aiming to provide a better understanding of the dominant theoretical frameworks in place to explain violent and homicidal behaviour.

As such, the first part of the book will provide the foundations for understanding homicide as a crime, both empirically and theoretically. It aims to provide the reader with the tools necessary for understanding this crime in relation to other crimes, as well as how homicide in Scotland fits into a larger, international picture. This part will also provide the methodological and theoretical underpinnings for understanding the second and third part of this volume, which will conduct empirical analysis of homicide as well as develop a new, theoretical framework to understand this crime. But first, we will begin with the basics in Chapter 2, exploring exactly how we may define a homicide.

DOI: 10.4324/9781003105282-2

2 What is homicide?

Introduction

While most of us probably think we have a good grasp of what homicide is, and is not, the exact definition of homicide is not always straightforward. What constitutes a homicide or a murder – which, as we will discover, is not always the same thing – may differ depending on country or jurisdiction, on how crime is recorded, or even the intent of the offender. To help navigate these complexities, this chapter aims to provide a legal definition of homicide in Scotland and to outline how this differs from corresponding crimes in England and Wales. This chapter will also explore how the definition of homicide may differ in research, and the consequences this may have. Finally, this chapter sets out to explore the database of homicide used in the studies throughout the book; the Scottish Homicide Database. We will explore the characteristics of homicide victims, offenders, and incidents, and compare these findings to previous studies to provide some context. As such, this chapter will provide the legal foundations for understanding homicide in Scotland, as well as the methodological underpinnings of forthcoming analysis.

We will begin, first, by exploring the legal definitions of homicide in Scotland and how this differs from the legal definitions in England and Wales.

Legal definitions of homicide

Exact definitions and boundaries of concepts are important regardless of what crime you are studying. This is also true in regards to homicide. Although the definition of homicide may seem obvious, legal definitions of this crime differ depending on various factors such as intent, culpability, or degree of preparation or planning for the crime. A homicide is therefore not always the same thing as a murder. Homicide may also include culpable homicide, corporate homicide, or manslaughter, depending on jurisdiction. Additionally, a homicide may not even always be a crime; homicides occurring on the battlefields of war or in the enactment of state capital punishment are lawful homicides that are not considered criminal.

DOI: 10.4324/9781003105282-3

10 *Understanding homicide*

To complicate matters further, legal definitions may also differ between countries, making international comparisons fraught with difficulty. While some countries, such as England and Wales, register infanticide (the killing of small children or infants) as a separate crime from other types of homicide, other countries do not. Similarly, abortions may also fit the definition of homicide in countries where the termination of pregnancy is illegal (Smit, De Jong, & Biljeved, 2012). Different countries furthermore have different counting rules when registering homicides, meaning that some countries register homicide incidents, while other countries register homicide offenders or homicide victims, leading to disparities in international homicide statistics. This underlines the fact that the criminal definition of homicide is a social construct, separate from the actual act of killing another individual. What constitutes the crime of homicide does not only differ between countries but also changes over time and is dependent on political and ideological influences. As such, there is no objective, conclusively legal definition of homicide. Rather, what constitutes a homicide is liquid; transient and shifting across time and place. It is therefore important to bear this in mind when comparing homicides between different countries or examining the change of homicide over time.

While Scotland is currently part of the United Kingdom, Scots law differs from the laws of England and Wales and Northern Ireland. This means that different laws dictate what constitutes a homicide in Scotland compared to the rest of the UK. While unlawful homicide may be classified as murder, manslaughter, or infanticide in England and Wales, criminal homicide in Scotland covers two principal crimes; murder and culpable homicide (see Figure 2.1). While infanticide is a separate legal category in England and Wales, this is not the case in Scotland, where this crime instead is included as either murder or culpable homicide, which is roughly comparable to manslaughter in England and Wales. Murder and culpable homicide are both common law offences in Scotland, meaning that, unlike in England and Wales, there is no statutory law for these crimes. Out of the two, murder is usually seen as the most serious crime, which also carries a mandatory life sentence in Scotland (Scottish Sentencing Council, 2021). In Scots law, murder is defined as 'any wilful act causing the destruction of life, by which the perpetrator either wickedly intends to kill or displays wicked recklessness as to whether the victim lives or dies' (Drury v HMA, 2001). This includes cases where the offender deliberately murdered the victim or where the offender demonstrated reckless disregard for the life of their victim.

Culpable homicide, on the other hand, refers to the killing of a victim in circumstances that are neither accidental nor justified, but where the requisites for murder are not met. This means cases where there is no 'wicked intent to kill' or 'wicked recklessness' demonstrated by the offender. Both murder and culpable homicide have the same *actus reus* (guilty act), meaning that both

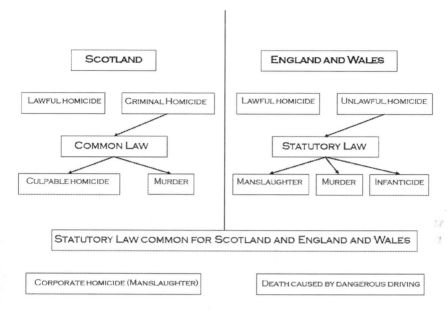

Figure 2.1 Flowchart of the legal framework for homicide in Scotland and England and Wales

crimes involves cases where the victim has been killed. These two crimes may, however, differ in regards to the *mens rea* (guilty mind). Where culpability in the form of intent or utter indifference to the consequences of the act are required for murder, this is not always so straightforward regarding culpable homicide. In fact, culpable homicide is often divided into two types: *voluntary culpable homicide* and *involuntary culpable homicide*. Voluntary culpable homicide includes cases that fulfil the *mens rea* requirements for murder but where mitigating circumstances are present, reducing the crime from murder to culpable homicide. Such mitigating circumstances include cases where the offender was provoked or where there was diminished responsibility of the offender (McDiarmid, 2018). Involuntary culpable homicide, on the other hand, refers to cases where the offender is culpable but where the offender did not intend to kill the victim. This could, for instance, include cases where death has been the unintended cause of an assault or where the victim has died from an overdose of drugs supplied by the offender. As such, involuntary culpable homicides may include cases where there is no act of violence involved. Unlike murder, there is a full range of sentencing options for culpable homicide, ranging from absolute discharge to life imprisonment (McDiarmid, 2018).

12 Understanding homicide

Case study: culpable homicide

Frank was owed a lot of money by his old friend Logan. Despite having made repeated requests and threats to Logan, he would not give Frank back his money. Growing increasingly angry, Frank decided to send Logan a message; one that would scare him enough to pay off his debt. Frank consequently filled a can with petrol and set fire to Logan's house. Frank did not have any intention of killing Logan; the motive behind the fire was to frighten, not to harm. Unbeknownst to Frank, Logan had spent the entire day drinking heavily, first with some friends and later alone. By the time the fire started, Logan was unconscious in a heavy, drunken stupor. As a result, Logan did not manage to get out of the house in time and died as a result of the fire. As Frank had killed Logan, yet without any culpable intent of doing so, this crime was classified as an involuntary culpable homicide according to Scots law.

Case study: murder

Liam and Catriona had been involved in a romantic relationship for almost five years. They lived together in a flat owned by Liam and they both had steady employment and a stable financial situation. Liam was often jealous and could quickly become very angry, especially if he had been drinking. Catriona had suffered physical as well as psychological abuse at the hands of Liam and despite wanting to leave the relationship on several occasions, Catriona and Liam had remained a couple. One night in December after an office Christmas party, they got into a fight, which quickly became violent. Catriona then declared her intention of finally leaving Liam, stating she had had enough and that she had met someone else. This sent Liam into a jealous rage, and he threatened to kill Catriona if she, in fact, were to leave him. As Catriona attempted to leave their flat, Liam grabbed a kitchen knife and stabbed his girlfriend four times in the back and chest. Even though Liam called an ambulance, Catriona later succumbed to her injuries and died a few hours later in hospital. As Liam had attacked Catriona with the intent of killing her, this crime was deemed to be a murder according to Scots law.

In accordance with their tenth programme of law reform, The Scottish Law Commission is currently undertaking a revision of the homicide law in order to examine the principles underlying the crimes of murder and culpable homicide as well as the boundaries between these two crimes (Scottish Law Commission, 2021). In the course of this revision, which was conducted between 2018 and 2022, the mental element required for these two crimes,

What is homicide? 13

currently defined by terms such as 'wicked', will be re-examined and potentially revised. In May 2021, the Scottish Law Commission released a discussing paper on the subject, opening up for comments on a number of different reform suggestions in relation to the homicide law, including the bipartite structure, the terminology (particularly the term 'wicked'), the possible defences, and whether a new crime of 'assault causing death' should be added (Scottish Law Commission, 2021). The Scottish Law Commission will consider the views of the discussion report, develop policy, and commence work towards publication of a report on the subject of homicide.

While both murder and culpable homicide are common law offences in Scotland, there are also two acts of killing that are regulated by statutory law. In addition to murder and culpable homicide, there is also a crime called corporate homicide, regulated by the Corporate Manslaughter and Corporate Homicide Act of 2007. This involves cases where an organisation, department, or company is organised or managed in such a way that it causes someone's death, either by negligence or deliberate decision-making. Examples of this could be deaths caused by unsafe working environments or by unsafe pharmaceutical products. Corporate homicide also includes death caused by the police force (Corporate Manslaughter and Corporate Homicide Act, 2007). The deaths of people caused by dangerous driving is another crime covered by statutory law in Scotland (The Road Traffic Act, 1991). Both of these crimes are regulated by the same laws in Scotland as in England and Wales. While these are serious crimes, they are not part of what usually constitutes 'homicide' in Scotland and will therefore not be considered further in this volume. Next, we will turn to how homicide may be defined in research projects, not unlike the one presented throughout the current book.

Homicide defined in research

While the legal definitions of homicide usually dictate how any country or region will register these crimes, various scholars or research projects may also have differing definitions of this crime depending on the aims of research. This will affect how homicide is measured but also how it is defined. For instance, research projects aiming to explore the victims of homicide will likely count every death individually, meaning that cases with multiple victims may be counted as separate crimes even though they were killed by the same offender. Similarly, studies that have a focus on homicide offenders will tend to use the perpetrators as the unit of measurement, even though any one homicide case may involve multiple offenders. Third, research that is interested in the homicide incident as a whole will probably use homicide cases as units of measurement, meaning there may be multiple deaths and multiple perpetrators in any single case to take into consideration. The unit of measurement is also often dependent on the type of data used in the research. While cause of death data from coroner offices or autopsy reports tends to be victim focused, police recorded data or court data is usually more focused on the incident or even the

14 *Understanding homicide*

offender. In addition to this, research projects that aim to explore homicide internationally are usually required to have a very inclusive definition of homicide in order to accommodate differing legal definitions between countries. For instance, researchers constructing the European Homicide Monitor (EHM) have attempted to find a cross-national definition of homicide that may be comparable across several European countries (Liem et al., 2013). By using the same definition of homicide, which was defined as 'an intentional criminal act of violence by one or more human beings resulting in the death of one or more other human beings' (Liem et al., 2013: 79), the EHM enables international comparison of homicide in a way that was previously not possible.

Exactly what constitutes a homicide is, in other words, not always so obvious or straightforward. There are many differing classifications of this crime and depending on jurisdiction, culpability, data source, or aim of a research project, the definition may vary. For the purposes of this book and the included studies, homicide will be defined as murder or culpable homicide in accordance with Scots law. This means that while both corporate homicide and death caused by dangerous driving are serious crimes resulting in people's deaths, they are in several ways different from murder and culpable homicide and will not be explored further in the context of this book. However, as will be explained below, the dataset used in the current study has some additional limitations to the definition of homicide. We will therefore now turn to a description of the dataset that has been used for the studies explored in this book.

The SHD – Scottish Homicide Database

The homicide data used in the studies of this book was collected from the Scottish Homicide Database (SHD), which is a live operational database held by Police Scotland. The SHD contains extensive information about all homicides coming to the attention of the police in Scotland, going back to the 1940s. This makes the SHD the most comprehensive and detailed data source of homicide in Scotland, and the SHD can therefore be considered a population dataset of homicide rather than a sample.

The development of the SHD was conducted over several years. The database was initially created during a Police operation called Trinity occurring in the early 2000s, which included the development of a database including all homicides of female victims occurring in Scotland from the 1960s and onwards. This smaller database, which would eventually become the SHD, was created in order to aid the investigation of a specific cold case in Scotland, often referred to as the World's End Murders. The case involved the homicides of two young women who were last seen outside a pub called *The World's End* in Edinburgh, murdered by the same male offender. The database was developed during Operation Trinity in order to assess whether there might be any other potential victims connected to this offender in other areas in Scotland.[1] The

1 For more information about this case, see Wood & Johnston (2008).

What is homicide? 15

database was subsequently developed further during another Police operation called Operation Phoenix, which included all homicides, not just homicides involving female victims. The data collection for Operation Phoenix, conducted between 2003 and 2009 by the legacy Strathclyde Police in collaboration with the Violence Reduction Unit, used the extended database as a tool to help identify similar cases across different forces in Scotland and to review unresolved cases. After 2009, the database was retained under various names until it was renamed the Scottish Homicide Database in 2012. Today, the SHD is a live database, designed as an investigative tool, connecting all aspects of a case such as suspects, evidence reports, and post mortems, accessible by any police officer working in Scotland.

As mentioned, the SHD includes homicide cases from as early as the 1940s and encompasses all significant deaths that have occurred in Scotland, including murders, culpable homicides, corporate homicides, and unexplained deaths. The data collection was based on police case files, information found in HOLMES,[2] Crown Office[3] records, and death certificates. However, cases prior to the year 2000 suffer from high levels of missing data. There are a few reasons for this missingness. As mentioned, the main bulk of the data was collected during Operation Phoenix, between 2003 and 2009. Homicide cases prior to this were recorded post hoc, meaning that the police had to input the information manually and that some information of these homicide cases was irretrievable at the time of data collection. The digitalisation process of the record system across the legacy police forces occurred at different rates and there were also some inconsistencies in accessibility of the records prior to 2000. Additionally, there was no great consensus between forces on how to code certain variables before the year 2000. This was particularly true regarding variables considered to be more 'subjective' in nature, such as motive or whether or not the offender was under the influence of drugs or alcohol. This led to the decision to only include cases from the year 2000 and onwards in the studies included in this book. Although the SHD is a live dataset when used by Police Scotland, meaning that the data is constantly being updated, the data extracted for use in the current book is static, meaning that it only contains the information that was available during data collection. This data collection was conducted between 31 March 2015 and 7 April 2016. Any possible updates to these cases that occurred after the last date of data collection will consequently not be included in the current studies.

It was furthermore decided to exclude culpable homicides from the data and only include cases that Police Scotland had recorded as murders. This was

---

2 HOLMES (Home Office Large Major Enquiry System) is the information storage and retrieval system used by all police departments in the UK (Brookman, 2015: 274; Holmes2, 2017). It allows for storage, indexing, and cross-referencing for all major enquiries.

3 The Crown Office and Procurator Fiscal Service is the prosecution service in Scotland, responsible for the decision of prosecuting someone based on reports about crime filed by the police and other crime reporting agencies (Crown Office, 2017a).

16 *Understanding homicide*

decided since culpable homicide, as previously discussed, also includes cases where the death did not result from a violent act of another person, such as, for instance, the self-administration of drugs. Since the principal aim of the current studies was to compare homicide with nonlethal acts of violence, it was decided to exclude any cases of homicide that did not involve violence.

The SHD database furthermore includes so-called unresolved homicide cases. While this may sound like homicides that have never been solved, the definition of unresolved homicides is a bit more comprehensive and technical. A homicide is considered to be resolved by Police Scotland if someone has been convicted of the crime or if someone is serving time in jail or in a mental institution. If the offender died by suicide or died before trial, the case could still be considered resolved if there is enough evidence that the offender killed the victim. Unresolved cases, on the other hand, refers to cases that are any of the following: the case remains undetected (as in no suspect is discovered); the case is considered detected but no further proceedings have been made; the case is awaiting trial; the case has proceeded to trial where the offender was found not guilty or the case was found not proven. Of all the 1344 cases of homicide, barely a fifth remained unresolved (18.5%, $n = 249$). This means that a case will still be counted as a homicide in the current studies even though the offender may not be found guilty further along in the criminal justice process. Since some of the cases included in the SHD might still be awaiting trial at the time of data collection, some cases might not be considered murders, or even homicides, after being tried in court.

The homicide dataset

Overall, the final dataset included 1344 cases of homicide that occurred between 2000 and 2015. All of these homicides were recorded as murders by Police Scotland, and about 19% of them were classified as unresolved. As mentioned earlier, any homicide case may, however, involve more than one victim as well as more than one offender. A homicide case for the purposes of this study was defined as an incident where at least one dead body (or parts of a dead body) was found within the context of the same crime scene, which the police considered to be murder. The homicide case may involve multiple offenders and/or multiple victims but if another victim was found outside the borders of the first crime scene, this would be regarded as another homicide case. Similarly, if an offender were involved in multiple homicides over time, these would be regarded as different cases.

In accordance with the Police and Fire Reform (Scotland) Act (2012), the previous eight police forces of Scotland were unified into one, centralised police force in April 2013: Police Scotland. This unification took place in an effort to render the police work more efficient as well as effective (MacAskill, 2011). Since the initiation of Police Scotland, the previous eight police forces have instead been divided into 13 Police Scotland Divisions. In order to provide an overview of where the homicide cases in the current studies took place,

What is homicide? 17

the 143 homicides that were committed in Scotland since 1 April 2013 were combined with the cases from the eight old police forces, allowing a cohesive comparison. As demonstrated in Table 2.1, the majority of the homicide cases were committed in Strathclyde. As the table also shows, this is the police force area with the largest estimated population, which includes Glasgow and nearby areas. A little more than a tenth of the cases were committed within the force of Lothian and Borders where Edinburgh is situated. As can be seen from Table 2.1, the larger the population estimate, the more homicides were committed.

As mentioned, any homicide case may involve more than one offender as well as more than one victim. In total, the 1344 homicide cases included 1366 victims and 1978 offenders (see Table 2.2). It was, in other words, more common for a case to involve more than one offender than more than one victim. In 13 cases (0.7%), the offender was unknown, and their characteristics

Table 2.1 Distribution of homicide cases in each legacy police force

Police force	Number	Percentage	Population estimate[a]
Strathclyde	857	63.8%	2 219 290
Lothian and Borders	174	12.9%	957 080
Tayside	86	6.4%	415 470
Grampian	78	5.8%	333 040
Fife	58	4.3%	402 600
Central	39	2.9%	294 430
Northern	30	2.2%	385 880
Dumfries and Galloway	22	1.6%	149 520

Note 1: Base: n = 1344.
[a] The population estimates are based on reported figures from Police Scotland (Police Scotland, 2017a) and the National Records of Scotland (NRS, 2017).
Source: SHD.

Table 2.2 Number of offenders and victims in homicide cases

Number of offenders	N	Percentage (%)	Number of victims	N	Percentage (%)
Uncertain	13	(1.0%)	1	1326	(98.7%)
1	950	(70.7%)	2	14	(1.0%)
2	235	(17.5%)	3	4	(0.3%)
3	85	(6.3%)			
4	39	(2.9%)			
5 or more	22	(1.6%)			
Total:	**1344**	**100%**		**1344**	**100%**

Note 1: Base: n = 1344.
Source: SHD.

18 *Understanding homicide*

Table 2.3 Cross-tabulation of number of victims and offenders

Number of offenders (% of total cases)	Number of victims (% of total cases)			Total
	1 victim	2 victims	3 victims	
Uncertain	11 (0.8%)	2 (0.1%)	0 (0.0%)	**13 (1.0%)**
1 offender	940 (69.9%)	9 (0.7%)	1 (0.1%)	**950 (70.7%)**
2 offenders	231 (17.2%)	2 (0.1%)	2 (0.1%)	**235 (17.5%)**
3 offenders	84 (6.3%)	0 (0.0%)	1 (0.1%)	**85 (6.3%)**
4 offenders	38 (2.8%)	1 (0.1%)	0 (0.0%)	**39 (2.9%)**
5 or more offenders	22 (1.6%)	0 (0.0%)	0 (0.0%)	**22 (1.6%)**
Total:	**1326 (98.7%)**	**14 (1.0%)**	**4 (0.3%)**	1344 (100%)

Note 1: Base: $n = 1344$.

Source: SHD.

were treated as missing. This would include cases where the police had found a dead victim but where no suspects were detected. While the majority of cases included one victim and one offender, the number of victims in a homicide case ranged from one to three and the number of offenders ranged between one and five. When we explore the distribution of victims and offenders using cross tabulation (see Table 2.3), we can see that while about 17% of the homicides involved two offenders and one victim, it was very uncommon for any one case to involve multiple offenders as well as multiple victims. The following sections will provide some descriptive information about the three different aspects of homicide cases: the victims, offenders, and incidents of homicide.

Victims of homicide

As mentioned, there were in total 1366 victims of homicide between 2000 and 2015 in Scotland. As can be seen from Table 2.4, the majority (79%) of these victims were male. Studies have repeatedly shown that violence, and particularly lethal violence, is a male affair, where men are overrepresented both as victims and as offenders (Connell & Messerschmidt, 2005; Hatty, 2000; Messerschmidt, 1999; Polk, 1994; Ray, 2011). As the data shows, this is also true in Scotland. We will discuss the connection between gender and homicide in more detail in Chapter 4 and in Chapter 9.

The mean victim age of the Scottish homicides was approximately 37 years old, which is slightly younger than in some other Northern European countries such as the Netherlands, Finland, Switzerland, and Sweden, where the most common age was 40–64 years old (Liem et al., 2016). When breaking down victim age into different categories, the data shows that 78 victims (5.7%) were under the age of 16, and may therefore be classified as child homicides. This is a rare type of homicide that we will explore further in Chapter 5. The

What is homicide? 19

Table 2.4 Victim variables of the SHD dataset

Victim variables		Valid N (%)	Missing (% of total)
Gender	Male	1079 (78.9%)	0 (0.0%)
	Female	288 (21.0%)	
Age	Mean victim age	36.7 years	2 (0.1%)
	Under 16 years old	78 (5.7%)	
	Between 16 and 30 years old	449 (32.8%)	
	Between 31 and 45 years old	446 (32.6%)	
	Between 46 and 60 years old	287 (21.0%)	
	Between 61 and 75	78 (5.7%)	
	76 years old and above	29 (2.1%)	
Ethnicity	White	1313 (97.8%)	24 (1.8%)
	Other than white	30 (2.2%)	
Residential status	Homeless	21 (2.2%)	393 (28.7%)
	Not homeless	953 (97.8%)	

Note 1: Base: *n* = 1367.
Note 2: Valid percentage was calculated based on the number of victims with the missingness excluded.

Source: SHD.

age of both offenders and victims of homicide is, however, quite dependent on gender. While the mean age of male victims was 36.1 years old, the mean age of female victims of homicide was noticeably higher at 38.9 years old.

The vast majority of all homicide victims in Scotland were of white ethnicity, which also reflects Scotland's ethnic distribution overall, where approximately 92% identifies as white (Scotland's Census, 2011). The data also shows that about a fifth of all victims of homicide were homeless at the time they were murdered. Homelessness is considered a risk factor for violence and homicide due to the vulnerability this means for the victim, including the lack of shelter such as doors or other means to block offenders and the engagement in high risk behaviours such as sex work, mental illness and substance abuse (Kushel, Evans, Perry, Robertson & Moss, 2003). Homelessness may also be indicative of socioeconomic status, as is unemployment; however, due to high levels of missingness in the unemployment variable, it was excluded from analysis.

Offenders of homicide

When we examine the 1978 offenders of homicide over the same time period, we can see that just like with the victims, male offenders are clearly overrepresented. As can be seen from Table 2.5, almost 90% of the offenders were male, meaning it was even more common for homicide offenders to be male compared with the victims. When the gender distribution of homicide offenders and victims was explored – that is, the proportion of victims killed by

20 *Understanding homicide*

Table 2.5 Offender variables of the SHD dataset

Offender variables		Valid N (%)	Missing (% of total)
Gender	Male	1753 (89.2%)	13 (0.7%)
	Female	213 (10.8%)	
Age	Mean offender age	30.0 years	45 (2.3%)
	Under 16 years old	61 (3.1%)	
	Between 16 and 30 years old	1110 (56.5%)	
	Between 31 and 45 years old	578 (29.4%)	
	Between 46 and 60 years old	180 (9.2%)	
	Between 61 and 75	34 (1.7%)	
	76 years old and above	3 (0.2%)	
Ethnicity	White	1911 (97.3%)	15 (0.8%)
	Other than white	53 (2.7%)	
Residential status	Homeless	21 (2.2%)	574 (29.0%)
	Not homeless	953 (97.8%)	
Offender Suicide	Offender committing suicide	20 (1.0%)	13 (0.7%)

Note 1: Base: $n = 1978$.
Note 2: Valid percentage was calculated based on the number of victims with the missingness excluded.
Source: SHD.

Table 2.6 Distribution of victim gender among male and female offenders

Victim		Offender	
		Male	Female
Male	Number (%)	1478 (75.2%)	169 (8.6%)
Female	Number (%)	274 (13.9%)	44 (2.2%)

Note 1: Base: $n = 1978$.
Note 2: Since the data is nested, meaning that the offenders are nested in homicide cases, these numbers are based on the number of offenders, not cases.
Note 3: In 13 cases, the offender was unknown and these cases were excluded from analysis.
Source: SHD.

male or female offenders – interesting patterns, however, emerge. As Table 2.6 demonstrates, the majority of all homicides are committed by male offenders against male victims. About 14% of the homicides were male offenders killing female victims and in approximately 9% of the homicides, a female offender murdered a male victim. The least common type of homicide was with both female victims and offenders, constituting about 2% of all homicides.

What is homicide? 21

The mean age of the offenders was 30 years, which is slightly younger than the victims (see Table 2.5). This is, however, consistent with other countries such as Switzerland, where offenders are slightly younger compared to the victims of homicide (Markwalder & Killias, 2013). When offender age is broken down into smaller categories as in Table 2.5, we can see that 61 offenders (3.1%) were under the age of 16 at the time of crime. Just as with homicide *of* children, homicide *by* children is very rare. In Scotland, it would also seem that homicides committed by children are decreasing. In 2000–2002, there were 14 homicide offenders under the age of 16, whereas this figure had dropped to 4 offenders in 2012–2015. As with the victims of homicide, offender age differs depending on offender gender. While the mean age of male offenders was 29.8 years, the female offenders tended to be older, with a mean age of 31.5 years old. The vast majority of the offenders were white, similarly to the victims, and the offender was homeless in approximately 2% of the cases (see Table 2.5).

In 20 cases (1%), the offender killed themselves after the homicide was committed. This rare type of homicide is usually considered its own category, often referred to as homicide–suicides in the research literature (see, for instance, Liem, Barber, Markwalder, Killias & Nieuwbeerta, 2011; Liem & Nieuwbeerta, 2010). This type of homicide usually involves male offenders killing a female intimate partner in a domestic setting before killing themselves. Sometimes these homicides also involves the murder of their children (known as a familicides) (Liem & Reichelmann, 2014). As mentioned, all forms of homicide–suicides are very rare, in most jurisdictions (Liem et al., 2011; Liem & Reichelmann, 2014). Of the 20 cases of homicide–suicides in Scotland, all but one included a male offender, and the majority of cases occurred inside in private settings. The victim was most commonly a female intimate partner of the offender, and all cases but one included only one victim.

Homicide incidents

While the information on homicide victims and offenders provides valuable insights to the nature of homicide, perhaps the variables concerning the incident itself can provide us with the most specific and detailed information pertaining to a homicide case. As Table 2.7 demonstrates, there are quite a number of variables explored in relation to the incident of homicide, which can provide us with information on what characterises Scottish homicides. The most common method of killing, sometimes also referred to as the *modus operandi*, was with the use of a sharp instrument. This would include knives, blades, or other forms of sharp weapons. As will be discussed further in Chapter 3, Scotland has quite a specific relationship to knife violence. The second most common method of killing, used in about a fifth of the cases, was physical assault, meaning that the offender beat or kicked the victim to death using their hands and feet. While about 18% of the homicides involved a blunt instrument, such as a baseball bat or a hammer, the use of firearms

22 Understanding homicide

was very rare; in only 4% of the cases did the offender use a gun to murder their victim. In contrast to countries such as the United States (Pizarro, 2008), firearms are rather uncommon in Scotland, making Scottish homicides more similar to Scandinavian homicides, including Swedish (Granath et al., 2011) and Finnish homicides (Lehti, 2014). Scotland even has a lower number of firearms-related homicides compared with England and Wales, where approximately 12% of all homicides were committed with a firearm in 2001/ 2002 (Brookman, 2005).

The most common relationship between offender and victim was an acquaintance, a friend, or someone known. Half of the homicide cases between 2000 and 2015 involved people who were known to each other. In 14% of the cases, the offender killed an intimate partner and in another 14% the victim was a relative of the offender. Only 8% of the cases involved strangers, meaning that the offender was someone unknown to the victim. In approximately 40% of the cases, the relationship between the offender and victim was, however, unknown or missing, meaning that there might be a substantial dark figure in regards to the relationship between offender and victim.

When the motive of the homicides was explored, the data showed that the most common motive for killing someone was because of a fight or an argument. More than half of the homicides fell into this category. This would include any homicide where the main motive of the murder was some sort of fight or quarrel between the victim and the offender. Feud was the recorded motive in about 8% of the cases, indicating longstanding rivalry between different factions, including gang-related incidents. In about 6% of the homicides, the motive was jealousy or revenge and in another 6% of the cases the motive was some sort of domestic argument. This would include cases of heated arguments between intimate partners which consequently led to the death of the victim. This variable also included a degree of unknowability; in almost a tenth of the cases the motive was coded as unknown and in another 12% of the cases, this variable was missing.

It has long been known in criminology that certain areas or locations figure as 'hot spots'; as areas which feature more frequently as locations for violent crime. This includes public houses or other similar venues where people get together and where alcohol or drugs are often involved. Areas surrounding these places, like nearby streets or alleyways, are often also considered hot spots, since fights that began inside the pub often continue and even escalate out on the street. While such public places figure quite commonly in Scottish homicides (46.3%), the data shows that it was more common for homicides to be committed in inside locations rather than outside locations (see Table 2.7). This may be explained by the fact that most homicides still occur in someone's home, whether it be the home of the victim, the offender, or an acquaintance to any one of them (Brookman, 2005).

In 48 of the homicides (4.8%), the offender destroyed evidence after the murder in some manner. This included cases where the offender had moved the body after the victim was killed or if the offender had buried, burned, or dismembered the body. This behaviour is usually indicative of forensic

What is homicide? 23

Table 2.7 Incident variables of the SHD dataset

Incident variables		Valid N (%)	Missing (% of total)
Method of Killing	Sharp instrument	759 (56.5%)	0 (0.0%)
	Blunt instrument	236 (17.6%)	
	Shooting or firearm	54 (4.0%)	
	Fire	21 (1.7%)	
	No weapon used	317 (23.6%)	
	Strangulation or ligature	84 (6.3%)	
	Physical assault	294 (23.3%)	
	Other[a]	143 (10.6%)	
Relationship between offender and victim	Known or acquaintance	401 (50.4%)	548 (40.8%)
	Relative (including parent)	115 (14.4%)	
	Rival	108 (13.6%)	
	Intimate partner	112 (14.1%)	
	Stranger	68 (8.5%)	
Motive	Fight, rage, or quarrel	659 (55.8%)	164 (12.2%)
	Financial (including theft)	76 (6.4%)	
	Insanity	30 (2.5%)	
	Jealousy or revenge	75 (6.4%)	
	Sexually motivated	27 (2.3%)	
	Domestic	71 (6.0%)	
	Feud	99 (8.4%)	
	Other[b]	70 (5.9%)	
	Unknown[c]	116 (9.8%)	
Public or private location	Public	381 (46.3%)	521 (38.8%)
	Private	442 (53.7%)	
Inside or outside location	Inside	530 (61.6%)	484 (36.0%)
	Outside	330 (38.4%)	
Evidence destruction	Whether the offender destroyed evidence after the homicide	64 (4.8%)	0 (0.0%)

Note 1: Base: *n* = 1344.
Note 2: Valid percentage was calculated based on the number of victims with the missingness excluded.
[a] Includes drowned as cause of death as well as when the cause of death or weapon was described as 'other'.
[b] Other includes mercy killings as well as homicides motivated by organised crime and motives that otherwise does not fit within any of the other categories.
[c] Unknown motive refers to the cases where Police Scotland could not establish the motive of the homicide
Source: SHD.

awareness (Skott, Beauregard, & Darjee, 2021) and it is overrepresented among sexually motivated homicides, which we will discuss further in Chapter 7.

Conclusions

This chapter has provided a description of the legal definitions of homicide in Scotland, outlining the difference between murder and culpable homicide as

24 *Understanding homicide*

well as having compared these crimes to the corresponding crimes in England and Wales. This chapter has also discussed the ramifications of differing definitions of homicide in a research context, highlighting the difficulty this entails for international comparisons. In order to provide the foundations for upcoming chapters in this volume, this chapter has also briefly described the Scottish Homicide Database, how it was created and how the data collection process occurred. This chapter has furthermore provided descriptive information on the homicide victims, offenders, and incidents that were committed in Scotland between 2000 and 2015.

Overall, most homicides committed in Scotland during this time occurred in Strathclyde, which is the area surrounding Glasgow, and most cases included a male offender killing a male victim. Most commonly, a homicide case involved one victim and one offender, but it was more common for a case to involve multiple offenders than multiple victims. The offenders tended to be younger than the victims, and females tended to be older than males, both as victims and offenders. Both victims and offenders of homicide were overwhelmingly white, and only a small proportion were homeless. The offender died by suicide in only 1% of the homicide cases, meaning homicide–suicide is a very rare type of homicide in Scotland. The most common method of killing was stabbing with the use of a sharp instrument such as a knife, and most homicides were motivated by some sort of fight or argument between offender and victim. Most offenders and victims were friends or acquaintances of some sort; only 8% of the cases involved strangers. While it was about as common for a homicide to occur in private settings as in public settings, the majority of homicides occurred indoors.

The next chapter will describe how homicide has changed over time in Scotland, exploring previous as well as current homicide trends. These trends will also be compared with international trends of homicide. The next chapter will also explore the Scottish context, providing a deeper understanding of the historical background and policy landscape relating to homicide occurring in Scotland.

3 Homicide in Scotland
Placing murder in context

Introduction

The changing trends in violence have been a subject of academic interest for well over a century (see, for instance, Quetelet, 1842). Dramatic decreases or increases in homicide have been studied as important social indicators of effects of major changes in society or even the functionality of social systems (Tonry, 2014). More recently, changes in crime trends have received specific attention in the context of the 'crime drop' – an internationally documented decline in most crimes across Western countries over the past two decades (Farrell & Brantingham, 2013). This declining trend marked the reversal of a previous increase in violence, prevalent since the 1950s (Tonry, 2014; Tonry & Farrington, 2005). While recent research has suggested that the crime drop may not be universal (Weiss, Renno Santos, Testa & Kumar, 2016), the decline in crime in most Western, industrialised countries since the early to mid-1990s, which includes homicide, cannot be denied (Aebi & Linde, 2010; Farrell, Tilley, Tseloni, & Mailley, 2010; LaFree, Curtis, & McDowall, 2015). This homicide decrease is evident in Canada and the US as well as in Western Europe, where homicide decreased in the latter half of the 1980s after having increased from the 1970s to the mid-1980s (Farrell & Brantingham, 2013; Haen Marshall & Summers, 2012; Selmini & McElrath, 2014). Homicide subsequently increased again, peaking in the early 1990s in most Western European countries (Aebi & Linde, 2012). A substantial decline followed, leaving the homicide rate at 24% lower in 2008 compared to 1970.[1] Very similar decreasing figures were found in Central and Eastern European countries (24% decrease in 2008 compared to 1985[2]).

The explanations for the overall decrease in homicide, and indeed other types of crime, are varied. Although various theories and hypotheses regarding the causes of the crime drop have been proposed such as changed

---

1 This was based on the geometric mean of the homicide rate per 100 000 people for 15 Western European countries (Aebi & Linde, 2012).

2 These figures were based on the geometric mean of the homicide rate per 100 000 people for 12 Central and Eastern European countries (Aebi & Linde, 2012).

DOI: 10.4324/9781003105282-4

26 *Understanding homicide*

crime justice policies and legislation, increased securitisation, and economical and societal change (Aebi & Linde, 2010; Farrell, 2013; Tonry, 2014), not many of them have been able to effectively explain why homicide has declined (Tonry, 2014). There is, furthermore, the issue of explaining changes in international crime trends using national variables such as increases in incarceration or legislative changes (Farrell et al., 2010). If we instead turn our gazes towards the change in homicide within a single country, this might mitigate some of the validity issues of comparing crime data across different countries (Aebi & Linde, 2010). Scotland is interesting for such an analysis mainly because of the vast changes in homicide that have occurred over time in this country. While Scotland has been described as one of the most violent countries in the developed world (BBC News, 2005; The Guardian, 2005), homicide and other violent crime have decreased to record low levels during the past decade. In order to explore this dramatic change, the following section will examine the existing literature on changes in trends in homicide in the specific context of Scotland.

Revisiting the 'murder capital of the world': exploring the homicide legacy of Scotland

More than 15 years ago, Scotland gained the unenviable reputation of being 'the most violent country in the developed world' (BBC News, 2005; The Guardian, 2005). Scotland was described as having the second highest murder rate in Western Europe, three times higher than the homicide rate in England and Wales, and Glasgow was described as the 'murder capital of Europe' (The Guardian, 2005). The core of the violence problem in Scotland has been centred around knife violence and gang violence, which has been especially prevalent in the west of Scotland (Carnochan, 2015; Damer, 1989; Fraser, 2015). As such, violence has been a deep-rooted problem, documented as early as in the 1920s and 1930s (Davies, 2007).

Despite this problem, going back for decades, only a handful of studies have examined violence on the aggregate level in Scotland. Two comparative studies exploring the rate of police-recorded violence in Scotland and in Sweden were conducted in the early 1990s by McClintock and Wikström (1990; 1992), concluding that all levels of violence, and homicide in particular, were considerably higher in Scotland. McClintock and Wikström (1990) also found that while the level of violence had increased in both countries since the 1960s, this increase was much more dramatic in Scotland. While McClintock and Wikström partially attribute this increase to improved recording practices, they argue that a real increase in crime most likely also occurred.

Comparing Scottish crime trends with the crime trends in England and Wales, Smith (2005) discovered that the trends in crime and punishment were substantially different in the two countries since the 1950s, despite the cultural similarities. Overall, the increase in police-recorded crime was substantially lower in Scotland, and while crime levelled off around the mid-1990s in England and Wales, this stabilisation occurred much earlier in Scotland, around 1980. Compared to most other crimes, which demonstrated a decrease, homicide had however demonstrated a slow increase in Scotland between 1981 and 1999 (Smith, 2005). As outlined in Chapter 2, such differences might, however, be related to differences in reporting and recording practices between Scotland and England and Wales. In order to examine the possible effects of such recording and coding differences, Soothill, Francis, Ackerley, and Collet (1999) compared the homicide rate in Scotland with England and Wales. They compared data from the Homicide Index from respective jurisdictions, exploring homicides committed between 1985 and 1994, revealing that there indeed was a real difference in homicide rates, and that these rates were significantly higher in Scotland compared with England and Wales. While the homicide rate was 19.15 per million population in Scotland, the corresponding figure was 11.28 homicides per million population in England and Wales. Soothill et al. furthermore estimated that the statistical differences relating to recording practices only contributed approximately 0.6 per million population to this difference.

However, when Soothill et al. (1999) explored different types of homicide they discovered that the difference between Scotland and England and Wales was not evident across all homicide types. When comparing homicides committed against male victims, Soothill et al. (1999) found that the Scottish homicide rate (28.84 per million population) was more than twice as high as the male homicide rate in England and Wales (13.40 per million population). When they compared homicides committed against female victims, Soothill et al., however, found that the level of homicides were approximately similar in the two jurisdictions (10.07 per million population and 9.25 per million population, respectively). There was also a significant difference in relation to age; the rates in Scotland were approximately twice as high as the rates in England and Wales for each age group of victims aged 15 years and older. The rates were, however, similar in the two jurisdictions regarding homicides involving victims aged younger than 15 (Soothill et al., 1999). While the modus operandi of homicide was similar in the two countries, Soothill et al. (1999) found that homicides more often were committed by the use of sharp instruments, blunt instruments, or with the use of no weapon at all in Scotland compared with England and Wales.

Despite the fact that Scotland had a higher homicide rate, Soothill et al. (1999) contrastingly found that the risk of experiencing nonlethal violence was overall much higher in England and Wales compared with Scotland. This was valid for domestic, acquaintance, and stranger violence, for male and female victims alike. These findings suggest that while the homicide rates were higher in Scotland, this was not true for all categories of violence. As such, the overall pattern of lethal and nonlethal violence appeared different in Scotland compared with England and Wales, involving a higher rate of male homicide victims killed by an acquaintance by the use of a sharp or blunt instrument but a similar or lower rate of other forms of nonlethal violence (Soothill et al., 1999).

28 *Understanding homicide*

More recent research has examined the change in violence in Scotland in the light of the recent crime drop. Exploring different types of crime, including nonsexual violence, Humphreys, Francis, and McVie (2014) identified two distinct peaks in violence in 1992 and 2003, subsequently followed by a consistent and rapid decline. In a similar vein, Norris, Pillinger, and McVie (2014) found that the overall likelihood of being a victim of crime had decreased between 1993 and 2010–2011 in Scotland. However, Norris et al. (2014) also found that there had been an increased inequality in victimisation. While the overall victimisation rates have decreased, the people who experience the most chronic levels of crime and violence remained at high risk of victimisation, largely unaffected by the crime drop. This group of victims, which suffered the highest number of assaults and threats, additionally experienced the largest increase in risk of violence over time (Norris et al., 2014). Confirming these findings in a later study, McVie, Norris, and Pillinger (2020) concluded that the crime drop in Scotland primarily reflected a decrease in nonviolent crime among victims who were already at low risk for being victimised. Meanwhile, there was no discernible reduction in either prevalence or incidence among victims who experienced repeated victimisation of violent crime. As McVie et al. (2020: 796) stated; 'indeed, against the prevailing trend of a crime drop, the incidence of violence increased among those at highest risk of victimization in Scotland'. In other words, while it would seem that violence has declined overall in Scotland, this decrease does not appear to have happened equally. This inequality in victimisation underlines the importance of examining the change in violence at a more detailed level. While the overall picture of violence is one of decline, a different pattern emerges when violence is disaggregated by other variables such as amount or type of victimisation.

While a rare crime, a few studies have examined sexual homicide in Scotland (Skott, Beauregard, & Darjee, 2019; Skott, Beauregard, & Darjee, 2021; Skott, 2019; Skott, Beauregard, Darjee, & Martineau, 2021), suggesting there are important differences between sexual and nonsexual homicides. While these findings will be explored further in Chapter 7 along with other studies exploring sexual homicide, these studies suggest that it is important to include sexual violence when comparing nonlethal violence to homicide. Approximately 5% of all homicides in Scotland recorded by the police between 2005 and 2015 were coded as sexually motivated[3] (Scottish Government, 2016b). Previous research has also found links between nonlethal sexual violence and homicide, as well as links between lethal and nonlethal sexual violence (Francis & Soothill, 2010; Grann & Wedin, 2002). This suggests that while sexual homicides remains rare, it is important to explore this crime in relation to nonlethal violence.

---

3 Additionally, between 13% and 24% of all homicide cases between 2004 and 2005 and 2015 and 2016 had an unknown motive (Scottish Government, 2016c), which may also include sexual cases.

Overall, while these previous studies on the change of homicide and related violence provide a good starting point, we need to explore the actual statistical trends of homicide in Scotland in order to get a better understanding of how this crime has changed over time. The following section will therefore examine aggregate statistics of homicide and violence published by the Scottish Government.

Trends in homicide over time

Every year, the Scottish Government produces annual crime statistics presented in an annual bulletin covering all national statistics of crimes and offences recorded and cleared up by the police. While these figures go back several decades, there are some difficulties with comparing such crime rates over time. While police-recorded crime usually is quite reliable, this measure does not reflect the true incidence of crime. Rather, police-recorded crime is a measure of the crime reported to and recorded by the police, regardless of how much crime that actually occurs. In fact, it has been approximated that only about 38% of all crime is reported to the police (Scottish Government, 2016d), a number that is likely to be even lower for crimes of a sexual nature (Daly & Bouhour, 2010; RCS, 2016). Sexual crimes are especially difficult to measure over time, not only because of the implementation of a wide range of legislative changes, altering the definition of criminal acts[4] (Scottish Government, 2016c) but also because of shifts in the public perception regarding sexual violence, which affects the number of crimes reported to the police. These crime statistics may also include older instances of sexual violence where the victim only now has dared to come forward and report this crime to the police. Overall, all types of police-recorded crime remain sensitive to changes in the practice of police recording or public reporting, as well as changes to legislature and laws. For instance, the Scottish Crime Recording Standard (SCRS) was implemented in 2004–2005 in order to improve crime recording consistency (Scottish Government, 2013). However, the introduction of the SCRS also meant that the requirement of corroborative evidence in order to record a crime was removed, resulting in an artificial increase in crime statistics (HMICS, 2008; Fraser, Burman, Batchelor, & McVie, 2010). As such, some scholars argue that police-recorded crime should be regarded as a measure of police activity rather than crime (Haen Marshall & Summers, 2012). Despite these limitations, police-recorded crime, however, remains a valuable reference point for the general level of crime within a society (Fraser et al., 2010), and is therefore often used when comparing different types of crime over time.

---

4 The implementation of the Sexual Offences Act 2009 in 2010 led to several changes in the sexual crimes, for instance a wider definition of rape (Scottish Government, 2016d).

30 *Understanding homicide*

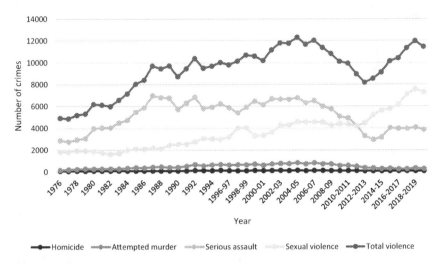

Figure 3.1 Absolute change in police-recorded violent crime 1976–2019/2020
Source: Scottish Government (2014b; 2016c; 2020)

In order to examine the long-term changes in homicide in Scotland, the trends of homicide and other police-recorded violent crimes since 1976[5] were examined. As can be seen from Figure 3.1, homicide (including murder and culpable homicide), attempted murder; serious assault and sexual violence[6] all follow similar trends over time, with some exceptions. When the trends are indexed in order to compare the relative change over time (see Figure 3.2), the data showed that all types of police-recorded violent crime, measured as 'total violence', increased steadily from the mid-1970s, peaking in 2004–2005 with an increase of about 150% compared to 1976, before decreasing until 2012–2013. A second increase was subsequently evident from 2013–2014 to 2019–2020. This meant that 'total violence' had increased by 132% in 2019–2020 compared to 1976 (see Figure 3.2). Exploring the relative change in trends in different types of crime, the data demonstrates that the trend in serious assault appeared to follow the trend in total violence quite closely. Since serious assault constituted the most common type of violence examined, and is therefore likely to be driving the trend of 'total violence', this is, however, not surprising (see Figure 3.1). Overall, serious assault had increased by 33% in 2019–2020 compared to 1976 (see Figure 3.2).

---

5 1976 is used as the first year since this is the first complete comparable year of recorded crime statistics (Scottish Government, 2014a). Data from 1975 is incomplete due to local government reorganisation, and can not be broken down into categories.
6 Sexual violence includes: rape and attempted rape, and sexual assault.

Homicide in Scotland 31

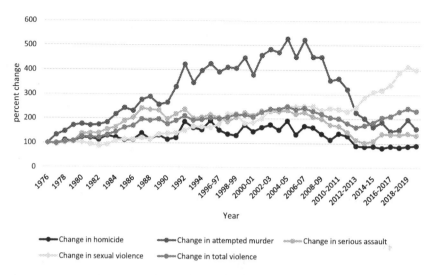

Figure 3.2 Relative change in police-recorded violent crime 1976–2019/2020
Source: Scottish Government (2014b; 2016c; 2020)

Looking more closely at the trend in homicide, we can see that homicide in Scotland appears to have two peaks; one in 1995–1996 (91% increase compared to 1976) and 2004–2005 (91% increase compared to 1976). Unlike the other types of violence, homicide decreased after the second peak in 2004–2005 until 2019–2020 without demonstrating another increase. In other words, the number of homicides has remained steadily low since 2012–2013, ranging between 59 and 64 homicides every year. The 64 homicides in 2019–2020 represents a 9% decrease from 1976, but the number of homicides has more than halved since the peak of 2004–2005 (see Figure 3.2). As can be seen from Figure 3.1, homicide remained the least common type of police-recorded violence examined. Similarly, attempted murder increased from 1976, peaking in 2004–2005 (with a 427% increase compared to 1976) before decreasing until 2019–2020. Despite this vast increase in attempted murder, this crime constituted a very small proportion of the trend in total violence (see Figure 3.1). Overall, attempted murder had increased by 60% in 2019–2020 compared with 1976.

The dramatic increase evident in attempted murder (see Figure 3.2) could be due to several factors. First, since the absolute number of attempted murders is quite small (see Figure 3.1), minor, year-to-year differences may generate large relative figures. Second, there might be a reduction in violence seriousness, meaning that fewer violent acts end in the death of the victim in the later years examined compared with the earlier years. This violence reduction might be related to improved medical care and emergency services. Since the difference between a murder and an attempted murder is partially

32 *Understanding homicide*

related to the attentiveness, availability, and accessibility of medical assistance (Smit, de Jong, & Bijleveld, 2012), the decline of homicide and simultaneous increase in attempted murder, may be related to the improvement of such emergency services evident in Western Europe over the past decades. As can be seen from Figure 3.2, homicide has decreased in Scotland while attempted murder and serious assault in fact has increased since 1976. Either of the factors mentioned above, or indeed, a combination of them all might explain this change in pattern over time. In other words, the decrease in homicide, in addition to reflecting an actual decrease, might also reflect the effects of improved medical care, leading to reduced violence seriousness. This medical care hypothesis has previously been discussed by other authors in relation to both Canada and USA (Farrell & Brantingham, 2013; Harris et al., 2002) as well as in regards to Western Europe overall (Aebi & Linde, 2010; 2012; Tonry, 2014). For instance, Tonry (2014) demonstrated that the proportion of all violent incidents ending lethally had decreased by almost half from 1999 to 2001.

Other scholars have, however, argued that improvements in medical care could not alone have caused the major declines in homicide, evident in Europe as well as elsewhere (Harris et al., 2002; Blumstein, 2000; Tonry, 2014). Looking at the Scottish data, there was also a strong[7] positive correlation between the long-term change in homicide and the long-term increase in attempted murder (*rho* = 0.81, *n* = 44, *p*<0.05), which would indicate that homicide and attempted murder have followed similar trends since 1976, despite the huge differences in magnitude. While there was no significant relationship between the trends in homicide and sexual violence, the relative trend in homicide also demonstrated a strong positive relationship with the relative trends of serious assault (*rho* = 0.72, *n* = 44, *p*<0.05). Since the trends in different violent crimes are correlated (with the exception of sexual violence), these findings would suggest that the medical hypothesis has limited explanatory value in regards to the homicide decline in Scotland.

If the homicide decline was explained by improved medical care, the numbers of attempted murder and serious assault would be expected to increase at the same time as the level of homicide decreased. However, as can be seen from Figure 3.2, homicide demonstrated a slow increase until the mid-1990s, after which homicide, attempted murder and serious assault all decreased. We will return to this hypothesis, along with other theories of violence and homicide, in the next chapter.

As mentioned, the trends in sexual violence is, however, somewhat of an exception. Although sexual violent crime gradually increased along with the other violent crimes examined, sexual violence continued to increase until 2018–2019. The increase in sexual violence was furthermore very steep in the last eight years measured, and as can be seen from Figure 3.1, sexual violence

---

7 Following Cohen's d criteria of weak (*r* = 0.10–0.29), moderate (*r* = 0.30–0.49) and strong (*r* = 0.50–1.0) correlations (Cohen, 1988).

surpassed serious assault as the most common type of police-recorded violence in 2012–2013. In 2019–2020, sexual violence had increased by 300% since 1976, demonstrating the largest increase of all violent crime. While this increase might be related to a real increase in sexual violence, as mentioned, the trends in sexual crimes are very different from other violent crimes due to the vast changes to the legislature and public opinion surrounding this crime. Overall, homicide was the only crime that had decreased in 2019–2020 compared to 1976, and this decrease also proved to be significantly lower than the change in attempted murder,[8] serious assault,[9] and sexual violence.[10]

Exploring the Scottish homicide trend has provided us with a clearer picture of how homicide and other types of violent crime has changed over time in Scotland. But how does this compare to homicide trends in other countries? In order to explore this, homicides in Scotland were compared to international homicide trends. As mentioned in Chapter 2, international comparisons are not always straightforward due to different definitions and legal frameworks. To facilitate comparison, homicide figures were taken from the United Nations Office of Drugs and Crime (UNODC), who define homicide as; 'unlawful death inflicted upon a person with the intent to cause death or serious injury' (UNODC, 2015: 17). Figure 3.3 shows the homicide rate per 100 000 population from 1990 to 2018 in Scotland and six other Western countries: England and Wales, the US, Germany, France, the Netherlands, and Sweden. As the data shows, Scotland had a higher homicide rate than all the other European countries explored from the mid-1990s onwards, being surpassed only by the US, who demonstrated the highest homicide rate of all countries. In 2012, the homicide rate in Scotland, however, declined below the homicide rate in France, and by 2018, the homicide rate in Scotland was on the same level as the other compared European countries. In fact, in 2017, the homicide rate in Scotland was lower than the levels of France, Sweden, and England and Wales (see Figure 3.3).

This demonstrates the vast changes that have occurred in Scotland in regards to intentional homicide over time. While Scotland consistently had a higher homicide rate compared to England and Wales up until the 2010s, this appears to be changing in the later years of the data. In order to explore this further, Figure 3.4 demonstrates the homicide rate per 100 000 population of only Scotland and England and Wales. As the data shows, the homicide rate was considerably higher in Scotland, with the peak in 2004 representing an almost twice as high homicide rate compared to the homicide rate in England and Wales. In 2012 however, the gap between the countries, decreased and by 2017, England and Wales had a higher homicide rate than Scotland.

---

8 According to a Mann Whitney U test between the trends of homicide ($Md = 126.4$, $n = 44$) and attempted murder ($Md = 282.2$, $n = 44$; $U = 1812.5$, $z = 7.05$ $p<0.05$, two-tailed).

9 According to a Mann Whitney U test between the trends of homicide ($Md = 126.4$, $n = 44$) and serious assault ($Md = 194.0$, $n = 44$; $U = 1539.5$, $z = 4.77$ $p<0.05$, two-tailed).

10 According to a Mann Whitney U test between the trends of homicide ($Md = 126.4$, $n = 44$) and sexual violence ($Md = 183.1$, $n = 44$; $U = 1429.5$, $z = 3.85$ $p<0.05$, two-tailed).

34 *Understanding homicide*

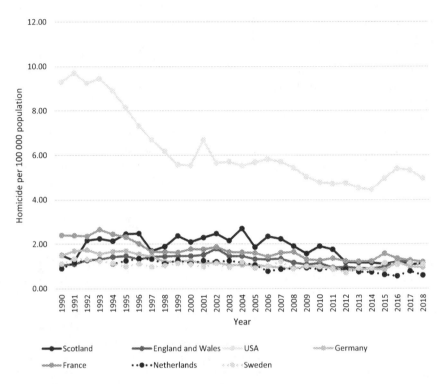

Figure 3.3 International homicide rates per 100 000 population, 1990–2018
Source: UNODC (2021)

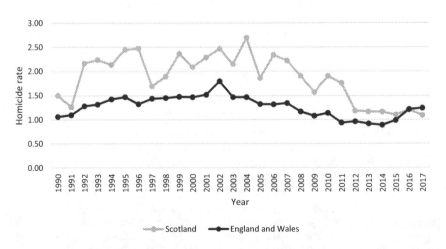

Figure 3.4 Homicide rate per 100 000 population, UK comparison, 1990–2017
Source: UNODC (2021)

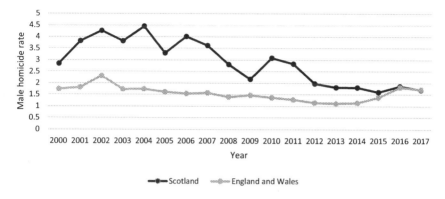

Figure 3.5 Male homicide victim rate per 100 000 population, 2000–2017
Source: UNODC (2021)

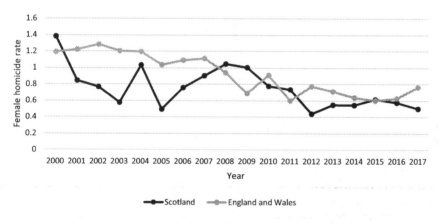

Figure 3.6 Female victim homicide rate per 100 000 population, 2000–2017
Source: UNODC (2021)

When these figures are broken down even further into homicides of male and female victims (see Figures 3.5 and 3.6), a slightly different pattern, however, emerges. While male victim homicide has been more prevalent in Scotland compared to England and Wales up until 2015, homicides of female victims have been more prevalent in England and Wales. As can be seen from Figure 3.6, Scotland has a lower rate of female victim homicides throughout most of the time series, including the final years of the data explored. This highlights the need of examining different types of homicide rather than just exploring homicide overall. As this descriptive analysis shows, the trends of homicide may vary depending on what types of homicide you are exploring.

36　*Understanding homicide*

Conversely, the overarching trends of homicide may conceal heterogeneity in the data, which has important implications for the interpretation of the results.

Scotland has consequently seen a dramatic change in the trends of homicide over time. It is within this context of decline that the studies in the following volume take place. In order to understand the Scottish context more fully, the next section will explore previous and current policies and interventions put in place in Scotland to reduce violence and homicide. This will be done to provide a description of how the problem of violence has been framed over time in Scotland as well as to provide a policy context of lethal and nonlethal violence in Scotland.

Policies and interventions of violence in Scotland

Knife violence, particularly among young men, has historically been one of Scotland's most pervasive problems, with documented gang-related violence going back to the 1920s (Davies, 2007). For instance, exploring the rising homicide rate between 1981 and 2003, Leyland (2006) found that the large increase (83%) was predominantly attributable to an increase in homicides using knives and other sharp instruments. This increase was also particularly prevalent among young men (Leyland, 2006). Responding to this massive increase in violence and knife crime observed by Leyland (2006) along with other researchers, Scottish police forces implemented several new initiatives to combat this trend in the early 1990s. Strathclyde Police Force was the largest force at the time, including approximately two thirds of all Scottish crime (Orr, 1998). Strathclyde also included Glasgow, which was a particularly problematic area in regards to violence but also in regards to issues with deprivation and poverty, including unemployment and substance abuse (Fraser, 2015; Orr, 1998). A series of operative initiatives were launched, including Operation Spur in order to recover criminally held firearms, Operation Turnkey to target housebreaking offences, and Operation Eagle in order to reduce the supply, dealing, and use of drugs (Orr, 1998). Among these was an initiative called Operation Blade, launched in 1993 in the Strathclyde Police force by Chief Constable Leslie Sharpe in an attempt to address the increased tendency of young people to carry and use knives (Bleetman, Perry, Crawford, & Swann, 1997). Building on a multifaceted approach, Operation Blade included a knife amnesty, an intensified stop and search campaign, improved CCTV and street lighting, but also conversations with knife retailers and pupils in secondary schools. While the early results of this campaign were mostly positive, Bleetman et al., however, did not find any significant difference in the number of victims before the implementation and after. As such, Bleetman et al., concluded that the impact of Operation Blade had not been sustained and such initiatives would need to be repeated with regular intervals in order to change the social attitudes in the longer term.

Homicide in Scotland 37

While the wide array of operative initiatives initially demonstrated positive results, including improved public support of the police, violent crime was still increasing (Orr, 1998; Scottish Government, 2014b). The public fear of violence during this time, including gang-related violence, was furthermore at a very high level. In order to further combat this issue, the new Chief Constable John Orr launched another operative initiative called Operation Spotlight in Strathclyde in 1996 (Murray & Harkin, 2016; Orr, 1998). Operation Spotlight aimed to dramatically decrease violent crime as well as to reduce fear of crime and disorder in the force area. Based on ideas of Broken Window theory (Kelling & Wilson, 1982), the focus of Operation Spotlight was to target minor crimes as a way to prevent serious crime, as well as to maximise officer presence on the streets (Orr, 1998). Described as a 'crack-down on crime' with a 'gloves off' approach (Orr, 1998: 106), it was perceived by many as a 'zero tolerance' policy for violence, even though it was explicitly stated that it was not (Orr, 1998: 106; Murray & Harkin, 2016). The implementation of Operation Spotlight, however, introduced a new style of policing, which was less focused on attempting to understand and explain the problem at hand, and more focused on police action and visibility, leading to massive increases in stop and search practices, often on a nonstatutory basis (Murray & Harkin, 2016). Different from the more multifaceted interventions initiated by Operation Blade, this was a 'Spotlight-style' of policing, illuminating certain problem areas at different times and aiming to ensure that 'the criminal would always be on guard!' (Orr, 1998: 118).

Violence, however, continued to increase in Scotland, despite these interventions, and by 2005, rates of both violence and homicide were at an all-time high (Scottish Government, 2014b). As a response to this seemingly unbreakable trend, Willie Rae, the Chief Constable of Strathclyde Police at that time, launched a new initiative to address the violence problem by establishing the Violence Reduction Unit. Unlike the crackdown, 'gloves off' approach advocated by Operation Spotlight (Orr, 1998), the Violence Reduction Unit framed violence as a public health problem, promoting early prevention strategies and multi-agency collaborations to reduce violence, teaming up with agencies in the field of health, education, and social work (VRU, 2016; 2017). By situating the issue of violence within the public health domain, the Violence Reduction Unit linked the violence problem to other problems of social deprivation, including homelessness and unemployment, examining the causes of crime and encouraging a 'bigger picture' response to violence (VRU, 2016; 2017).

The Violence Reduction Unit was rolled out as a national unit in 2006, and was predominantly focused on preventing knife violence (VRU, 2016). There was a very prevalent public concern about knife carrying, especially among youths, in Scotland around this time. Youth violence remained at the centre of the public debate, leading to an escalating moral panic around youth crime and antisocial behaviour, which in turn evolved into a crackdown on this type of behaviour, advocated by the Justice Minister at the time, Cathy

38 *Understanding homicide*

Jamieson (McAra, 2010). However, due to a lack of available data, not much was known about the nature or prevalence of violence committed (Fraser, Burman, Batchelor, & McVie, 2010). While the long-term trends in criminal convictions for violent crimes among young people indicated an increase in violence and handling offensive weapons, there was an overall decrease in robbery convictions, which more closely resembled trends in property crime (Fraser et al., 2010). Other studies indicated that most young people who carried knives tended to do so very infrequently rather than persistently, indicating that there was a 'core' of youths engaging in repeated weapon use responsible for a huge part of all incidents (Bannister et al., 2010; McVie, 2010). As such, the issue was not increased weapon use across the board, but rather a small but persistent group of young violent offenders, often suffering from multiple aspects of deprivation and vulnerability.

Multiple prevention strategies were initiated by the Violence Reduction Unit in order to tackle this problem, including the Community Initiative to Reduce Violence (CIRV), Medics Against Violence in 2008, and the Ask, Document, Validate, Refer (ADVR) intervention for domestic violence aimed at dentists in 2009 (VRU, 2016). The Mentors in Violence Prevention (MVP) school programme was launched in 2011, aiming to empower students to speak out against all types of violence, including bullying, abuse, and sexual violence (VRU, 2021). More recent interventions include the Navigator programme launched in 2015, which aims to support people who want to move away from a violent lifestyle (VRU, 2021). The Navigator programme works in collaboration with emergency services, aiming to break the cycle of violence as well as easing the pressure on the NHS caused by violence. The establishment of the VRU marked yet another new direction for violence policy in Scotland. The Cabinet Secretary for Health declared violence to be a public health problem in 2007 and the No Knives Better Lives initiative (NKBL, 2014), aiming to raise awareness about the consequences of knife carrying, was established in 2009. The same year also saw the launch of the Scottish Government flagship initiative aimed to reduce the number of victims in Scotland called the Building Safer Communities Program (BSC, 2016; Scottish Government, 2017b; VRU, 2016). Advocating a holistic approach, Building Safer Communities was a collaborative program with both national and local partners aimed at reducing the number of victims of crime as well as to reduce unintentional injury.

While public violence involving knives, mostly committed by young men, continued to be a strong policy focus in Scotland, new policies aimed at domestic violence were also developed during this time. In 2009, the Scottish Government published their approach to combat violence against women called Safer Lives, Changed Lives, forming the basis for their strategies and focusing on prevention and early intervention (Scottish Government, 2009; Scottish Government, 2017a). The prevention and reduction of domestic violence was also one of the main priorities of the new Chief Constable of Strathclyde Police, Stephen House, appointed in 2007 (Murray, 2016).

Scholars have, however, criticised the policy development process as well as its implementation in Scotland, arguing that this process reinforces gendered and social hierarchies (Hearn & McKie, 2010). Hearn and McKie (2010) argue that a failure to actively gender the representation of the problem as well as a reinforcement of the demarcation between the public and the private has resulted in an individualised and a-gendered response to gendered violence, framing the problem as one of 'atypical men' (Hearn & McKie, 2010: 149).

Equally Safe, a complete strategy for preventing and eradicating violence against women and girls, building on the Safer Lives, Changed Lives approach, was initiated in 2014 (Scottish Government, 2014a; 2016a). The Equally Safe strategy, updated in 2016, was developed by the Scottish Government in collaboration with COSLA[11] and other public and third sector organisations (Scottish Government, 2016a). Focusing on all forms of violence committed against women, including domestic, sexual, and honour-based violence, this strategy links violence against women and girls to deep-rooted issues of inequality and prioritises preventative strategies as well as multi-agency and multi-sector responses to combat this type of violence. This includes the establishment of the Violence Against Women and Girls Joint Strategic Board, aiming to identify emerging issues as well as to provide leadership on this issue. The Equally Safe Strategy also included the launch of Multi-Agency Tasking and Co-ordinating Groups (MATAC) by Police Scotland, which aims to target serious as well as serial offenders of domestic violence (Scottish Government, 2016a). Public health guidance was also developed within the framework of the Equally Safe strategy in order to support the implementation of the strategy within the NHS. Another program launched to reduce domestic violence include The Caledonian System which has been in operation since 2011. The Caledonian System aims to reduce reoffending among men convicted of domestic abuse, as well as providing integrated services for women and children (Ormston, Mullhulland & Setterfield, 2016; Scottish Government, 2017e).

The legal framework surrounding sexual violence has also been developed over the last few years in Scotland. This includes the implementation of the Sexual Offences Act (2009), which for the first time introduced a legal definition of rape, and the Criminal Justice and Licencing Act (2010), which introduced stalking as a statutory offence as well as removing the requirement for a public element to the offence. The Abusive Behaviour and Sexual Harm Act was also introduced in 2017, modernising the law on domestic and sexual abuse, which, for instance, increased the power of the courts to make nonharassment orders and introduced an offence for sharing private intimate images without consent (commonly referred to as 'revenge porn') (Scottish Government, 2017d). A Domestic Abuse Act (2018) was passed in

---

11 COSLA stands for Convention Of Scottish Local Authorities and is a national association of Scottish councils (COSLA, 2017).

40   *Understanding homicide*

2018 and enacted in 2019, which criminalised psychological domestic abuse as well as coercive and controlling behaviour. The act also takes into account the possible harm inflicted on children in an abusive relationship, including this aspect as a statutory sentencing aggravation. The Scottish Government has also provided funding to educate Independent Domestic Abuse Advisers (IDAAs) in order to provide support for high-risk domestic abuse survivors as well as to help guiding them through the legal system (Scottish Government, 2017d).

Since the unification of the eight Scottish police forces in 2013, Police Scotland has maintained a strong focus on preventing and reducing domestic abuse with the formation of the National Domestic Abuse Task Force and specialist domestic abuse investigation units in every local policing division in Scotland (Scottish Government, 2015). Police Scotland has also emphasised prevention as well as risk and harm reduction in their strategic program for the forthcoming ten years, 'Policing 2026', where the tackling of crime is linked to inequality and enduring problems in communities (Police Scotland, 2017b).

Conclusions

This chapter has provided an overview of the changes in homicide trends in Scotland over time. Previous research on homicide in Scotland has been examined, and the trends of homicide have been put in local context by comparing them to other types of violent crimes within Scotland such as attempted murder and serious assault. Scottish homicide has also been compared to international homicide trends to provide a wider perspective. While the homicide rates in Scotland consistently has been higher than other European countries, including England and Wales, the levels of homicide in Scotland has decreased dramatically over the past decades. In the most recent years explored, the homicide rate in Scotland is even lower than the levels in England and Wales. Scotland has furthermore consistently had a lower rate of homicide committed against females compared to England and Wales.

This chapter has also explored the violence polices in Scotland in order to examine how the problem of violence has been framed in this country. The current policies to tackle violence in Scotland have shifted into framing violence as a public health problem, connected to wider issues of deprivation, inequality, and social context. There is a strong focus on building an evidence base around these issues and to examine and gain a deeper understanding of the problem at hand. There is little trace in current policies of the crackdown, 'gloves-off' approach advocated during the mid-1990s. Instead, violence in Scotland is tackled within a 'bigger picture' perspective, which is trying to get at the causes of violence as well as reducing it. As mentioned, the current policy response to reduce and prevent violence can broadly be divided into two main foci: action against violence more generally, which has a specific focus on youth violence and knife crime; and action against domestic violence and violence against women, including sexual violence.

Homicide in Scotland 41

The next chapter will provide a comprehensive overview of the main theories explaining homicide, as well as examining the impact of gender on homicide and the role of homicide in the media. This will provide a deeper understanding for homicide, including the question of why someone would commit this crime. This will also be done to provide some theoretical underpinnings to the forthcoming analysis of the later chapters in this volume.

4 Theories of homicide

Introduction

As the previous chapter examined how homicide in Scotland has changed over time, providing an empirical foundation for the forthcoming analysis, this chapter will provide the theoretical foundations for understanding homicide. While there is an abundance of criminological theories out there aiming to explain why individuals commit various forms of crime, criminologists usually divide these theories into three families: biological theories, psychological theories, and sociological theories. As with all classifications, this taxonomy is not perfect and does contain some overlap; however, it is usually a good starting point when trying to sort through all the various theoretical frameworks. This chapter will therefore begin by outlining these three families of theories. The chapter will then move on to explore the relationship between gender and homicide. As will be explained, violence in general, and homicide in particular, is a masculine affair. While there indeed are women who commit violent acts, including homicide, the vast majority of all homicide offenders, and victims, are men. This naturally begs the questions of what it is about being a man that seems so conducive of violence. In order to attempt to clarify and explain the association between gender and homicide, this chapter will therefore explore this relationship in depth.

Following the section on homicide and gender, this chapter will then turn to one of the newer, more critical perspectives in criminology, namely Gothic criminology. While a relatively new theoretical perspective, Gothic criminology stems from cultural and feminist criminology, and explores the Gothicity of crime in modern society (Picart & Greek, 2007). This includes the study of 'the other', both in real-life crime as well as in fictionalised media, and the study of the monstrous. To demonstrate the usefulness of this emerging perspective when studying homicide, one specific type of homicide will be explored with a Gothic lens: serial killing. While exceedingly rare, serial killers figure heavily in popular culture and have a prominent impact on the public imaginary of homicide as a crime. The final section of this chapter will therefore briefly explore the construction of the serial killer in popular culture using a Gothic lens. However, first this chapter will explore the dominant

DOI: 10.4324/9781003105282-5

theories of homicide, beginning with the biological explanations for homicidal behaviour.

Dominant theories to understand homicide

The following sections will outline the most influential theories used to explain homicide and violent behaviour. The theories delineated here are by no means an exhaustive list but a sample of the most commonly used theories to explain violence. It is also important to acknowledge that something as complex as human behaviour may not be caused by simply one factor, be it biological, psychological, or sociological. Many students, at the commencement of their studies, mistakenly believe that there is one indisputable theory of crime that may explain all sorts of violent and criminal behaviour within the same, neat framework. Reality is unfortunately less well ordered. The theories laid out here are all contrasting but complementary frameworks that may be explored and applied to increase our understanding of homicide and violent behaviour. I do not claim that any of these theories may solely explain all violence. There is no 'crime gene' or 'violence gene'; there is no personality disorder that may perfectly explain why some individuals commit violence, and there is not one societal phenomenon that perfectly predicts homicide. Instead, this chapter aims to provide a wide-ranging view of the current theories used to explain homicide and violence in order to provide a deeper understanding for the mechanisms behind this type of behaviour.

It is also important to point out that some, if not most, of the theories explored below are concerned with the explanation of violent behaviour generally rather than homicide specifically. While homicide and nonlethal violent acts may differ in some respects, many times they are only differentiated by outcome. Whether or not the victim dies as a result of the violence inflicted upon them may be a matter of chance. For this reason, most theories attempting to explain homicide therefore also tend to include violence. But for now, let us turn our focus towards the biological theories attempting to explain violent and homicidal behaviour.

Biological theories

Some of the earliest criminological theories to explain violence and homicide are biological theories. This family of theories places the causes or explanations of crime within the biological makeup of an individual. This also means that this family of theories, alongside the psychological theories that will be covered within the following section, most commonly have an individual focus. This is mainly due to their theoretical roots in individual positivism, stemming from theorists like Beccaria (1767/1995), and indeed Lombroso (Lombroso & Ferrero, 1893/2004), who explained violent and criminal behaviour as an effect of biological or genetic deficits. While such

44 *Understanding homicide*

deterministic branches of biological theory have been discredited in later years, there are some modern theories attempting to explain violent crime using biological explanations using new, cutting-edge research in genetics and neuroscience. This section will outline a few of these theories and their application to explain homicide and violent behaviour.

Intelligence and self-control

A few theories, such as Gottfredson and Hirschi's (1990) *A General Theory of Crime* and the biologically based theory by Wilson and Hernstein's (1985), relate criminal and violent behaviour to low levels of intelligence and self-control. Low levels of intelligence, usually measured verbally as well as behaviourally, has been linked to offending, including the perpetration of homicide (Templer, Connelly, Lester, Arikawa, & Mancuso, 2007). The correlation between violence and low intelligence is, however, hotly debated. While some researchers believe the relationship to be direct and causal, where low levels of intelligence limits the individual's capacity to noncriminal solutions, other researchers refute this relationship, arguing that the tests to measure intelligence are biased against ethnic minorities and lower social classes (Jolliffe & Farrington, 2010). Other studies have found an intermediate relationship between low levels of intelligence and violent offending. Low intelligence may, for instance, lead to school failure, which in turn has a knock-on effect on employment opportunities, which then results in offending. Lower levels of intelligence could also lead to higher levels of impulsivity in an individual, which is also related to violent offending.

Impulsivity, or low self-control, has been the centre of many modern criminological theories to explain violence, including Gottfredson and Hirschi's (1990) theory and theories by Farrington (1989) and Wikström (2019). Impulsivity, or low self-control, has also been linked to the perpetration of homicide, specifically (Salfati, 2003). Impulsivity is a wide concept, encompassing a variety of traits such as risk-taking behaviour, sensation seeking, poor ability to delay gratification, and being inconsiderate of the consequences of one's actions. All of these traits have been found conducive of crime, including violence. As with intelligence, some researchers argue for a direct relationship, while others believe impulsivity to be a mediator between, for instance, school failure or poor parenting and the perpetration of violence. Impulsivity is also part of some neurodevelopmental disorders such as ADHD (Attention Deficit Hyperactivity Disorder), which also has been linked to the perpetration of violence (Gonzalez, Kallis & Coid, 2013). The association between ADHD and homicide has, however, been found to be mediated by substance and alcohol abuse (Kouichi, 2016), which tends to exacerbate ADHD symptoms, such as impulsivity. The association between the use of drugs and alcohol and violence, including lethal violence, has also been widely established through a range of studies (see for instance Yarvis, 1994).

Theories of homicide 45

Genetic predispositions to crime

The advancement of science and the study of genetics has resulted in a range of new tools available for the exploration of criminality. Adoption studies as early as in the 1970s and 1980s demonstrated that having criminal parents increased the child's risk of becoming criminal as well, regardless of having law-abiding foster parents (Baker, Tuvblad & Raine, 2010). While this attests for the general heredity of crime, new neuroscientific studies have been able to link specific genes with the perpetration of crime and violence. This includes the MAO-A gene, which, when functioning properly, breaks down excessive neurotransmitters in the brain (Baker et al., 2010). Low-acting versions of this gene have, however, been shown to result in ineffective functioning of certain neurotransmitters, such as the ones necessary for impulse control, which has been associated with aggressive and violent behaviour. This association has, however, only been found in men who had been the victims of childhood abuse (Caspi et al., 2002), demonstrating that the genetic links to violent behaviour are contingent on environmental factors. This is important to bear in mind since no specific gene alone has been proven to cause violence or criminal behaviour.

Other research has explored neurological links to aggression and homicide using brain imaging such as reduced prefrontal grey brain matter (Raine, Lencz, Bihrle, LaCasse, & Colletti, 2000), abnormal activities of the amygdala (Raine, Buchsbaum & LaCasse, 1997), or other structural or functional deficits of the prefrontal cortex (Yang & Raine, 2009). The genetic and environmental effects on crime are, however, complex, and while many of the studies have found hereditary evidence for property crime, this is less valid for violence (Baker et al., 2010). When it comes to biological explanations of crime, there is also an issue of direction of relationship. For instance, while researchers have not been able to find a conclusive link between testosterone and violence, the studies that have found evidence for this association cannot be certain that high levels of testosterone are causing the violent behaviour and not the other way around (Archer, 1991). This 'chicken and egg' conundrum is a problem of most biological theories attempting to explain aggression or violence, and underlines the importance of caution in relation to these ideas.

There are consequently a number of different biological explanations of violent behaviour. As Brookman (2005) notes, it seems that biological explanations are particularly attractive when trying to explain extreme violence such as serial killing or sexual homicide, cementing these crimes as monstrous or made by the 'Other'. It is, however, important to underline that biological predispositions *cannot alone* explain why some individuals commit violent acts and others do not. Linking criminality to predisposed biological traits may open up dangerous deterministic avenues that could have detrimental effects on how individuals who commit crime are regarded. Such a framing also has important implications for agency; if violence is merely the effect of one's genetic makeup, where does that leave these individuals

46 *Understanding homicide*

in terms of choice, or in terms of responsibility? As mentioned, none of the theories explored in this chapter claim to have the full answer as to why some individuals engage in violence and others do not, but in no other family of theories is this perhaps more important to acknowledge than in the family of biological theories. While there is sufficient research affirming the biological aetiology of crime to warrant exploration, it is important to exercise caution when making implications from this research. Moving on to the next, adjacent family of theories, the following section will explore the psychological theories of violence and homicide.

Psychological theories

Stemming from the biological field of theories, a range of psychological explanations for crime and violence developed towards the end of the nineteenth century, led by psychoanalysts such as Sigmund Freud and Carl Jung. Psychological theories of violence share their individualistic, positivist focus with the biological theories, placing the factors relating to crime within the individual rather than without. This most commonly also entails the perspective of the criminal or violent perpetrator as different from other, nonviolent individuals, and many of the theories aim to find the mechanism that can explain this difference. This section will explore a few psychological theories that specifically looks at violent behaviour, starting with evolutionary psychology.

Evolutionary psychology

Evolutionary psychology is, similarly to the biological theories, based on the idea of behaviour as inherited in a Darwinian sense, meaning that 'every organism acts (consciously or unconsciously) to enhance its inclusive fitness – that is, to increase the frequency and distribution of its "selfish" genes in future generations' (Brookman, 2005: 79). In other words, according to evolutionary psychologists, adaptive behaviour is selected in the process of evolution, influencing the individual's physiology and genes as well as psychology. Regarded this way, violence can be seen as something evolutionary advantageous; as something that provided strategic solutions to problems and even enabled survival. Daly and Wilson (1988) developed a theory of homicide based on the notion of evolutionary psychology, suggesting that this idea of inclusive fitness is the reason most homicides are committed against genetically nonrelated individuals (including friends, strangers, or spouses). The idea here is that individuals would be less inclined to kill someone to whom they are related in order to ensure the survival of one's lineage. While there are a few exceptions to this, such as the murder of one's child, Daly and Wilson (1988) argue that homicide statistics support their evolutionary theory in several ways, even in these cases. First, they argue that step-parents constitute a much higher risk in regards to killing a child compared to biological parents. Second, they

Theories of homicide 47

argue that mothers killing their children are more likely to be single parents who lack social support, and third, mothers who kill their biological children are more commonly young, which means they still have time to have more children. These conclusions are, however, not supported by data in all countries. As Brookman (2005) points out, it is more common for children to be murdered by their biological parents than by stepparents in England and Wales, casting some doubt on Daly and Wilson's (1988) conclusions.

Other evolutionary psychologists focusing on violence more broadly rather than homicide specifically have also found explanations for different types of violence, including domestic violence. For instance, Roach and Pease (2013) argued that domestic violence committed by men was motivated by a desire to restrict sexual behaviour of the partner in order to ensure the reproduction of genes. As such, evolutionary psychology is inherently connected to biological theory and the field of biocriminology (Ray, 2018), meaning that much of the implications of evolutionary psychology should, similarly to the theories explored above, be made with caution. Many of the claims made by evolutionary psychologists are also contingent on other environmental factors, such as unemployment or problems with abuse.

Mental disorders or personality disorders

While there are some links between mental disorders and the perpetration of violence (see, for instance, Shaw et al., 2006), the vast majority of individuals who suffer from some form of mental illness do not have a propensity for violence. Due to the conflation of dangerousness and disorder in the nineteenth century, exacerbated by the strong influence of the medical profession (South, Smith, & Green, 2006), the misrepresentation of mentally disordered individuals as violent still persists. Similarly, there is also a lingering assumption that one has to be 'mad' in order to be able to commit an act such as homicide. Generally speaking, there is no affirmed personality disorder or mental illness that may explain the difference between violent and nonviolent individuals. Rarely, individuals with mental disorders engage in violence and in some instances, violent offenders suffer from mental illness; however, there is no definitive or causal link between the two. In fact, while the circumstances of some homicides may sometimes be so extraordinary and incomprehensible that they defy all rational explanation, the vast majority of homicides occur in rather mundane and relatable circumstances. Yet, within the family of psychological theories, personality disorders or other forms of mental illness frequently arise as potential explanations for violent behaviour. This section will therefore explore the relationship between mental illness and violence and go through some of the disorders most frequently associated with violent or homicidal behaviour.

One of the most misrepresented mental disorders in relation to violence is psychotic disorders such as schizophrenia. These disorders involve an altered, often morphed view of reality and may often include delusions, hallucinations,

48 *Understanding homicide*

and disorganised thought and speech (Nolan-Hoeksema, 2011). Due in part to many misconceived portrayals of 'insane' or maniacal murderers in popular culture, there is a persistent, erroneous idea of individuals suffering from psychotic disorders as dangerous, overly violent, and even homicidal. This is very far from the truth. In fact, research has shown that individuals suffering from psychotic disorders such as schizophrenia are only marginally more likely to engage in violence compared to control groups (Arsenault et al., 2000; Walsh et al., 2004). Research also shows that individuals suffering from schizophrenia are far more likely to hurt themselves than someone else (cf. Haw et al., 2005). Additionally, research has shown that comorbidity in terms of substance abuse is very common in cases where schizophrenic individuals engage in violence, which is also true for individuals with any type of mental disorder (Nolen-Hoeksema, 2011).

Another very common mental disorder connected to violent behaviour is antisocial personality disorder or psychopathy. While these two diagnoses are similar, the terms are not interchangeable. Individuals with antisocial personality disorder have a blatant disregard for the rights of others, manifested in a behavioural pattern of deceitfulness, impulsivity, aggressiveness, recklessness, and lack of remorse (American Psychiatric Association, 2013). Similarly, a psychopathic individual also displays these personality traits, with the addition of callousness, shallow emotions, superficial charm, grandiose self-worth, manipulative traits, and a lack of empathy (Hare & Neumann, 2006). There is consequently a significant overlap between these two constructs, and while diagnostic manuals such as the ICD-10 or the DSM-5 specify antisocial personality disorder, psychopathy is not currently listed within the main diagnostic manuals. Instead, alternative diagnostic tools have been developed to measure the disorder, such as the Psychopathy Checklist (Hare, 1980; Hare, 1996; Hart, Cox, & Hare, 1995). These diagnostic manuals are used as guiding tools by clinicians and medical care professionals when diagnosing mental illness and various disorders. While the manuals are being updated periodically in order to accommodate new research findings and paradigmatic shifts in thinking about mental disorders,[1] it is important to bear in mind that the psychiatric profession such as the American Psychiatry Association creates these manuals. This means that the psychiatric profession dictates what classifies as a mental disorder, and what behaviours fall outside this definition, highlighting that mental disorder, just as homicide, is a social construct.

A significant body of research has arisen exploring psychopathy and its relationship to violence. Such research has established that there is a clear link between psychopathy and the perpetration of violence, demonstrating that individuals with this disorder are more likely than nonpsychopaths to commit violent acts, including homicide (Cornell et al., 1996; Laurell et al.,

---

1 As an example, homosexuality was listed as a mental disorder in older versions of the DSM, but was removed in 1973 for the second edition (Drescher, 2015).

Theories of homicide 49

2010; Williamson, Hare, & Wong, 1987; Woodworth & Porter, 2002). In a meta-analytic review of the relationship between psychopathy and homicide, Fox and DeLisi (2019) also discovered that homicide offenders demonstrate significantly higher levels of psychopathy compared to nonoffenders. Fox and DeLisi furthermore found that psychopathy was particularly prevalent in sexual, sadistic, and serial homicides. Homicides committed by psychopathic individuals furthermore tend to be more instrumental and premediated in nature compared to homicides committed by individuals without the disorder (Woodworth & Porter, 2002).

As such, it would seem that psychopathy offers a reasonable explanation for why some individuals commit homicide and others do not. Many of the personality traits used to define psychopathy seems conducive to violence, such as lacking empathy, shallow emotions, lack of remorse, and callousness. However, far from all homicide offenders are psychopaths and not all psychopaths commit violence. The construct of psychopathy as a disorder has furthermore been contested, both from within the psychological field and from sociological and criminological perspectives. For instance, it has been shown that individuals identified as psychopaths were viewed more negatively and treated more severely by mock jurors both in comparison to individuals with other disorders or no disorder (Edens, Desforges, Fernandez, & Palac, 2004). Due to the stigmatic effect the diagnostic label of psychopathy can have, both in relation to the legal system and among mental health professionals, suggestions have been made to abandon the diagnostic label of psychopathy all together (Edens & Petrila, 2006).

In a similar vein, the lack of concern for social or environmental factors when disaggregating psychopathy has also led to critique. Psychopathy is considered a disorder that is unaffected by socioeconomic or societal factors, which removes society's implication in the aetiology of the disorder. Federman et al. (2009) furthermore argues that psychopathy has become a construct of power – a socio-medical label of dangerousness applied to a wide range of individuals, underpinned by the belief that the perpetration of crime is a personal choice, unaffected by the effects of social structures. This modern-day 'pathology of the monstrous' (Foucault, 1978: 5) serves to further conflate criminality and mental illness, and as Federman et al. (2009) argue, the label 'psychopath' has become the modern-day equivalent of the 'monster', further linking psychopathy with biological dangerousness.

The psychopathic label is thus not a straightforward one. Although there is a vast number of studies attesting to the relationship between psychopathy and the perpetration of violence, this relationship is problematised further by the fact that the perpetration of crime is one of the factors used to diagnose psychopathy. As such, the construct of psychopathy is to some degree circular, where previous violence is used to predict future violence. While research has consistently linked psychopathy to the perpetration of violence and homicide, it is, however, important to acknowledge the limitations of the construct.

50 *Understanding homicide*

Social learning theory

A more environmentally oriented psychological theory explaining violence is social learning theory, developed by Bandura (1973) and later by Akers (1998). The theory stipulates that behaviour such as violence or aggression is learned through a social process of interaction with others. This learning process may be both direct, as in having experienced violence first hand, or indirect, meaning that individuals learn to act violently through observation. In these cases, what is observed could be anything from violence occurring between family members, peers, or even violence happening on TV. The aggressive behaviour is then reinforced by either internal reinforcement, such a sense of pride or achievement, or external reinforcement, such as favourable or positive effects in association with violence.

The idea of violence as something that is learned has been an important cornerstone to the wide-held criminological idea of the intergenerational transference of violence, where children learn to be violent from their parents or other family members. While this theory represents a radically different way to explain the heredity of violence in comparison to the biological and evolutionary theories, it is not without its limitations. As with many other theories, social learning theory fails to provide a satisfactory explanation as to why some children who grow up in violent homes later engage in violence themselves, why others do not.[2] Acknowledging this problem, Collins (2008: 567) developed a micro-sociological explanation of violence based on social learning theory, exploring 'why violence fails to come off in many – indeed a majority – of the situations in which it threatens, and what is distinctive about the dynamics of situations which proceed more and more deeply into the tunnel of violence'. Exploring the situational dynamics of violence, Collins argued that violent offenders use techniques of emotional dominance, controlling their own fear and confrontational tension in order to get the upper hand on their victims. Individuals who are unsuccessful at these techniques also 'fail' at violence, and eventually desist from using violence as a tool to resolve conflicts.

Taking a slightly different social psychological approach to theorising homicide, Katz (1988) explored the exhilarating and even seductive aspects of violence. In his seminal work *The Seductions of Crime* (1988) Katz argues that it is the emotional and sensual attractions of criminality rather than any response to external deprivations that drive individuals to commit violence. Focusing on what it 'means, feels, sounds, tastes or looks like' to commit lethal violence, Katz (1988: 3) argues that most 'typical homicides' are justified from the perspective of the offender, even though the circumstances might seem

---

2 The Swedish term *Maskrosbarn*, roughly translated into 'Dandelion children', is often used in political and social Scandinavian contexts to describe children who grew up in violent or otherwise abusive homes, yet who themselves appear resilient to such a lifestyle. They were termed 'Dandelion children' due to the flower's tenacious ability to push through asphalt.

incomprehensible for any outsiders. The offenders consider their own actions as righteously good, defending themselves against attacks on their values, honour, or beliefs. As such, the emotions experienced by the offender just before the 'righteous slaughter' takes place compels him or her (although, in Katz own admission, mostly him) to respond violently as the offender 'takes humiliation and turns it into rage; through laying claim to a moral status of transcendent significance, he tries to burn humiliation up' (Katz 1988: 312). Providing a contextualised meaning of violence, Katz's theory moves away from the idea of homicide as inherently senseless and instead posits interesting, albeit provocative, questions about the motives and causes of homicide. While Katz's theory has been criticised for ignoring structural background factors relevant to the perpetration of violence (Young, 2003), the idea of violence as exhilarating and seductive has been developed further by for instance Lyng (1990) in his theory of Edgework and other more culturally oriented criminologists. Such theorists, including Ferrell (1997) and Young (2007), are most appropriately placed within the sociological or structural theories of homicide, to which we will turn next.

Sociological theories

Unlike both biological and psychological theories of violence, sociological theories emphasises structural and cultural factors when exploring the causes of violence. Rather than looking to find explanations *within* the individual, these theories tend to look *outside* the individual person, to societal issues and changes that may affect people to commit violent acts. This include large cultural theories attempting to explain international shifts in crime perpetration, such as the crime drop theories, but also small-scale theories attempting to explain why any one individual may be socialised into violent behaviour. While the entire body of sociological theories attempting to explain violence or criminal behaviour is too large to be sufficiently covered in this volume, this section will explore two main types of theories within the sociological field; crime opportunity theories and cultural theories. While these theories can be applied on both macro and micro levels, we will mainly explore these theories on the macro level in this section to provide a balance to the inherently micro-level perspectives of the biological and psychological theories explored earlier in this chapter. We will begin examining the crime drop theories, starting with macro theories looking to explain the crime drop.

Theories explaining the crime drop

While some cultural theories argue that society overall has become more infused with violence (see the next section), most violence scholars agree that the amount of violence and homicide has decreased over time along with almost all other types of crime. Within the context of this crime drop, some scholars such as Elias (1939) and Pinker (2011) argue that violence

52 Understanding homicide

has decreased due to a 'civilisation process', where centuries of societal change have encouraged individuals to develop a higher level of control, decreasing impulsive and rash behaviour that would otherwise lead to violent altercations. In this shift from medieval to modern society, where violence has been constructed as morally wrong and hence become monopolised by the state, a greater interconnectedness between individuals has arisen, which has increased our sense of empathy. All of these factors have, according to Elias (1939), led to an overall decrease of violence in our modern society.

While both Elias (1939) and Pinker (2011) explore the change in violence from a very long-term perspective, other theorists have attempted to explain the more recent drop in crime evident in the latter half of the twentieth century. While many theories have been developed in order to explain the crime drop, including explanatory factors such as shifts in crime justice policies, increased securitisation, and changes to the economic and social societal structure (Aebi & Linde, 2010; Farrell & Brantingham, 2013; Tonry, 2014), the empirical support for these theories has been varied. Furthermore, there is the issue of using national variables such as increased incarceration or legislative changes to explain international crime trends (Farrell et al., 2010). Farrell et al. therefore proposed a theory attempting to explain the crime drop called the Security Hypothesis, drawing on crime opportunity theories. Providing an explanation for the declining trends in crime, especially property crime, Farrell et al. (2010; 2014) argued that increased and improved measures of securitisation have led to a decrease in available targets for crime, which in turn has led to a decrease in crime rates. While the Security Hypothesis mainly explains the falling rates in property crimes such as car theft and burglary, the securitisation process would also affect trends in violent crime. As Farrell et al. (2010; 2014) explain, such property crimes are referred to as 'debut crimes', often constituting the start of a criminal career. Preventing these debut crimes would also prevent young people from engaging in criminal careers, which most likely will involve violent crime. In other words, the Security Hypothesis and the Debut Crime Hypothesis (Farrell et al., 2011; 2014) both propose that violence and homicide would decrease as a result of increased securitisation and decreased availability to offend. While these hypotheses provide an explanation for the changing pattern of public violence, they do not explain any change in violence occurring indoors, such as domestic violence.

Another theoretical explanation for the decrease in violent crime is the Medical Care Hypothesis (Blumstein, 2000; Harris et al., 2002; Smit et al., 2012). As discussed briefly in the previous chapter, this theory proposes that homicide and violence are demonstrating different trends over time due to improvements in emergency services and medical care. As these improvements lead to fewer deaths as a result of violent injuries, homicide trends would decrease while trends in nonlethal violence would increase. As such, the Security Hypothesis and the Medical Care Hypothesis provide contradicting explanations for the relationship between trends in homicide and violence, based on contrasting assumptions about how these crimes change over time.

Theories of homicide   53

In order to tease out these contradictions a bit further, we will return to this issue in Chapter 8 after we have explored the empirical trends of lethal and nonlethal violence in Scotland.

The two crime drop theories mentioned above are both based on the ideas of Situational Crime Prevention (Clarke, 1983; Clark, 1995) and Routine Activities Theory (Cohen & Felson, 1979). As part of classical criminological theory, these perspectives postulate that crime occurs whenever three different elements converge: a motivated offender, a suitable target, and the absence of a capable guardian. Neither perspective aims to provide an explanation as to why individuals commit crime; instead, propensity to crime is understood as given, and focus is centred on the social structures that allow individuals to translate criminal inclinations into action (Cohen & Felson, 1979; Felson & Cohen, 1980). Situational Crime Prevention usually involves measures directed at specific crime types, where the immediate environment is permanently and systematically manipulated, managed, or designed in order to reduce crime opportunities as well as increase the perceived risk by the offenders (Clarke, 1983). This approach has, however, been criticised for merely displacing crime, not preventing it (Guerette & Bowers, 2009). When prevention strategies, such as increased surveillance or control of public spaces, are implemented without combatting the underlying propensity to commit crime, crime may simply be moved; existing somewhere else in another shape or form (Clarke, 1983). The evidence for the extent of crime displacement is, however, mixed, with some scholars arguing that such implementations still have beneficial effects (Guerette & Bowers, 2009).

As such, changes occurring in the pattern of homicide and violence over time may be related to a shift of daily routine activities. Routine Activities Theorists such as Cohen and Felson (1979) and Meier and Meithe (1993) define routine activities as any activity that is part of everyday life, such as work, social interaction or leisure, and theorise that changes in crime trends, including that of homicide, are related to the structural change of routine activities within a society. According to this perspective, the evident decrease in homicide over time might therefore be related to the change of routine activities within Western countries. As such, this theory postulates that the changed circumstances of our everyday lives also have changed the way people kill. In line with this perspective, Aebi and Linde (2010) argue that the evident decrease of lethal and nonlethal violence may be related to decreased interactions in public locations. As particularly young people spend more time indoors, by computers and other forms of entertainment, increasingly less time is spent in public places, leading in turn to fewer opportunities to engage in violence (Aebi and Linde, 2010). The location of the crime has also been linked to socioeconomic status and marginalisation, particularly in regards to youth crime as access to a reliable internet connection and accessibility to entertainment systems and video games are dependent on the socioeconomic status of the offender's family (Aebi & Linde, 2010). As Aebi and Linde (2010) argue, young people who spend less time in public places tend to be

54   *Understanding homicide*

individuals coming from more privileged socioeconomic households. While the relationship between the quality of internet connections and decreased violence has been contested (Farrell et al., 2014), the relationship between marginalisation and violent crime has been widely proven (see, for instance, Brookman, 2005; Land, McColl & Cohen, 1990; Polk, 1994).

Other scholars have also argued that violence has become privatised; meaning that violence has become increasingly more private and less public in nature (Cooney, 2003). As Cooney argues, instances of violence has become considerably more individualised in modern societies compared to earlier societies, occurring more often between just two or a few individuals. Violence has also become more intimate, occurring more commonly between people who know each other well, such as family members or intimate partners (Cooney, 2003). This increased intimacy of violence also means that there has been a steady decrease in violence occurring between strangers, particularly among unrelated men. Cooney argues that these two parallel processes, where violence has become both more intimate as well as more individualised, together have led to a privatisation of violence, where violence in general is being perpetrated in private contexts more often than in public ones. Cooney relates this privatisation of violence to the modernisation process, which has not only contributed to the increased intimacy and individualisation of violence, but which has also reinforced the link between marginalisation and violence. Taken together, these crime opportunity theories including Routine Activities Theory and the privatisation of violence provide relevant insights for theorising the change in lethal and nonlethal violence over time. We will now turn to the second type of theories explored in this section; the cultural theories.

Cultural theories

The change in homicide trends has since long been related to various societal shifts such as cultural and social changes. One of the first scholars to link the change in homicide trends to cultural or social development was Durkheim (DiCristina, 2004; Durkheim, 1951 [1897]; Durkheim, 1957 [1900]). According to Durkheim, rates of lethal violence decrease when the collective bonds tying society together disintegrate. This is because this cultural change increases our 'moral individualism', which in turn increases our respect and value for human life. The disintegration of collective bonds also encourages tougher legislation designed to prevent homicide, which then results in further decreases of homicide. As Durkheim argued, the waning significance of collective bonds in society are symptomatic of a more socially advanced, 'higher' society, relating changes in homicide trends to societal and cultural change.

Contrastingly, Durkheim also argues that 'lower societies' possessing strong, collective bonds along with an intense commitment to family, religion, and other collective institutions instead tend to have higher rates of lethal violence (DiCristina, 2004; Durkheim, 1951 [1897]; Durkheim, 1957

Theories of homicide 55

[1900]). Durkheim relates this to the fact that these societies do not value individual life as much as 'higher' societies. Instead, offences against collective institutions in these 'lower' societies were considered to be 'sacrileges', and could therefore act as 'stimulants to murder' (DiCristina, 2004; Durkheim, 1951 [1897]; Durkheim, 1957 [1900]). Durkheim also argued that increases in suicide or homicide can be traced to the presence of 'anomie', a sense of inability to satisfy one's desires caused by changes in the opportunity structure. Anomie may occur during periods involving great social or economic change, which further links changes in the pattern of homicide and violence to societal changes.

Many scholars have continued to explore the relationship between changes in lethal and nonlethal violence and societal change since Durkheim. These studies have not only explored how the trends in homicide and violence have changed but also how the construction of these crimes have changed over time, as well as what implications these changing constructions have. These scholars often relate the construction of violence to the development of late modernity, which has been described as a society characterised by risk, globalisation, and technical advancements. Late modernity also promotes individualism, creativity, and generation of lifestyle (Young & Hayward, 2012). Young (2007) argues that late modernity is permeated by both paradoxical and contradictive influences, giving rise to both liberative and repressive potentials for all the major institutions. Young furthermore argues that late modernity has caused societal as well as individual feelings of disembeddedness, where norms become dissolved and normative boarders blur and detach. This gives rise to a feeling of ontological insecurity and precariousness, something that Young (2007) refers to as the *Vertigo of Late Modernity*. According to Young (2004; 2007), we are currently living within a Paradigm of Violence, where violence is not only neutralised rather than condemned but which also provides narratives for when and where violence is justified. As Hatty (2000) argues, narratives about violence, as well as the discourses underpinning these narratives, are central to how violence is patterned in society. According to the Paradigm of Violence theorised by Young (2004; 2007), violence is not only overt and explicit but glorified in late modern society. Within this paradigm, modern individuals experience an ontological insecurity – 'an identity in crisis' (Young, 2007: 35) – which gives way for a process of othering as a mechanism to enforce one's own identity. This othering in turn both promotes and facilitates violence (Young, 2007). As such, these ontological and vertiginous insecurities, created by late modernity, can be regarded as conducive to violence.

Building on similar ideas, Giroux (Evans & Giroux, 2015; Giroux, 2013) argues that we are living in a Culture of Violence, where violence, both real and symbolic, has become pervasive and ubiquitous. Symbolic violence can be defined as violence that is usually not recognised as violence, legitimising and confirming inequality structures in society (Bourdieu, 2000). According to the theory by Giroux and Evans (Evans & Giroux, 2015; Giroux, 2013),

56 *Understanding homicide*

human suffering and violent imagery have been turned into spectacles of violence, where the commodification and framing of violent acts renders some lives meaningful, while others are dismissed as disposable, eroding social bonds (Evans & Giroux, 2015). In line with other studies on late modernity (Garland, 2001; Giddens, 1991; Giroux, 2013), the Culture of Violence also works to increase our sense of fear, which also increases measures of control. According to Giroux (2013), the fear induced by the Culture of Violence is particularly pertinent in public places and especially targeted towards youth. This construction of violence has resulted in dramatic increases in securitisation and surveillance measures, while issues of collective security and social welfare has been neglected (Beck, 1992; Evans & Giroux, 2015; Giroux, 2013).

While these cultural perspectives provide a very critical view of societal reactions to violence, measures to decrease violence and other crime in public places have been implemented in most countries in the Western world over the past decades, including Scotland (Scottish Government, 2017f). Both the Paradigm of Violence (Young, 2007) and the Culture of Violence (Evans & Giroux, 2015 Giroux, 2013) relate the construction of violence to issues of identity as well as current power structures in society. Additionally, the Culture of Violence connects violence to masculinity and reaffirms violent acts as an expression of masculinity (Giroux, 2013). The next section will therefore examine the link between gender and violence, including homicide.

Gender and homicide

> The social construction and performance of masculinities are central to understanding violence.
>
> (Ray, 2011: 195)

While there are many different theories concerning homicide and violence, gender has been given particular attention in this volume for several reasons. First, since both homicide and violence are overwhelmingly male activities (Connell & Messerschmidt, 2005; Hatty, 2000; Polk, 1994; 1999), understanding the connection between the construction of masculinity and the perpetration of violence is vital if the changes in these crimes are to be understood. Second, certain aspects of these mechanisms underpinning the construction of masculinity have been shown to increase the lethality of violence. Polk (1994), for instance, argued that violence taking place in the presence of a social audience has a greater risk of ending lethally due to the way masculinity is constructed within this particular context. Third, the link between masculinities and violence seems to have been prominent within the Scottish culture (Fraser, 2015), which highlights the need to examine this link in the current study. Not only has violence been integral to the construction of gender identities in Scotland in the past, evident for instance through the notion of 'the hardman' or 'the fighting man' (Fraser, 2015: 68), but violence and the construction of masculinity is still very much linked in Scotland

Theories of homicide   57

(Fraser, 2013; 2015). This link is particularly evident in gang-related violence (Fraser, 2013; 2015). The social context in which violence and masculinity are expressed is therefore important for understanding how patterns of homicide and violence have changed over time and for explaining any difference between lethal and nonlethal violence. This section will therefore explore the relationship between gender and violence, with a particular focus on the perpetration of homicide.

Many scholars have identified the connection between violence and gender, and the expression of masculinity in particular (Connell & Messerschmidt, 2005; Hatty, 2000; Messerschmidt, 1999; Kreiger & Dumka, 2006; Polk, 1994; Polk, 1999; Ray, 2011; West & Zimmermann, 1987). Overall, it has been widely established in the literature that gender is something we 'do' rather than 'is', and that gender is constantly recreated within different social contexts, affected by social and structural constraints (Butler, 2006; Connell & Messerschmidt, 2005; West & Zimmerman, 1987). Gender identities are therefore changeable, heterogeneous, and fluid – processes rather than products (Hatty, 2000). Masculinities, as part of many different gender identities, are performative, and it is generally considered that there is not just one type of masculinity, but multiple versions, structured by class, social position, and age (Butler, 2006; Hatty, 2000; Ray, 2011). Violence, then, can be seen as a way of expressing or 'doing' masculinity, to solve interpersonal disputes but also to reaffirm the cultural definition of manliness (Butler, 2006; Hatty, 2000; Messerschmidt, 1999; Polk, 1994). In fact, violence has even been described as 'integral to masculinity' (Hatty, 2000: 120). As Hatty argues, the form of masculinity and how masculinities take its expression is related to current male anxieties and worries in society, as ways of overcoming anxieties about issues such as unemployment, sexuality, or identity. The erosion of these boundaries therefore leads to a crisis around the construction of masculinity and a crisis in relation to the boundaries of these constructs. Violence can then function as a demarcation or reaffirmation of such boundaries (Hatty, 2000; Ray, 2011). But violence is also intrinsically linked to marginalisation and a sense of powerlessness (Ray, 2011). Any change in the levels of violence might therefore be an indicator of changing patterns or expressions of masculinities, which is why it is important to examine the link between the two.

Making the link between violence, gender, and class, Polk (1994; 1999) argued that violence is not only masculine but also occur in marginalised circumstances. Violence as an expression of masculinity appears especially prevalent among marginalised men who find themselves cut off from the conventional routes of resolving issues (Messerschmidt, 1999; Polk, 1994). While homicide and violence occurs among people of any social class, marginalised individuals may often find themselves in situations that only seem solvable through violence. As Polk (1994) argues, physical prowess and aggression might no longer be as necessary for the economically advantaged male to reaffirm and express his masculinity. However, for the marginalised male who possess fewer of these resources, violence, including ultimately lethal violence,

58   *Understanding homicide*

might be called into play in order to face challenges of status and to reaffirm their masculinity (Polk, 1994; 1999). This might be one of the reasons why some men do and some men do not use violence as a tool of affirming their masculinity. As Polk argued, scenarios of male homicide are not only masculine, but also distinctly working- or underclass in nature.

A large body of research has focused on the role the construction of masculinity plays into the perpetration of domestic violence, most commonly perpetrated by a sexual partner (Dobash & Dobash, 2011; Connell & Messerschmidt, 2005; Hatty, 2000; Polk, 1994; Polk, 1999; Ray, 2011). When this violence turns lethal, the victim has often separated from the offender, and the violence occurs in an attempt to control the victim or to prevent them from leaving. However, when women kill within the context of a sexual relationship, the murder is often committed in the context of self-defence (Polk, 1994). Research has found that the victim is more likely to be a family member, such as an intimate partner, compared to when men kill, and there is often signs of abuse in such cases (Polk, 1994). In other words, homicides motivated by possession, jealousy and control are emphatically masculine in nature.

Despite the fact that violence and homicide have been defined as predominantly masculine activities (Hatty, 2000; Ray, 2011), research tends to overlook that men most commonly are the victims of this violence as well (Polk, 1999). As Polk (1994; 1999) argues, these male-on-male homicides often emerge as a response to a perceived threat to their status or masculinity. Such 'honour contests' or 'bar brawls' often involve some sort of provocation from either the victim or offender, which may seem insignificant or even trivial to an outsider, such as an insult or spilling a drink. However, if this provocation is viewed as a challenge to one's honour or status, a fight is usually triggered, muddling the lines between victim and offender (Polk, 1999). Other studies have labelled this type of homicide as 'victim participated homicides' (Wolfgang, 1958).

Most of these 'honour contests' are perpetrated in public locations such as pubs or bars, restaurants, or even on the street (Polk, 1999). As Polk describes, the social setting conducive for this type of homicide most commonly includes both a social audience of young male peers, making the honour contest public, as well the presence of alcohol (Polk, 1999). Previous research has also identified the presence of a social audience as a contributing factor to homicide. For instance, Luckenbill (1977: 177), drawing on Goffman's (1967) ideas of 'character contests', argued that homicides involve joint contributions of both the offender and victim who attempt to 'establish or save face at the other's expense', often in front of a social audience. Similarly, Ganpat et al. (2013) demonstrated that the presence of third parties in violent altercation can increase the risk of violence becoming lethal. Homicides involving honour contests have also been described as a 'young male syndrome' (Polk, 1999: 11; Daly & Wilson, 1988), since most of the victims and offenders are relatively young.

However, as Hatty (2000) argues, contemporary society tends to split masculinity into a dichotomous construction of 'the respectable' and 'the dangerous'.

Theories of homicide 59

While fathers, families and individuals in the home tends to be constructed as respectable forms of masculinity, dangerous forms of masculinity are relegated to strangers, sexual predators, and the unknown. As a new 'pathology of the monstrous' (Foucault, 1978: 5), not unlike what we discovered earlier in relation to psychopathy, Hatty argues that this construction creates a misleading dichotomy of violent men. This act of Othering violence masculinity, dividing masculinity into an intrafamilal and extrafamilial dichotomy, works to distract society from violent actions of ordinary men by relegating 'the monstrous to the zone beyond the family, outside the domestic' (Hatty, 2000: 66). This process of Othering violence and violent men perpetuates the construction that only a small minority of the population resemble these violent 'monsters'. The study of the monstrous and how that relates to crime and criminal justice has been explored further in a relatively new branch of criminological study. This emerging Gothic criminology explores not only how the monstrous is constructed but how this relates to our understanding of crime and criminality and the effects this might have on criminal policy. In order to examine how such concepts may be useful to help us get a deeper understanding of homicide, it is to this new perspective we will turn next.

From murderer to monster: exploring serial homicide in popular culture

While the exploration of the 'monstrous' might sound like something belonging to film or literature studies rather than the study of criminality, there is an emerging field within criminology that concerns itself with the study of the Gothic in relation to crime. This Gothic criminology aims to examine the Other as well as the societal construction of the monstrous in both 'real' and 'reel' worlds in order to prompt a critical response (Picart & Greek, 2003). While mentions of the Gothic may bring to mind 'the graveyard, and the convent, the moats and the drawbridges, dungeons, towers, mysterious trap doors and corridors, rusty hinges, flickering candles, burial vaults, birthmarks, tolling bells, hidden manuscripts, twilight, ancestral curses' (Picart & Greek, 2007: 23), the Gothicity of crime transgress these themes. The Gothic permeates contemporary society. The late modern Gothic is mirrored not only in fanciful art or literature but in the way we 'story' transgressive behaviour such as violence and turn it into discourse (Sothcott, 2016). Gothicity is thus prevalent in real-life tales of transgression, ranging from corruption within the police force, the modern day Mr Hydes emerging behind the cracking facades of celebrities and entertainers, and sensationalist reports of serial killers, whose cold and blood-thirsty figures blur into that of the gothic vampire (Picart & Greek, 2007; Sothcott, 2016).

As such, Gothic criminology studies what, and who, we construct as 'monstrous' as well as what effects this may have on discourse, policy-making, crime prevention, and the understanding of crime in general. Such studies include the exploration of the uncanny and abject aspects of the prison in

60   *Understanding homicide*

autobiographical prison literature, reimagining the prison as a monstrous–feminine institution (Fredriksson, 2019), the zombification and normalisation of police violence (Linneman, Wall, & Green, 2014), and the monstrification of intimate partner violence offenders in narratives by professionals working to prevent such violence (Skott, Nyhlén, & Giritli-Nygren, 2021). Gothic criminology does, however, also include the study of how crime and criminality is portrayed in different mediums, such as films, television shows, and even video games. Steinmetz (2018) did, for instance, explore carceral themes of retribution and confinement within the video game series of *Silent Hill*, arguing that the games are expressive of cultural anxieties relating to increased 'securitization and prisonization of society and everyday life' (Steinmetz, 2018: 265). Fawcett and Kohm (2019) furthermore examined the elision of crime and madness in the video games *Batman: Arkham Asylum* (2009) and *Batman: Arkham City* (2011), arguing that the excessive violence prevalent in the game both celebrated aggression while simultaneously offered a visceral critique against excessive punishment. Additionally, Skott and Skott Bengtson (2021) explored carceral violence in the video game *Majora's Mask* (2000), arguing that the themes of carceral violence evident within the text were symptomatic of a deep, haunting disillusionment of carceral justice within the contexts where the game was created. As such, Gothic criminology 'recognises the complementarity of critical academic and aesthetic accounts of deviant behaviour as intersecting with public policy in complex, non-reductive ways' (Picart & Greek, 2007: 11–12).

This also relates to what is known as Popular Criminology (Rafter, 2007: 404), a framework that argues that we need to explore the representation of crime and punishment in its own right, as 'a discourse parallel to academic criminology and of at least equal social and intellectual significance'. According to the perspective of Popular Criminology, the cultural imagination surrounding crime and justice is an important source in order to identify and trace public discourses of criminality and get a deeper understanding of society's attitude towards crime overall. As such, if we are to fully understand homicide in modern society, part of that understanding comes from the exploration of how homicide offenders (and victims) are constructed in popular culture. The following section will therefore examine the construction of homicide in popular culture, using an extreme but mythicised form of homicide: serial killing. By exploring how serial killers are constructed in popular culture, creating a discourse that both forms and is informed by the popular imaginary of serial killers, this section aims to demonstrate the relevance of Gothic and Popular Criminology when attempting to theoretically understand homicide.

Serial killers in popular culture: monstrous humans or humane monsters?

Our modern-day popular culture is fascinated with violence, from taut psychological thrillers and gory horror films to real-crime documentaries; our

Theories of homicide   61

modern society seems to revel in violent crime. One of the most intriguing offenders characterised in these mediums is the serial killer. As Oleson (2005: 186) describes; 'at the pinnacle of this infatuation with crime towers the serial killer'. More than just a fascination, Oleson (2005: 187) argues that this infatuation has inverted the idea of the serial killer, turning them from villains into 'strange heroes'. But as the serial killer motif appears in films, books, and TV shows again and again, we can also see that the way these offenders are depicted has changed; that they are increasingly taking on Gothic expressions. Slowly, the image of the serial killer begins to blend together with that of another cinematic monster haunting our screens; the vampire (Picart & Greek, 2003). Not only do they both have an uncontrollable compulsion to kill, but they both also hold a certain allure; a monstrous power that allows them to break and bend societal conventions and beliefs. As the narrative of the serial killer moves across and converges with fictional narratives, a Gothicisation of serial killing occurs, where the behaviour of these 'real men' are explained using Gothic tropes in the shape of vampires and monsters (Picart & Greek, 2003). As such, the 'contemporary cinematic characterizations of serial killers have appropriated gothic vampire conventions' (Picart & Greek, 2003: 43). One of the most telling examples of this elision of vampire and serial killer in popular culture is Hannibal Lecter in the 1991 film *The Silence of the Lambs*. Inspired by real-life serial killers such as Ed Kemper and Ted Bundy, Lecter still manages to eclipse the notoriety of all 'real' killers, fictional as he may be (Oleson, 2005). This highlights an interesting fusion of fiction and fact in relation to serial killers. As Picart and Greek (2003: 63) state, just as writers of crime fiction such as Thomas Harris spend 'considerable time interviewing profilers and reviewing their case files', profilers themselves also 'rely upon crime fiction'. The idea of serial killers thus becomes a construction – an amalgamation of fiction and fact. As the real influences the reel and vice versa, it becomes increasingly difficult to discern where the true-life serial killers end and the imaginary of the serial killer begins. This furthermore enables a Gothicisation of the serial killer, infusing this construction with vampiric and monstrous elements, such as in the case of Dr Hannibal Lecter. While there is obvious mirroring of the vampire in Lecter's cannibalism, meaning he literally consumes other humans (albeit flesh rather than blood) the vampiric elements to Lecter's character are also evident in his hypnotic stare, supernatural intelligence, and aristocratic elegance (Picart & Greek, 2003). He is dangerous, powerful; almost not human. Described as our 'number one villain' (Oleson, 2005: 191), Lecter is more than just an evil monster that needs to be cast out; his monstrosity is alluring, and it is this appeal that brings Clarice (and the audience) back for more (Picart & Greek, 2003). It is the dangerously sympathetic depiction of this character as brilliant, refined, and even gallant towards the main protagonist, very much in line with our twenty-first century romanticisation of the vampire (Crawford, 2014), which epitomises the Gothic shift in narrative surrounding the male serial killer.

62   *Understanding homicide*

By contrast, female serial killers are often described in rather different monstrous terms. In stark opposition to descriptions of male serial killers such as Ted Bundy, female serial killers such as Aileen Wuornos are depicted as a 'pitiful and ugly outcast, the Frankensteinian Monster' (Picart, 2016: 174). Instead of being described as ruthless, alluring, and intelligent, Wuornos tended to be described as someone in desperate need for love and companionship, who tragically sacrificed everything for a lover who eventually betrayed her (Picart, 2016). By contrasting the fictionalised depictions of Aileen Wuornos in *Monster* (Picart, 2016) and the depictions of the eponymous *Ed Gein* and the (almost) entirely fictional Hannibal Lecter (Picart & Greek, 2003), Picart (2016) demonstrates how the construction of the serial killer is dependent on gender as well as race and sexuality. While their monstrosity takes different expressions, the fictionalised versions of Aileen Wuornos and Ed Gein are, however, both characterised by Gothic tropes.

As such, the Gothicisiation of serial killers in the media renders their narratives more sympathetic and much less the 'other', placing 'the monstrous other as a site for identification' (Picart, 2006: 13). Serial killers are no longer evil others that must be cast out of society; rather, they are the inevitable product of that society, an evil already lurking within. This type of narrative further moves the responsibility from the individual onto society itself, as 'society, rather than the individual, emerges as a primary site of horror' (Picart, 2006: 13). As Picart (2006) states, this increased use of Gothic narratives in relation to serial killers is often underlined by the simultaneous use of the Gothic Doppelgänger trope, where the detective manages to apprehend the villain only by over-identifying with the killer, sparking questions of whether the possibility of violence and corruption exist within us all. The Doppelgänger motif was made particularly prevalent in the NBC re-adaptation *Hannibal* (2013–2015), where the titular Dr Hannibal Lecter is continuously doubled with FBI analyst Will Graham, merging the monstrous and humane until the monster and his pursuer becomes indistinguishable (Abbott, 2018; Carroll, 2015). As such, *Hannibal* pushes the Gothic narratives around monstrosity further, prompting complex questions not only in regards to whether separation of monster and human is possible, but whether the human can even survive without the monstrous at all. As argued by Carroll (2015), this ambivalent characterisation of the serial killer–monster reveals both increasing societal insecurities in relation to the identification of threatening figures but also a realisation that the monster is more complicated than we perhaps would like him to be. As Carroll poignantly asks; 'if, as popular scholars suggest, we create monsters to kill them, what should we make of the need to keep them alive?' (Carroll, 2015: 59).

Overall, the use of Gothic tropes and narratives in relation to serial killers has created a shift in the way serial killers are conceived. Not only monstrous humans, but humane monsters, this character blurs the boundaries between self and other, criminal and cop, and becomes an alluringly repulsive mirror image of ourselves. This fictitious, verisimilar construction, while distorting the line between victim and villain, raising issues with the romanticisation of murder, simultaneously problematises the role of the monstrous 'other', warning against demonisation and opens up questions of the role of the humane within the monstrous. While these constructions offer little theoretical understanding of why individuals commit multiple homicides, they provide a deeper understanding of the popular imaginary of serial killers, which in turn helps to inform discourses of these offenders, and indeed, even academic and professional understandings of serial killers. As such, the exploration of these Popular Criminology discourses, framing serial killers as powerful yet humane monsters, is important in order to get a full understanding of homicide.

Conclusions

This chapter has provided an overview of the dominant theories explaining homicide and violent behaviour, outlining biological, psychological, and sociological theories of crime. While the criticism of particularly biological explanations of homicide in this chapter may appear biased, a central theme of the current book is the cultural and social construction of violence as well as how this affects interpersonal relationships. While perhaps other criminologists within the biocriminological field would find evidence supporting the genetic aetiology of violence, this volume primarily concerns itself with the exploration of the construction of violence in society and the power structures that enable this construction.

This chapter has also provided a closer examination of the relationship between gender and homicide, exploring why men seem to be overrepresented both as victims and offenders of homicide. As the chapter has shown, violence, and sometimes lethal violence, is used as a means to express and affirm masculinities, to 'do' gender. The relationship between violence, masculinity, and marginalisation demonstrated in this chapter is relevant for the understanding of homicide for several reasons. First, since both homicide and violence are overwhelmingly male activities (Connell & Messerschmidt, 2005; Hatty, 2000; Polk, 1994; 1999), understanding the connection between the construction of masculinity and the perpetration of violence is vital if homicide is to be fully understood. The link between masculinities and violence furthermore seems to have been particularly prominent within the Scottish culture (Fraser, 2015). The social context in which violence and masculinity are expressed is therefore important for understanding how patterns of homicide have changed over time and to gain a deeper understanding of homicide.

This chapter has also examined homicide through a Gothic lens, using serial killing as an example. By examining how homicide is constructed in popular culture we can get a better understanding of the discourses shaping the public imaginary of homicide, which in turn affects criminal justice policies and our understanding of this crime. While the theories covered in this chapter can be regarded as the most dominant theories of homicide, this is by no means an exhaustive list. No theory, mentioned here or otherwise, can fully

64 *Understanding homicide*

explain why some individuals commit murder and others do not. The greatest problem that all of these theories must face is the fact that most people do not commit violence. While the possibility of violence exist within us all, the vast majority of people do not inflict serious violence or death upon others. This means that any theory attempting to explain the perpetration of violence must also take into account why the vast majority of people do not engage in violent behaviour. A problem that is not so very easily solved.

This chapter concludes the first part of the volume, where we have laid out the foundations for understanding homicide. As we move on to the second, empirical part of the book, the descriptions and perspectives examined here will hopefully provide a useful foundation for the examination of different types of homicide.

Part II

Different types of homicide

The first part of the book has provided a foundation for understanding homicide. We have explored what really constitutes homicide, how homicide is defined legally, and how this definition differs depending on jurisdiction. We have given particular focus to the differences between the legal definitions in Scotland and in England and Wales and highlighted the issues of comparing homicide transnationally. The dataset used in the following chapter of this volume has also been described in greater detail, and a brief overview of homicide, including previous and current homicide trends describing how this crime has changed over time, has been provided. This section of the book has also contextualised homicide in Scotland by exploring the historical background of this crime; how Scotland went from being 'the murder capital of Europe' to one of the countries with the lowest homicide rates in Europe. Finally, this part of the book has examined different theoretical approaches to understanding homicide. We have explored the most dominant theories used to explain homicide but also examined the link between gender and homicide, as well as explored homicide using a Gothic lens.

The following part of the book will continue to provide a deeper examination at homicide by exploring different types of homicide. This will be done in several ways. Chapter 5 will explore homicides disaggregated by gender and age, examining homicide committed by men, homicides committed by women, homicide committed against children, and homicide committed by children. This will provide a deeper understanding for the heterogeneous nature of homicide, demonstrating that not all homicides are the same. There are, however, many different ways to disaggregate homicide and, as will be discussed in Chapter 6, there are some issues with the *a priori* disaggregation most commonly used. Chapter 6 will therefore propose a new, data-driven approach to homicide disaggregation and these inductive subtypes are presented in this chapter along with how they have changed over time. Finally, the second part of the book will also take a closer look at a very rare but extreme type of homicide: sexual homicide. Drawing on four studies on the subject, Chapter 7 will explore sexual homicide committed by male offenders, homicide committed by female offenders, and homicide committed against child victims before subtypes of sexual homicide will be explored using the

DOI: 10.4324/9781003105282-6

66 *Different types of homicide*

same explorative method outlined in Chapter 6. As such, the second part of the book aims to provide an in-depth analysis of homicide by exploring different types of homicide in Scotland and placing these types in international context. Drawing on the foundations of homicide research laid out in Part I, Part II provides the empirical enquiry and analysis that enables the theoretical framework developed in the final part of the book.

5 Different types of homicide in Scotland

Introduction

Exploring all homicides committed, such as described in Chapter 2, provides a valuable overview of homicide generally in a particular jurisdiction. When homicides are compared internationally, they are often also examined in this aggregate form, including all different types of homicide. However, all homicides are not the same. Homicides may differ radically depending on where they are committed, when, or by whom. For instance, a homicide occurring between two intimate partners after a long time of abuse is very different from a murder taking place between two strangers outside a pub after too much drinking on a Friday night. However, if we examine homicide generally, in aggregate form, we treat all homicides as if they are the same, clustering them all together in the same group. When exploring homicide in this way, any differences between different *types* of homicide are obscured and lost in the analysis. In order to take these differences into account, researches have therefore begun to disaggregate homicide in order to identify and explore different subtypes of this crime. When examining homicide in this way, various differences between types emerges, which would otherwise have remained hidden.

Recent developments in homicide research have underlined the limitations of measuring homicide as a unidimensional construct (Blumstein, 2000; Lehti, 2014; Messner & Savolainen, 2001; Roberts & Willits, 2015; Thompson, 2015). Studies have previously demonstrated that different types of homicide vary across covariates and other variables, and have pointed to the necessity of disaggregation in order to provide a full understanding of this crime (Blumstein, 2000; Block & Block, 1995; Kubrin, 2003; Kubrin & Wadsworth, 2003; Lehti, 2014; Mares, 2010; Messner & Savolainen, 2001; Tapscott, Hancock, & Hoaken, 2012; Thompson, 2015).

This also relates to crime trends. By breaking down homicides by other variables and examining these different types in detail, different patterns than the overall trend can be revealed (Chilton & Chambliss, 2015; Norris et al., 2014). While the overall trend might be one of decrease, there might be hidden countertrends in the data; some types of homicide that have remained

DOI: 10.4324/9781003105282-7

68 *Different types of homicide*

stable, or even increased over time. For instance, when disaggregating homicide in Finland, Lehti (2014) discovered hidden counter-trends obscured by the greater homicide drop. While the overall decline in lethal violence appears to have been driven by a decline in alcohol-related homicides most commonly committed by working-age men, homicides committed by young female offenders had increased (Lehti, 2014). This trend only became apparent when homicide was disaggregated and divided into types. Previous research has also demonstrated that similar underlying patterns might emerge when homicide is disaggregated into subtypes, even though there may be differences on the bivariate level (Messner & Savolainen, 2001; Skott, Beauregard, Darjee, & Martineau, 2021). Blumstein (2000) has similarly argued that aggregate homicide rates can be the product of several, distinct trends that needs to be explored separately in order to explain major shifts in homicide.

It has therefore become widely accepted among international homicide researchers that homicide is a multidimensional phenomenon that needs to be disaggregated if we are to fully understand this crime (Lehti, 2014). There is furthermore an argument in crime trends research which states that changes in aggregate rates may reflect different and potentially opposite trends for different heterogenous subgroups in the population (Hox, 2002; Lindley & Novick, 1981). Exploring these subgroups together, treating them as if they were the same, can lead to erroneous conclusions and data inaccuracies, known as 'Simpson's Paradox' (Hox, 2002: 3; Lindley & Novick, 1981). In other words, even though violent crimes decrease at the aggregate level, this does not mean that all *subtypes* of violence are falling equally. In fact, while some subtypes of lethal violence are decreasing in line with the general trend, other types may remain stable, or might even increase over time. However, if such hidden trends are to be identified, homicides must be disaggregated into subtypes. While the disaggregation of lethal and nonlethal violence would prevent Simpson's paradox, it would also operationalise homicide and violence as multidimensional constructs in line with current homicide research (Blumstein, 2000; Lehti, 2014; Roberts & Willits, 2015; Thompson, 2015).

There are, however, many different ways of disaggregating homicide, ranging from simply grouping murders together based on a single variable to the application of advanced statistical techniques. These various processes, their advantages and disadvantages, will be discussed further in Chapter 6 of this volume. For now, this chapter will take a very simple approach and explore homicide disaggregated by gender and age. First, we will take a closer look at the most common type of homicide – homicides committed by male offenders against adult victims. We will then explore a significantly more rare form of homicide; homicides committed by female offenders, also against adult victims. We will then explore homicides committed against children, regardless of offender gender and lastly, we will examine homicide committed by child offenders. We will explore the characteristics of each of these four homicide types, exploring the victim, offender, and incident variables, as well as how these homicide types have changed over time.

Different types of homicide in Scotland 69

Homicide committed by men

The most common type of homicide by far is homicides committed by men. Between 2000 and 2015 in Scotland there were 1344 cases of homicide committed. These cases involved 1978 offenders in total, of which 1631 offenders, or 83%, were male adults.[1] In other words, the vast majority of homicide cases in Scotland involved a male offender. In order to explore the characteristics of these murders, this section will only examine homicides committed by a male offender.

As can be seen from Table 5.1, the vast majority of victims of male-perpetrated homicides were also men. While 85% of the victims were male, only 15% of the victims were female. This means that the most common type of homicide overall are homicides committed by men against other men. This can be related back to what we discussed in Chapter 4 in relation to gender theories, as homicides has been described as distinctly masculine in nature. The mean victim age of male-perpetrated homicide was 37 years old, and about 40% of the victims were between 16 and 30 years old. The vast majority of the male victims were of white ethnicity and only 2% of the victims were homeless. Homelessness is generally associated with increased risks for violence (Calvo et al., 2021), and individuals who are without a recorded home address tend to be in a more vulnerable position. It is usually therefore

Table 5.1 Victim variables of homicide committed by men

Victim variables		Valid N (%)[a]	Missing (% of total)
Gender	Male	1391 (85.0%)	0 (0.0%)
	Female	245 (15.0%)	
Age	Mean victim age	36.78	27 (1.7%)
	Under 16 years old	0 (0.0%)	
	Between 16 and 30 years old	665 (40.8%)	
	Between 31 and 45 years old	561 (34.4%)	
	Between 46 and 60 years old	306 (18.8%)	
	Between 61 and 75	74 (4.5%)	
	76 years old and above	31 (1.9%)	
Ethnicity	White	1599 (98.0%)	0 (0.0%)
	Other than white	32 (2.0%)	
Residential status	Homeless	27 (2.2%)	401 (24.6%)
	Not homeless	1230 (97.8%)	

Note 1: Base: $n = 1631$.
[a] Percentages may exceed 100% since the data is based on the incident-level.
Source: SHD.

1 All offenders under the age of 16 have been removed, as well as all victims under the age of 16.

70 *Different types of homicide*

Table 5.2 Offender variables of homicide committed by men

Offender variables		Valid N (%)	Missing (% of total)
Age	Under 16 years old	0 (0.0%)	0 (0.0%)
	Between 16 and 30 years old	962 (59.0%)	
	Between 31 and 45 years old	484 (29.7%)	
	Between 46 and 60 years old	152 (9.3%)	
	Between 61 and 75	30 (1.8%)	
	76 years old and above	3 (0.2%)	
Ethnicity	White	1594 (97.7%)	0 (0.0%)
	Other than white	37 (2.3%)	
Residential status	Homeless	35 (3.0%)	463 (28.4%)
	Not homeless	1133 (97.0%)	
Offender suicide	Offender committing suicide	18 (1.1%)	0 (0.0%)

Note 1: Base: n = 1631.

Source: SHD.

measured in relation to violent crime to get a better understanding of victim and offender characteristics.

When the offender variables were examined (see Table 5.2), the data showed that the most common age category of the offenders was, similarly to the victims, 16–30 years old, with almost 60% of the offenders falling in this age bracket. As with the victims, the vast majority of the offenders of male-perpetrated homicide were white and had a recorded home address. Eighteen of the offenders killed themselves after the homicide. Overall, this means that the victims and offenders were very similar in male-perpetrated homicide.

While there are other variables to explore that are relevant when examining homicide, such as employment status, social class, and status of intoxication of offenders and victims, these variables did unfortunately also include high levels of missingness. Since the data used comes from the police, cases can include missing values due to coding errors, unsolved cases, or simply because the officers did not have the time to fill out all of the information. Previous research has, however, shown that there is a clear link between social class, economic inequality, and homicide (Jacobs & Richardson, 2008: Polk, 1994; 1999). While unemployment may be regarded as a type of proxy variable for marginalisation, studies have also found a direct relationship between unemployment and homicide (Ritter & Stompe, 2013). Even though homicides occur in all social strata, there consequently appears to be a particularly strong relationship between marginalisation, inequality, and homicide. This also relates to gender inequality and not just economic inequality (Moore, Heirigs & Barnes, 2021). The link between alcohol and substance use and homicide has also been widely established, where studies have found that alcohol and drug consumption among both offenders and

Different types of homicide in Scotland 71

victims increases the risk of serious violence and homicide (Bye, 2008; Hohl et al., 2017; Lester, 1995).

When the incident variables were examined (see Table 5.3), we can see that the most common method of killing was with the use of a sharp instrument such as a knife or a blade. More than half of all male-perpetrated homicides involved the use of a sharp instrument. A blunt instrument, such as a hammer or a baseball bat, was used in almost a fifth of the cases and a firearm was used in approximately 5% of the cases. While the most common method of killing someone in a male-perpetrated homicide was by the use of a sharp weapon, no weapon was used in about a fifth of the cases. In another quarter of the cases, the victim was killed using physical assault, such as acts of kicking or punching. Death by strangulation or asphyxiation occurred in about 5% of the cases. As we will discuss in Chapter 7, strangulation is quite common in sexual homicide cases but is otherwise not a very common method of killing. Finally, in about 10% of the cases, the method of killing was coded as 'other'. This include cases where the victim was drowned, killed in a fire, or where circumstances were described as 'other'. This could, for instance, involve the use of an unusual weapon (such as a pillow or accelerant) or method of killing (such as hypothermia or an act of defenestration) which does not fit in any other category.

It was most common that the offender of male-perpetrated homicide knew the victim (see Table 5.3). In more than half of the cases, the victim was a friend or acquaintance of the offender. In about 6% of the cases the offender was a relative (such as a parent, child, or sibling) to the victim and in another 10% the victim and offenders were intimate partners. In about a fifth of the cases the victim was a rival of the offender. This is often related to gang-related homicides, where the victim and offenders are feuding with one another. The victim was a stranger in only 9% of the cases, meaning that contrary to popular belief, the vast majority of homicides occur between people who know one another.

The most common motive of male-perpetrated homicide was some sort of fight or argument (see Table 5.3). More than half of the cases were motivated by some sort of quarrel or rage between victim and offender. The second most common motive (14%) was feuding, which, as mentioned above, is most commonly related to gang-related homicides. A financial motive to the murder was evident in about 7% of the cases, and in another 6% of the cases the motive was coded as jealousy or revenge. Only about 4% of the cases was motivated by a domestic dispute, which often involved intimate partners. As mentioned before, sexual homicides are very rare; only about 2% of all the male-perpetrated homicides were sexually motivated. Insanity as a motive for murder was also exceedingly rare; barely 2% of the cases were recorded with this motive. Finally, 'other' as recorded motive, which includes mercy killings, killings in relation to organised crime, and motives that otherwise do not fit within any of the other categories, constituted little more than 5% of cases. In approximately 7% of the cases, the motive was unknown. This may happen

72 Different types of homicide

Table 5.3 Incident variables of homicide committed by men

Incident variables		Valid N (%)	Missing (% of total)
Method of Killing	Sharp instrument	940 (57.6%)	0 (0.0%)
	Blunt instrument	315 (19.3%)	
	Shooting or firearm	90 (5.5%)	
	No weapon used	348 (21.3%)	
	Strangulation or ligature	80 (4.9%)	
	Physical assault	393 (25.6%)	
	Other[a]	170 (10.4%)	
Relationship between offender and victim	Known or acquaintance	533 (54.6%)	654 (40.1%)
	Relative (including parent)	61 (6.2%)	
	Rival	212 (21.7%)	
	Intimate partner	96 (9.8%)	
	Stranger	87 (8.9%)	
Motive	Fight, rage, or quarrel	800 (56.1%)	206 (12.6%)
	Financial (including theft)	101 (7.1%)	
	Insanity	24 (1.5%)	
	Jealousy or revenge	98 (6.0%)	
	Sexually motivated	26 (1.8%)	
	Domestic	58 (3.6%)	
	Feud	200 (14.0%)	
	Other[b]	73 (5.1%)	
	Unknown[c]	103 (7.2%)	
Weapon selection	Weapon improvised	250 (28.4%)	752 (46.1%)
	Weapon brought to scene	429 (48.8%)	
	Weapon selection other	30 (3.4%)	
	Weapon selection unknown	119 (13.5%)	
Public or private location	Public	568 (54.7%)	605 (37.1%)
	Private	541 (52.7%)	
Inside or outside location	Inside	574 (52.7%)	541 (33.2%)
	Outside	586 (53.8%)	
Evidence destruction	Whether the offender destroyed evidence after the homicide	78 (4.8%)	0 (0.0%)

Note 1: Base: $n = 1631$.
[a] Includes drowned and fire as cause of death as well as when the cause of death or weapon was described as 'other'.
[b] Other includes mercy killings as well as homicides motivated by organised crime and motives that otherwise do not fit within any of the other categories.
[c] Unknown motive refers to the cases where Police Scotland could not establish the motive of the homicide

Source: SHD.

in cases where no offender was identified or went unsolved, or if the offender never provided an explanation for their behaviour.

In the homicide cases where a weapon was used the police also recorded how that weapon was selected in relation to the crime (see Table 5.3). In most

Different types of homicide in Scotland 73

cases of male-perpetrated homicide, close to 50% where a weapon was used, the offender brought the weapon with them to the scene of the crime. This could indicate a level of planning or premeditation to the homicide. In little more than a quarter of the cases, the offender took whatever weapon was at hand in an improvised fashion, which would indicate that the crime was not planned in advance. About as many male-perpetrated homicides were committed in a public place (55%) as in a private place (53%), which was also true for crimes occurring inside (52%) and outside (54%). In about 5% of the cases, the evidence of the crime was destroyed. This included cases where the body had been moved, where the body had been covered or buried, where the body had been burned or where the body had been dismembered. Attempting to destroy evidence after the murder may also be seen as a sign of premeditation (in cases where preparations had been taken to dispose of evidence) or forensic awareness on behalf of the offender (Skott, Beauregard, & Darjee, 2021).

Overall, male-perpetrated homicides most commonly involved very similar offenders and victims; white males between 16 and 30 years old who were known to one another. These murders were usually committed using a sharp instrument, most commonly a knife, and were often motivated by some sort of fight or argument. The offender usually brought the weapon to the scene of the crime and it was equally common for homicides to take place in private indoor locations as in public outdoor locations. This type of homicide bear much resemblance to what previous research refer to as 'male-on-male' or 'masculine' homicide (Brookman, 2005). The findings here also resemble what other research has found in different countries. For instance, Hääkänen-Nyholm et al. (2009) found that homicides committed by male offenders in Finland were most commonly committed against male victims who were acquaintances or friends of the offender. The male-perpetrated homicides were most commonly committed with the use of a sharp instrument and the murder was most commonly motivated by some sort of fight or quarrel (Hääkänen-Nyholm et al., 2009). These characteristics of male-perpetrated homicide was also found in Sweden (Trägårdh, Nilsson, Granath & Sturup, 2016), and in England and Wales (Henderson, Morgan, Patel & Tiplady, 2005). While the motive and the relationship between offender and victim was the same in the US, the most common type of weapon used in male-perpetrated homicide was a firearm (Fox & Fridel, 2017). Similarly, while South Korean male-perpetrated murders usually involved acquaintances using a sharp weapon motivated by some sort of argument, it was more common for men to kill other women in South Korea than for men to kill other men (Sea, Young, & Tkazky, 2019). As such, while there are some cultural differences, most male-perpetrated homicides display similar characteristics internationally.

Overall, the characteristics of male-perpetrated homicides are similar to the characteristics of homicide at the aggregate level as described in Chapter 2. This is simply because male-perpetrated homicides constitute the majority of all homicides, and it is therefore this type of homicide which

74   *Different types of homicide*

shape the description of homicide when we look at this crime at the aggregate level. This further highlights the need for disaggregation. Less common types of homicides, such as homicides committed by female offenders, are obscured when homicide is explored at the aggregate level. We will now therefore examine female-perpetrated homicides in order to explore whether there are any differences between these two types of homicide.

Homicide committed by women

About 9% (*n* = 185) of the homicides committed between 2000 and 2015 in Scotland involved an adult female offender killing an adult victim. The majority of these homicides were, similarly to the male-perpetrated homicides, committed against a male offender. As can be seen in Table 5.4, little more than 80% of all the victims were male. The mean age of the victims was 39 years old, and the most common age group was 31–45 years old, which was slightly older compared to homicides committed by men. The vast majority of the victims of female-perpetrated homicides were white and had a recorded home address. The most common age bracket for the women who killed was 16 to 30 years old and the vast majority of offenders were of white ethnicity and had a recorded home address (see Table 5.5). Overall, both the victims and offenders of female-perpetrated homicides were very similar to the victims and offenders of homicides committed by male offenders.

When the incident variables were explored (see Table 5.6), the data showed that the most common method of killing in female-perpetrated homicides

Table 5.4 Victim variables of homicide committed by women

Victim variables		*Valid N (%)*[a]	*Missing (% of total)*
Gender	Male	151 (81.6%)	0 (0.0%)
	Female	35 (18.9%)	
Age	Mean victim age	39.03	1 (0.5%)
	Under 16 years old	0 (0.0%)	
	Between 16 and 30 years old	58 (31.4%)	
	Between 31 and 45 years old	64 (34.6%)	
	Between 46 and 60 years old	52 (28.1%)	
	Between 61 and 75	12 (6.5%)	
	76 years old and above	1 (0.5%)	
Ethnicity	White	179 (96.8%)	0 (0.0%)
	Other than white	6 (3.2%)	
Residential status	Homeless	5 (3.4%)	39 (21.1%)
	Not homeless	141 (96.6%)	

Note 1: Base: *n* = 185.
[a] Percentages may exceed 100% since the data is based on the incident-level.
Source: SHD.

Different types of homicide in Scotland 75

Table 5.5 Offender variables of homicide committed by women

Offender variables		Valid N (%)	Missing (% of total)
Age	Under 16 years old	0 (0.0%)	0 (0.0%)
	Between 16 and 30 years old	95 (51.4%)	
	Between 31 and 45 years old	68 (36.8%)	
	Between 46 and 60 years old	19 (10.3%)	
	Between 61 and 75	3 (1.6%)	
	76 years old and above	0 (0.0%)	
Ethnicity	White	205 (97.2%)	0 (0.0%)
	Other than white	5 (2.7%)	
Residential status	Homeless	7 (5.0%)	44 (23.8%)
	Not homeless	134 (95.0%)	
Offender suicide	Offender committing suicide	0 (0.0%)	0 (0.0%)

Note 1: Base: *n* = 185.

Source: SHD.

was with the use of a sharp weapon, constituting approximately 65% of the cases. A blunt instrument was used in about 16% of the cases and in almost a fifth of the cases, no weapons were used at all. With the exception of shooting as method of killing, which was slightly less common in female-perpetrated homicides, the distribution of method of killing was very similar to that of male-perpetrated homicides. There were, however, some prominent differences between male and female-perpetrated homicide when it came to the relationship between offender and victim. While the most common relationship was someone known, such as a friend or acquaintance, more than a fifth of the female offenders killed an intimate partner. This was more common compared to the male-perpetrated homicides, where only about 10% of the offenders killed their intimate partner. As previous studies have found, victims of female-perpetrated homicides are more likely to be a family member, such as an intimate partner, compared to when men kill, and there are often signs of abuse in such cases (Polk, 1994). It was also less common for female homicide offenders to kill a rival compared with male offenders; only 12% of the cases involved rivals in female-perpetrated homicides whereas a fifth of the male-perpetrated homicides occurred between rivals. Finally, while it was about as common for male and female offenders to kill a relative, it was also less common for female homicide offenders to kill a stranger; while only 4% of the female-perpetrated homicides were committed against someone unknown, nearly 9% of the male homicide offenders killed a stranger.

When the motives of female-perpetrated homicides were examined (see Table 5.6), the most common motive was revealed to be some sort of fight or argument (56%), similar to male-perpetrated homicides. It was, however, more common for female-perpetrated homicides to be motivated by some sort of domestic dispute compared to male-perpetrated homicides; while only 4%

76 *Different types of homicide*

Table 5.6 Incident variables of homicide committed by women

Incident variables		Valid N (%)	Missing (% of total)
Method of killing	Sharp instrument	120 (64.9%)	0 (0.0%)
	Blunt instrument	29 (15.7%)	
	Shooting or firearm	2 (1.1%)	
	No weapon used	36 (19.5%)	
	Strangulation or ligature	6 (3.2%)	
	Physical assault	38 (21.6%)	
	Other[a]	22 (11.9%)	
Relationship between offender and victim	Known or acquaintance	65 (57.0%)	71 (38.4%)
	Relative (including parent)	10 (8.8%)	
	Rival	14 (12.3%)	
	Intimate partner	25 (21.9%)	
	Stranger	5 (4.4%)	
Motive	Fight, rage, or quarrel	92 (55.8%)	20 (10.8%)
	Financial (including theft)	13 (7.9%)	
	Insanity	2 (1.2%)	
	Jealousy or revenge	11 (6.7%)	
	Sexually motivated	4 (2.4%)	
	Domestic	20 (12.1%)	
	Feud	9 (5.5%)	
	Other[b]	9 (5.5%)	
	Unknown[c]	12 (7.3%)	
Weapon selection	Weapon improvised	49 (53.3%)	93 (50.3%)
	Weapon brought to scene	32 (34.8%)	
	Weapon selection other	3 (3.3%)	
	Weapon selection unknown	4 (4.3%)	
Public or private location	Public	34 (31.5%)	77 (41.6%)
	Private	80 (74.1%)	
Inside or outside location	Inside	84 (74.3%)	72 (38.9%%)
	Outside	34 (18.4%)	
Evidence destruction	Whether the offender destroyed evidence after the homicide	12 (6.5%)	0 (0.0%)

Note 1: Base: $n = 185$.
[a] Includes drowned and fire as cause of death as well as when the cause of death or weapon was described as 'other'.
[b] Other includes mercy killings as well as homicides motivated by organised crime and motives that otherwise do not fit within any of the other categories.
[c] Unknown motive refers to the cases where Police Scotland could not establish the motive of the homicide

Source: SHD.

of the male homicides were recorded with this motive, more than a tenth of the female-perpetrated homicides were related to domestic disputes. It was also less common for female-perpetrated homicides to be motivated by a feud; while only about 5% of the women killed because of this motive, the corresponding figure in male-perpetrated homicide was 14%.

Different types of homicide in Scotland 77

In cases were a weapon was used, the weapon was most commonly improvised at the crime scene by the female offenders (53%) (see Table 5.6). Unlike in male-perpetrated homicides, where the offender most commonly brought the weapon to the crime scene, female homicide offenders most commonly used whatever weapon was available at the time of the murder. This could indicate that most of the female-perpetrated homicides were unplanned or impulsive. It was furthermore more common for female-perpetrated homicides to be committed indoors (74%) in private settings (74%) compared with homicides committed by male offenders. While still uncommon, a slightly higher percentage (7%) of the female homicide offenders destroyed evidence after the murder compared to male homicide offenders (5%).

Overall, female-perpetrated homicides were most commonly committed against white male victims between 31 and 45 years old. The offenders were most commonly white and between 16 and 30 years old and very few of both victims and offenders were homeless. The most common method of killing was with the use of a sharp instrument, and when a weapon was used, this choice of weapon was most commonly improvised at the crime scene and rarely brought to the scene by the offender. While nearly half of the female-perpetrated homicides were committed against a friend or an acquaintance, little more than a fifth were committed against an intimate partner. Most of the homicides committed by women were motivated by some sort of fight or argument, and a tenth of the murders was motivated by some sort of domestic dispute. The vast majority of the female-perpetrated homicides were committed indoors in a private location.

These characteristics are also congruent with international research. For instance, studies examining female-perpetrated homicide in the US found that women most commonly killed intimate partners or family members, that they most commonly used a sharp instrument, and that the motive most commonly was some sort of argument (Fox & Fridel, 2017). This pattern was also found in Sweden as well as in England and Wales, where intimate partner homicide constituted the most common type of female-perpetrated homicide (Brookman, 2005; Trägårdh et al., 2016). South Korean female-perpetrated homicides also followed this pattern, where the victims most commonly was a family member (spouse or child) (Sea et al., 2019). While most female-perpetrated homicides in Finland were also committed with a sharp instrument, the most common relationship was, similarly to Scotland, an acquaintance or friend (Hääkänen-Nyholm et al., 2009). Women who killed in Finland were furthermore most commonly motivated by a domestic dispute. Overall, Scottish female-perpetrated homicides appear to be similar to homicides committed by female offenders in other countries. While approximately 20% of the Scottish homicides committed by women was committed against an intimate partner, this was, however, not the most common relationship between victim and offender. Instead, female-perpetrated homicides committed against a friend of acquaintance appear to be slightly more common in Scotland.

78 *Different types of homicide*

While there are some differences between female and male-perpetrated homicides, mainly pertaining to the relationship between victim and offender, motive, and crime setting, there are also many similarities between these two types of crime. This opens up questions of whether there may be other ways of disaggregating homicide that may reveal deeper differences than those apparent here. We will return to the question of how to best disaggregate homicide in later chapters, but first, we will explore the third type of homicide – homicides committed against child victims.

Homicide committed against children

Homicides committed against children often provoke much public outrage and may be considered one of the most disturbing types of homicides. In Scotland, homicides committed against children constituted nearly 5% of all homicides committed between 2000 and 2015 ($n = 93$). While this type of homicide is unusual, it carries a profound emotional impact on communities where they occur. While the definitions of child homicide varies, a child in the current chapter is considered to be any individual aged between 0 and 15 years old.

Children who were victims of homicide in Scotland were most commonly male; close to 70% of all the victims were boys (see Table 5.7). While all victims were under the age of 16, the mean age of the victims was 7 years old. The vast majority of the child victims were white and none of them were homeless at the time of the murder. The offenders of child homicides were most commonly male; 73% of the cases involved a male offender (see Table 5.8). The most common age of the offenders was between 16 and 30 years old, and although the vast majority of the offenders were white, this type of homicide includes a higher degree of nonwhite offenders compared with homicides committed against adults. The vast majority of the offenders of child homicides had a recorded home address at the time of murder, and in only one case did the offender kill themselves after the homicide.

Table 5.7 Victim variables of homicide committed against children

Victim variables		Valid N (%)[a]	Missing (% of total)
Gender	Male	62 (66.7%)	0 (0.0%)
	Female	37 (39.4%)	
Age	Mean victim age	7.28	0 (0.0%)
Ethnicity	White	87 (93.5%)	0 (0.0%)
	Other than white	6 (6.5%)	
Residential status	Homeless	0 (0.0%)	28 (30.1%)
	Not homeless	65 (100.0%)	

Note 1: Base: $n = 93$.
[a] Percentages may exceed 100% since the data is based on the incident-level.
Source: SHD.

Different types of homicide in Scotland 79

Table 5.8 Offender variables of homicide committed against children

Offender variables		Valid N (%)	Missing (% of total)
Gender	Male	68 (73.1%)	1 (1.1%)
	Female	24 (25.8%)	
Age	Under 16 years old	4 (4.3%)	1 (1.1%)
	Between 16 and 30 years old	53 (57.0%)	
	Between 31 and 45 years old	25 (26.9%)	
	Between 46 and 60 years old	9 (9.7%)	
	Between 61 and 75	1 (1.1%)	
	76 years old and above	0 (0.0%)	
Ethnicity	White	81 (88.0%)	1 (1.1%)
	Other than white	11 (12.0%)	
Residential status	Homeless	2 (3.2%)	31 (33.3%)
	Not homeless	60 (96.8%)	
Offender suicide	Offender committing suicide	1 (2.2%)	0 (0.0%)

Note 1: Base: $n = 93$.

Source: SHD.

Unlike in homicides committed against adults, homicides committed against children seldom involved the use of a weapon (see Table 5.9). In almost half of the cases, no weapon was used, and in another quarter of the cases, the victim was killed as a result of physical assault. In a third of the cases, the method of killing was recorded as 'other', a third of which involved fire as cause of death. The most common relationship between victim and offender was a relative, often a parent; in more than 60% of the cases, the child was killed by a relative. The offender was also more likely to be the parent if the child was killed by a woman. While most of the children who were killed in Scotland were killed by a male offender, women who killed children most commonly killed their own child whereas men who killed children most commonly killed someone else's child. The children who were killed by female offenders often tended to be younger (mean age 2 years old) than children killed by men (mean age 9 years old). A stranger killed the child in little more than 16% of the cases. While a fight, rage, or quarrel was the most common motive of child homicide (26%), a fifth of the motives was recorded as 'other' and another fifth was recorded as 'unknown'. This highlights the fact much still remains unknown about homicides committed against children.

In the cases that involved a weapon, the offender most commonly brought the weapon with them to the murder scene (see Table 5.9), which could indicate a level of planning. Similarly to female-perpetrated homicides, the majority of homicides against children were committed indoors (63%) in private locations (70%) which suggest that these murders most commonly occur in the home. In a tenth of the cases, the offender destroyed the evidence after the homicide was committed, which also could indicate a level of planning.

80 *Different types of homicide*

Table 5.9 Incident variables of homicide committed against children

Incident variables		Valid N (%)	Missing (% of total)
Method of killing	Sharp instrument	23 (24.7%)	0 (0.0%)
	Blunt instrument	15 (16.1%)	
	Shooting or firearm	2 (2.2%)	
	No weapon used	45 (48.4%)	
	Strangulation or ligature	11 (11.8%)	
	Physical assault	25 (26.9%)	
	Other[a]	31 (33.3%)	
Relationship between offender and victim	Known or acquaintance	13 (15.3%)	8 (8.6%)
	Relative (including parent)	53 (62.4%)	
	Rival	4 (4.7%)	
	Intimate partner	2 (2.4%)	
	Stranger	14 (16.5%)	
Motive	Fight, rage, or quarrel	24 (25.8%)	0 (0.0%)
	Financial (including theft)	6 (6.5%)	
	Insanity	5 (5.4%)	
	Jealousy or revenge	3 (3.2%)	
	Sexually motivated	3 (3.2%)	
	Domestic	1 (1.1%)	
	Feud	6 (6.5%)	
	Other[b]	19 (20.4%)	
	Unknown[c]	21 (22.6%)	
Weapon selection	Weapon improvised	7 (26.9%)	67 (72.0%)
	Weapon brought to scene	15 (57.7%)	
	Weapon selection other	1 (3.8%)	
	Weapon selection unknown	2 (7.7%)	
Public or private location	Public	23 (40.4%)	36 (38.7%)
	Private	40 (70.2%)	
Inside or outside location	Inside	37 (62.7%)	34 (36.6%)
	Outside	22 (37.3%)	
Evidence destruction	Whether the offender destroyed evidence after the homicide	10 (10.8%)	0 (0.0%)

Note 1: Base: $n = 93$.

[a] Includes drowned and fire as cause of death as well as when the cause of death or weapon was described as 'other'.

[b] Other includes mercy killings as well as homicides motivated by organised crime and motives that otherwise do not fit within any of the other categories.

[c] Unknown motive refers to the cases where Police Scotland could not establish the motive of the homicide

Source: SHD.

Overall, homicides committed against child victims demonstrate substantial differences from homicides committed against adults. While the offender characteristics are quite similar to adult homicides, with the exception of offender ethnicity, the incident variables differ substantially. Not only are most children killed without the use of any weapon, unlike adult homicide where

Different types of homicide in Scotland 81

a sharp instrument most commonly is used, children are most commonly murdered by blood relatives rather than acquaintances or strangers. There is furthermore less known about the motive behind child homicides compared to adult homicides, even if many homicides against children are motivated by a fight or argument, similarly to adult homicide. Child homicides most commonly occur in private, indoor locations, most likely the home, and the characteristics of this type of homicide would indicate that they often involve some degree of planning by the offender. Considering these differences, it is not surprising that many studies regard homicides committed against children as a separate type of homicide (Azores-Gococo, Brook, Teralandur, & Hanlon, 2017; Skott, 2019).

Previous studies of this type of homicide have argued that homicide committed against children is one of the least understood categories of homicide (Azores-Gococo et al., 2017). Research conducted in England and Wales as well as the US has found that homicide committed against children is often committed by a male offender and is often intrafamiliar in nature (Azores-Gococo et al., 2017; Pritchard, Davey, & Williams, 2013). In these instances, it was most commonly the parent who killed the child. A Dutch study also showed that child homicides may sometimes be part of multiple family homicides, or familicides, where one parent, often a father, kills the spouse before killing the children (Liem & Reichelmann, 2014). When the victim is the child of the perpetrator (filicide), the reported motive may be altruism (relieve the child of real or imagined suffering), acute psychosis, that the child was unwanted, unintentional murder due to abuse, or spousal revenge (Azores-Gococo et al., 2017; Bourget & Gagné, 2002). Research has also shown that there are significant differences between intrafamilial and extrafamilial homicides, where extrafamilial murders tended to involve male offenders, slightly older victims, strangulation, and sexual motivation (Alder & Polk, 2001; Cavanagh, Dobash, & Dobash, 2005). As such, although much remains unknown, it would seem that there are some international similarities when it comes to homicide against children, which includes Scotland.

Homicide committed by children

The fourth and final type of homicide that will be discussed here is homicide committed by young people. Just as with the previous type of homicide, children or young people are here defined as individuals between 0 and 15 years old. In total, there was $n = 61$ homicides committed by children in Scotland between 2000 and 2015, which constituted 3% of all homicides. This is, in other words, a very rare type of homicide. The majority of child-perpetrated homicides were committed against a male victim; 77% of the cases involved a male victim (see Table 5.10). The most common age span of the victims was 16 to 30 years old, meaning that homicides committed by children were usually committed against someone older than the offender. As with the other homicide types, the vast majority of both the victim and offenders were of white ethnicity and none of the offenders or victims were homeless (see Tables 5.10

82   Different types of homicide

Table 5.10 Victim variables of homicide committed by children

Victim variables		Valid N (%)[a]	Missing (% of total)
Gender	Male	47 (77.0%)	0 (0.0%)
	Female	14 (23.0%)	
Age	Mean victim age	33.41	3 (4.9%)
	Under 16 years old	4 (6.6%)	0 (0.0%)
	Between 16 and 30 years old	27 (44.3%)	
	Between 31 and 45 years old	20 (32.8%)	
	Between 46 and 60 years old	5 (8.2%)	
	Between 61 and 75	4 (6.6%)	
	76 years old and above	1 (1.6%)	
Ethnicity	White	57 (93.4%)	0 (0.0%)
	Other than white	4 (6.6%)	
Residential status	Homeless	0 (0.0%)	16 (26.2%)
	Not homeless	45 (73.8%)	

Note 1: Base: $n = 61$.
[a] Percentages may exceed 100% since the data is based on the incident-level.
Source: SHD.

Table 5.11 Offender variables of homicide committed by children

Offender variables		Valid N (%)	Missing (% of total)
Gender	Male	57 (93.4%)	0 (0.0%)
	Female	4 (6.6%)	
Age	Mean offender age	14.6	0 (0.0%)
Ethnicity	White	58 (98.3%)	2 (3.3%)
	Other than white	1 (1.7%)	
Residential status	Homeless	0 (0.0%)	25 (41.0%)
	Not homeless	36 (100%)	
Offender suicide	Offender committing suicide	0 (0.0%)	0 (0.0%)

Note 1: Base: $n = 61$.
Source: SHD.

to 5.11). The vast majority of the offenders of child-perpetrated homicides was male; 93% of the offenders were boys, and only $n = 4$ offenders (7%) were girls. While all the offenders were under the age of 16, the mean offender age was 14.6 years old, meaning that the majority of offenders were between 14 and 15 years old at the time of crime. None of the offenders committed suicide after the homicide was committed.

Exploring the incident variables of child-perpetrated homicide (see Table 5.12), nearly half of the homicides involved the use of a sharp instrument, such as a knife. In nearly 45% of the cases, the victim was killed using

Different types of homicide in Scotland 83

Table 5.12 Incident variables of homicide committed by children

Incident variables		Valid N (%)	Missing (% of total)
Method of killing	Sharp instrument	30 (49.2%)	0 (0.0%)
	Blunt instrument	15 (24.6%)	
	Shooting or firearm	1 (1.6%)	
	No weapon used	16 (26.2%)	
	Strangulation or ligature	0 (0.0%)	
	Physical assault	24 (43.6%)	
	Other[a]	6 (9.8%)	
Relationship between offender and victim	Known or acquaintance	14 (60.9%)	38 (62.3%)
	Relative (including parent)	2 (8.7%)	
	Rival	10 (43.5%)	
	Intimate partner	0 (0.0%)	
	Stranger	2 (8.7%)	
Motive	Fight, rage, or quarrel	29 (53.7%)	7 (11.5%)
	Financial (including theft)	5 (9.3%)	
	Insanity	0 (0.0%)	
	Jealousy or revenge	4 (6.6%)	
	Sexually motivated	5 (9.3%)	
	Domestic	0 (0.0%)	
	Feud	6 (11.1%)	
	Other[b]	2 (3.7%)	
	Unknown[c]	3 (5.6%)	
Weapon selection	Weapon improvised	14 (50.0%)	33 (54.1%)
	Weapon brought to scene	11 (39.3%)	
	Weapon selection other	0 (0.0%)	
	Weapon selection unknown	1 (3.6%)	
Public or private location	Public	27 (73.0%)	24 (39.3%)
	Private	12 (34.3%)	
Inside or outside location	Inside	14 (35.0%)	21 (34.4%)
	Outside	28 (70.0%)	
Evidence destruction	Whether the offender destroyed evidence after the homicide	1 (1.6%)	0 (0.0%)

Source: SHD.

Note 1: Base: $n = 61$.

[a] Includes drowned and fire as cause of death as well as when the cause of death or weapon was described as 'other'.
[b] Other includes mercy killings as well as homicides motivated by organised crime and motives that otherwise do not fit within any of the other categories.
[c] Unknown motive refers to the cases where Police Scotland could not establish the motive of the homicide.

physical assault, which would include instances of kicking or punching, and in a quarter of the cases, no weapon was used at all. In approximately 10% of the cases, the method of killing was coded as 'other', which included drowning, killing by fire, and methods of killing that did not fit any of the other categories.

84 *Different types of homicide*

The most common relationship between offender and victim was someone known, like a friend or an acquaintance (see Table 5.12). More than 60% of the offenders were friends or acquaintances with their victims, and in 44% of the cases, the victim was a rival to the offender. In approximately 9% of the cases, the victim was related to the offender. Another 9% of child-perpetrated homicides was committed against a stranger. The most common motive for children who killed was some sort of fight or argument with more than half of the cases falling into this category. More than a tenth of the cases was motivated by some sort of feud between victim and offender, and in 7% of the cases, the motive was jealousy or revenge. In 9% of cases, the motive was reported as sexual. This was considerably higher than any of the other homicide types, where only around 2–3% of the cases were sexually motivated. Although the percentage was quite high, this still only involved five offenders. It was equally common for the homicide to be financially motivated, such as be related to a theft or robbery, as it was to be sexually motivated. If a weapon was used in the homicide, the offender had most commonly brought it with them to the crime scene, which, as in previous types, could indicate planning or premeditation. Only one case, however, involved evidence destruction, which also could be consider a sign of premeditation. Most of the cases occurred in public locations (73%) outdoors (70%).

Previous research examining child-perpetrated homicide in other jurisdictions such as the US have found that most young offenders who commit homicide are male, and they are likely to have used drugs or alcohol and to commit the murder using a firearm (Farrington, Loeber & Berg, 2012; Heide, 2003; Heide, Solomon, Sellers, & Chan, 2011). Research has also shown that the most common relationship between victim and offender in child-perpetrated homicide was a stranger, followed by an acquaintance, and that most homicides were motivated by some sort of fight or conflict (Heide et al., 2011). Studies have also shown that young people who kill often had both a previous criminal record of violence as well as were likely to have been the victims of violence themselves (Farrington et al., 2012; Heide, 2003). While there are some obvious differences to child-perpetrated homicides in Scotland, such as, for instance, the prevalent use of firearms in the US, there are also some similarities between jurisdictions. Overall, child-perpetrated homicides is a very rare type of homicide on which we currently have very little information. In the Scottish data, it would furthermore appear that this small group of offenders primarily consisted of younger teens rather than small children. There were many similarities between child-perpetrated homicides and male-perpetrated homicides, which may be related to the fact that the vast majority of the child homicide offenders were male. As previous research has found clear differences between young male and young female homicide offenders, particularly in regards to the relationship between offender and victim and method of killing, it would seem that gender is important for the characterisation of young homicide offenders (Heide, Roe-Sepowitz, Solomon & Chan, 2012). The same study also found similarities between young female and adult female-perpetrated homicide, as well as similarities between young and adult male-perpetrated homicides, suggesting that gender might be more relevant than age when disaggregating homicide. Research has, however, also shown that the characteristics of child-perpetrated homicides are dependent not only on offender gender, but offender age (Heide et al., 2011). Homicides committed by child offenders aged 6–12 years old demonstrated differences compared to homicides committed by offenders aged 13–17 years old, particularly in regards to relationship between offender and victim, where younger offenders tended to kill an acquaintance and slightly older offenders tended to kill a stranger. This would also suggest that simply disaggregating homicide based on gender and age may be inadequate for gaining a deeper, more comprehensive understanding of homicide. We will return to this matter in Chapter 7 for further discussion. The final section of this chapter will, however, explore how these different types of homicide have changed over time.

Change in homicide types over time

In order to explore how the different types of homicide has changed over time in Scotland, the data was divided into four time periods: 2000–2003, 2004–2007, 2008–2011, and 2012–2015. This was done due to the low number of homicides in each type of homicide per year. The data was indexed at the first time period, which means that all other time periods are compared against the first one. As can be seen from Figure 5.1, the number of all homicides has decreased over time in Scotland. In fact, homicide overall has decreased by 42% in 2012–2015 compared to 2000–2003. Overall, all homicide types with the exception of female-perpetrated homicides increased in the second time period (2004–2007), before demonstrating a marked decrease (see Figure 5.2). Female-perpetrated homicide instead increased in the third time period

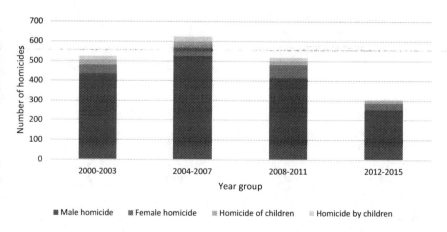

Figure 5.1 Number of types of homicides over time 2000–2015

86 *Different types of homicide*

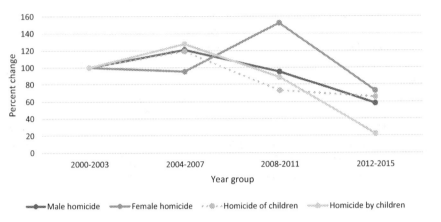

Figure 5.2 Percentage change in homicide types over time 2000–2015

(2008–2011), demonstrating a dramatic 52% increase in comparison to 2000–2003. Female-perpetrated homicide subsequently decreased in 2012–2015, demonstrating a decrease of 27% compared to the first time period. Overall, this homicide type demonstrated the smallest decrease over time.

After the peak in male-perpetrated homicide in 2004–2007, this type of homicide subsequently declined, demonstrating a total decrease of 42% in 2012–2015 compared to 2000–2003 (see Figure 5.2). Similarly, homicide committed against children decreased after the peak of 19% in 2004–2007, demonstrating a total decline of 35% from the first time period to the last. Child-perpetrated homicides demonstrated the largest decline over time. Peaking in 2004–2007 by 28%, this homicide type subsequently demonstrated a dramatic decline of 78% in 2012–2015 compared to the first time period.

Overall, this analysis suggests that while all types of homicide identified here had decreased over time, the largest decrease was evident in cases where a young person committed homicide. The data also shows that while most homicide types increased in 2004–2007, female-perpetrated homicides peaked a little later, in 2008–2011 before declining along with the other types of homicide. It is, however, important to note the vast differences in number of homicides. While female-perpetrated homicides and homicides committed by children demonstrate the most extreme variations over time, these two types of homicide had quite a low number of cases, meaning that even small changes in number lead to large proportional changes. The most common type of homicide by far was male-perpetrated homicide, which also had demonstrated a marked decrease over time (see Figure 5.2).

Conclusions

This chapter has explored different subtypes of homicide based on offender gender and age. Male-perpetrated homicide, which constituted the vast

Different types of homicide in Scotland 87

majority of all homicides committed in Scotland, was predominantly committed against a male victim between 16 and 30 years old who were known to the offender. These murders were usually committed using a sharp instrument and were often motivated by some sort of fight or argument. The offender usually brought the weapon to the scene of the crime, and it was equally common for homicides to take place in private indoor locations as in public outdoor locations. Homicides committed by female offenders, while similar in certain aspects to their male counterparts, differed from male-perpetrated homicides in regards to relationship, motive, and locus. It was noticeably more common that female-perpetrated homicides occurred in the context of intimate partner violence, where the victim was an intimate partner, the motive was a domestic dispute and the homicide took place inside a private setting.

This chapter has also explored homicides committed against child victims. This type of homicide differed substantially compared to adult homicide. Not only were most children killed without the use of any weapon, unlike adult homicide where a sharp instrument most commonly was used, but children were most commonly murdered by blood relatives rather than acquaintances or strangers. Child homicides most commonly occurred in private, indoor locations, and the characteristics of this type of homicide would indicate that they often involved some degree of planning by the offender. The fourth and final type of homicide that was explored was homicides committed by child offenders. While exceedingly rare, this type of homicide, predominated by teenaged male offenders, was very similar to adult homicides committed by men. This suggested that offender gender might be more important when disaggregating homicide compared to offender age. Finally, this chapter explored how these homicide types have changed over time. While all types of homicide had demonstrated marked decreases over time, homicides committed by child offenders demonstrated the largest decline, decreasing by nearly 80%.

As we have now explored different types of homicide based on gender and age of the offender, what have we learned so far? While there are some distinct differences between different types of homicide, as demonstrated here, this chapter has also established the limitations of this type of disaggregation. For instance, while male-perpetrated homicide differed from homicides committed by women, particularly in regards to location of the crime and relationship between offender and victim, there were also many similarities between these two types of homicide. While one of the reasons for this result may be that male and female homicide offenders are very similar, another explanation may also be that any potential differences are still obscured. For instance, the male-perpetrated homicides explored here are most commonly committed against male victims, and are best described as what Brookman (2005) refers to as 'masculine' or male-on-male homicides. However, a smaller subset of these offenders commit homicide against intimate partners, yet they are obscured in this group since the male-on-male homicides are so much more frequent. Similarly, there appears to be a subset of homicides perpetrated by women who kill their intimate partner (21%) and a close relative (9%), which

88 *Different types of homicide*

might have been better as separate homicide types. This opens up the question of how to disaggregate homicide in order to provide the most specified, yet still generalisable homicide types possible. As this is an important question, and directly relevant to the main argument of this volume, the next chapter will therefore discuss this matter further.

6 Disaggregating homicide
Explorative subtypes

Introduction

As discussed in the previous chapter, there are many different ways of disaggregating homicide into subtypes. We attempted to disaggregate homicide based on gender and age in the previous chapter, and while the results were interesting, the findings demonstrated that this basic typology did not cover all the different nuances necessary for disaggregating homicide. For instance, while there seemed to be underlying differences between female and male perpetrated homicide, these differences were obscured by the rather crude method of disaggregation used in the previous chapter. This chapter will therefore explore another explorative method of disaggregation, which takes the data's own structure into account. Before this, we will however explore different typologies of homicide identified in previous research in order to get a better understanding of various ways to identify homicide typologies, as well as what variables that may be important for homicide disaggregation.

Typologies of homicide in previous research

There are many different typologies of homicide that overall appear to be more diverse than similar (Polk, 1994: 20). Wolfgang (1958) was among the first scholars to examine different types of homicide and his work remains influential to this day (see, for instance, Brookman, 2005; Ganpat et al., 2013; Polk, 1994). Wolfgang (1958) was not only among the first scholars to argue that victims and offenders should be examined together as social actors of the same event but also among the first researchers to note that homicide most commonly occur among people who know one another. Even though Wolfgang's study included variables relating to the victim, offender and the incident of homicide, many of the earliest developed homicide typologies were based almost exclusively on classification variables concerning the incident, including the organised/disorganised typology developed by Hazelwood and Douglas (1980). Other typologies have focused solely on the offender, such as the instrumental/expressive typology (Block & Block, 1995; Salfati, 2000), or the victim, such as the typology of Pizarro, Zgoba, and

DOI: 10.4324/9781003105282-8

90 *Different types of homicide*

Jennings (2011), focusing on the victim's criminal lifestyle. There is, however, an argument that examining the aspects of homicide separately does not offer a clear overall picture of the context in which this crime takes place, and that any comprehensive analysis of this crime should take all three aspects of a homicide case into account (Beauregard & Proulx, 2007; Meier, Kennedy & Sacco, 2001). More recently, typologies exploring all three of these aspects have therefore been developed, and it is to this body of research that we will now turn.

Typologies based on offender, incident, and victim variables

When exploring homicide typologies based on the incident, the offender, and the victim, five typologies in previous research were identified. Morton, Runyan, Moracco, and Butts (1998) proposed a typology of homicide–suicides involving female victims older than 15 years old. Based on US data between 1988 and 1992, the typology was based on more than 100 variables relating to the victim, the offender, and the incident of homicide (see summary in Table 6.1). Three types were identified in Morton et al.'s (1998) homicide–suicide typology: Type I (characterised by a history of conflict between the offender and victim, sometimes with additional nonfamilial victims); Type II (which included children as additional victims, sometimes even the entire family); and Type III (which included elderly victims of declining health, very similar to 'mercy killings' in previous literature).

Wood Harper and Voigt (2007) also proposed a typology of homicide–suicides based on US data. Five types were identified based on variables measuring the relationship between offender and victim, the motivation of the offender, type of fatal injury, location of the event, and characteristics of the offender and the victim: *Intimate or Domestic Lethal Violence–Suicide*; *Family Annihilation–Suicide*; *Mercy Killing–Suicide*; *Public Killing Spree–Suicide*; and *Mistaken or Accidental Homicide–Suicide. Intimate or Domestic Lethal Violence–Suicides* took place between intimate partners, most commonly a male partner against a female partner, where most cases involved the use of a gun. The offender was often unemployed and the homicide–suicide often seemed unplanned. *Family Annihilation–Suicides* were most commonly committed by a family member against another relative, most often a child, was often planned, and included both female and male offenders. *Mercy Killing–Suicides* were most commonly committed by older (75 years and older) offenders against victims of a similar age where the victim was suffering from a chronic critical illness. *Public Killing Spree–Suicides* were most commonly committed by male offenders, often occurring in the workplace or in schools. The last type of homicide–suicides described by Wood Harper and Voigt (2007) was the *Mistaken or Accidental Homicide–Suicide*, which was characterised by a mistaken homicide, followed by the suicide of the offender due to the guilt of the crime. Although homicide–suicides are considered rare, many of the variables used by Wood Harper and Voigt (2007)

Disaggregating homicide 91

Table 6.1 Homicide typologies based on victim, offender, and incident variables

Typology	Name of types	Classifying variables[a]
Bijleveld & Smit, 2006	Business/personal; and personal-settlement-impersonal escalation/angry brawl	(*Motivation of the offender; Relationship to victim*[b]); offender characteristics; victim characteristics; method of killing; locus; previous criminal record; premeditation
Morton et al., 1998	Type I; Type II; Type III	Offender characteristics, victim characteristics; relationship to victim; method of killing; motivation of the offender; presence of other victims; and locus
Pridemore & Eckhardt, 2008	Neither drinking; offender drinking; victim drinking; and both drinking	(*Intoxication*); Offender characteristics; victim characteristics; relationship to victim; method of killing; and context (day, time, season).
Pizarro, 2008	Domestic; drug; robbery; interpersonal dispute; and other	(*Motive*); Offender characteristics; victim characteristics; relationship to victim; method of killing; locus; and context (day, time, season)
Wood Harper & Voigt, 2007	Intimate/domestic; family annihilation; mercy killing; public killing spree; and mistaken/accidental	Offender characteristics; victim characteristics; relationship to victim; method of killing; motivation of the offender; and locus

[a] These variables were summarised into these more general themes.
[b] Variables put in brackets indicates that these variables were used to define typologies *a priori*.

are used in the development of other homicide typologies, suggesting their relevance for homicide disaggregation.

Based on alcohol use of both the offender and victim, Pridemore and Eckhardt (2008) developed a typology of homicide events in a Russian context. Four types were identified: *Neither Participant Drinking; Offender Drinking; Victim Drinking;* and *Both Drinking*. These types were then compared on 11 variables measuring victim, offender, and event characteristics (Pridemore and Eckhardt, 2008). The study demonstrated that there were significant differences between all four types of homicide events but also between alcohol and nonalcohol-related homicides. Alcohol-related homicides were more likely to occur at night, on weekends, and to result from acute arguments, and less likely to occur between strangers, to be profit motivated, to be premeditated, and to be committed in order to hide other crimes. Pridemore and Eckhardt consequently found that the distribution of several homicide characteristics on the incident level varied significantly based on the absence or presence of

92 *Different types of homicide*

alcohol, which would strongly suggest that alcohol is an important variable when disaggregating homicide.

Similarly to Pridemore and Eckhardt (2008), Pizarro (2008) examined the situational covariates of different homicide subtypes based on US data. Five subtypes were identified *a priori* based on the motive of the offender: *Domestic* homicide, *Drug* homicide, *Robbery* homicide, *Interpersonal Dispute* homicide, and *Other* homicide. *Domestic* homicides were most commonly committed within a residence, and often occurred as part of a pattern of abuse against an intimate partner or family member. As such, a subset of the victims in this subtype were child victims. While this type of homicide most commonly involved male victims, this subtype included the highest number of female victims compared to the other types. The *Drug* homicides most commonly involved men who were known to each other, such as friends or acquaintances, and were predominantly committed in a public setting in the context of the sale or distribution of illegal drugs. While the *Robbery* homicides also tended to be committed in public, this type of homicide was predominantly committed in the context of a robbery. The *Robbery* homicides most commonly involved male victims as well as male offenders. Similarly to the *Drug* homicides, the *Interpersonal Dispute* homicides were most commonly committed between male friends or acquaintances in public locations outdoors with a higher than average level of intoxication among both victims and offenders. Unlike the *Drug* homicides, the *Interpersonal Dispute* homicides were, however, motivated by some sort of conflict that was not related to drugs or domestic disputes. The fifth and final type Pizarro (2008) identified was the type labelled *Other*, including all remaining homicides. The homicides in this type was most commonly perpetrated in a public location, often with the use of a firearm, and most commonly occurred between male friends or acquaintances. Despite being disaggregated by offender motivation, the subtypes in Pizarro's (2008) typology were quite similar. However, when comparing the subtypes regarding temporal aspects, event characteristics and variables relating to the victim and the offender, the study found significant differences that confirmed the need to examine homicide in a disaggregated manner.

Lastly, Smit, Bijleveld, and van der Zee (2001) created a typology of 11 subtypes of homicides based on both the motive of the offender and the relationship between the offender and the victim: *Criminal Background* (divided into contract killing, drug-related, and other); *Sexual*; *Robbery*; *Dispute* or a *Fight* (divided into intimates, acquaintances and strangers); *Psychotic*; *Other*; and *Unknown*. Developing this typology further, Bijleveld and Smit (2006) used a method called multiple correspondence analysis in order to examine the relationship between these 11 identified types and 17 other variables measuring the relationship between victim and offender, the cause of death, the location, and characteristics of the victim and offender. This study demonstrated that although homicides can be structured meaningfully, the homicides could not be separated into clearly defined categories or types. Instead, the homicide types should be interpreted dimensionally along two axes measuring business/personal, and personal settlement–impersonal escalation/angry brawl. Although Pridemore and Eckhardt (2008), Pizarro (2008), and Bijleveld and Smit (2006) all used homicide typologies that had been developed *a priori*, the results of this research demonstrate that situational covariates differ between subtypes of homicide. This indicates that both the variables used to classify homicide as well as the situational covariates examined would be relevant to include in a homicide typology.

Towards an exploratory approach to disaggregation

There are consequently several variables relating to the victim, offender, and the incident of homicide that are relevant for the disaggregation of homicide. As can be seen from Table 6.2, a total of 23 variables were identified as important across these five studies. Although the identified subtypes differed between typologies, the variables on which the types were based were very similar. While this raises questions regarding the validity (both internal and external) of the types themselves, the persistent inclusion of these variables when disaggregating homicide has demonstrated their value. In light of these findings, these 23 variables were used as a starting point for the identification of subtypes in this chapter. As this review of previous typology literature has demonstrated, the method of disaggregation is quite diverse, ranging from identifying subtypes based on a single variable to using distance-based clustering techniques.

As explained in Chapter 1, one of the aims of the current volume is to examine the changing characteristics and patterns of homicide in Scotland and to determine the extent to which changes in homicide reflect the changing characteristics and patterns in nonlethal violence. As argued in the previous chapter, homicide and violence should also be regarded as heterogeneous

Table 6.2 Classifying variables in typologies in Table 6.1

Victim variables (n studies)	Offender variables (n studies)	Incident variables (n studies)
Age at time of crime (4)	Age at time of crime (4)	Method of killing (5)
Gender (4)	Gender (5)	Relationship between offender and victim (5)
Employment status (3)	Employment status (3)	Motive (5)
Ethnicity (4)	Ethnicity (4)	Locus (5)
Influenced by alcohol or drugs (2)	Influenced by alcohol or drugs (4)	Premeditation of the offence (1)
Residential status (1)	Residential status (1)	Context (day, time, or season) (2)
Previous criminal record (1)	Previous criminal record (2)	
Victim precipitation (2)	Suicide of the offender (2)	
	Mental illness (1)	

94 *Different types of homicide*

constructs which need to be disaggregated in order to be fully understood. Otherwise, the multifaceted aspects of lethal and nonlethal violence may be lost, and hidden trends in the data may go undetected. In order to fulfil this aim, subtypes of both homicide and violence need to be identified and explored over time. In order to be able to disaggregate lethal and nonlethal violence based on victim, offender and incident-level variables, some form of statistical clustering technique was necessary. As demonstrated by the previous section, various methods have been employed to identify such subtypes in previous research. Some studies, such as the research conducted by Morton et al. (1998) and Wood Harper and Voigt (2007), disaggregated homicide into subtypes by conducting a qualitative examination of different variable groupings on a case-by-case basis. While very data sensitive, this method is quite subjective and, as the types identified were very much at the discretion of the researchers, potentially not very replicable on a larger scale.

Other researchers have identified homicide subtypes with the use of one single variable, such as motive or gender, before comparing these subtypes regarding other variables using regression analysis. For instance, Pizarro (2008) divided homicides into different subtypes based on the motive of the offender and Pridemore and Eckhardt (2008) used the influence status of both the victim and the offender to identify subtypes of homicide. While this method remains common in typology research, it is a less inductive approach to identifying subtypes compared to other available methods. As we have demonstrated in the previous chapter, this method may furthermore still obscure hidden types and trends in the data. By utilising an inductive, explorative methodology we can not only get results that are closer to the actual data, but this will also allow for the identification of new or previously unknown subtypes. Studies using a deductive approach, identifying subtypes *a priori* based on previous theory (see for instance Pizarro, 2008; Pridemore & Eckhardt, 2008) may only identify subtypes that are already known to the researchers. While important in order to test the validity of different subtypes, the deductive method may consequently miss important subtypes that exist in the data, leading to biased results. The *a priori* approach does furthermore not enable the examination of different combinations of important variables when disaggregating lethal and nonlethal violence. As indicated by the review of the typology literature above, motive and the influence of alcohol both appear to be important variables when disaggregating homicide. However, if subtypes are disaggregated using these variables separately, the effect of the empirical combination of these variables, or indeed, the combination of any other variables, remains unknown. As such, it is important to utilise an explorative, inductive approach to the identification of subtypes if a deeper understanding of homicide is to be obtained.

Using such an inductive approach, there are other, statistically more sophisticated methods used in typology research to identify subtypes of homicide and violence. Such studies have, for instance, used different forms of distance-based clustering techniques in order to identify subtypes of homicide, such as multiple correspondence analysis (Bijleveld & Smit, 2006), smallest space analysis (Salfati, 2000; Salfati & Canter, 1999), or two-step cluster analysis (Liem & Reichelmann, 2014). While slightly different approaches, these three clustering techniques all have the common aim to identify subsets in the data that are as similar as possible within the groups but as different as possible between groups (Rokach & Maimon, 2010). By using a statistical technique such as cluster analysis, the researcher also has the advantage of using multiple variables when identifying subtypes. However, there are some issues with distance-based clustering techniques. While useful and relatively straightforward, these methods are designed to identify similarities between cases based on their proximity using measures of distance, such as for instance Euclidian distance (Ketchen & Shook, 1998; Romesburg, 1984), making them sensitive to the scale of the variables. Although the variables could be standardised (converted into z-scores), this reduces variability and the distance between clusters, risking biasing the results (Cornish, 2007; Ketchen & Shook, 1998; Romesburg, 1984). As the research in the current volume involves categorical data, techniques using distance-based measures, which are mostly used with continuous data, are furthermore less suitable. Distance-based techniques classify cases into groups based purely on their proximity, without making any assumptions about the underlying distribution of the data or any underlying relationships between the variables. This however constitutes a problem in the current study since the data used is quite complex. The homicide dataset, described briefly in Chapter 2, is hierarchical, meaning that since the offenders (and victims) are nested in cases, data exists on two different levels. The data furthermore has issues relating to missingness. This type of data thus requires a disaggregation technique that is capable of taking these complexities into account. One such technique, called Latent Class Analysis (LCA), assumes that the subtypes of homicide are latent constructs that explains the heterogeneity in the data. A latent variable can be described as a construct that cannot be observed directly, but which measures an underlying concept and which usually affects observed variables. Latent constructs can furthermore be used to simplify or reduce data and identify underlying patterns. In this study, subtypes of homicide are taken to be latent constructs since these subtypes are assumed to be 'heuristic devices' (Sampson & Laub, 2005; Skardhamar, 2009) and not representative of distinctive groups of people or cases in the population.

There has been a debate in previous research regarding the problematic theoretical implications of classifying individuals into specific types or groups, specifically when these types imply causal differences (see, for instance, Nagin & Tremblay, 2005; Sampson & Laub, 2005; Skardhamar, 2009). In light of this debate, it is important to clarify that any subtypes identified in the current volume merely represent one of many possible descriptions when conducting complex modelling on imperfect data. As such, this study does not make any causal inferences. Instead, the subtypes identified in the current study may be regarded as a summary of complex data, conducted in order to provide

96 *Different types of homicide*

a deeper understanding of homicide overall, as well as to understand the relationship between trends in lethal and nonlethal violence in Scotland over time. When conceived this way, the subtypes are considered to be latent constructs in the data that can be measured through other observed variables. As such, the statistical technique used to identify subtypes in the current study is required to be robust enough to handle the practical issues with the data (such as missingness) as well as be able to model the underlying latent structures in the data. LCA is one such technique, and the following section will provide a brief overview of LCA as a technique and how it was used in the current study.

Disaggregating homicide using MLCA

LCA uses a probabilistic model to describe the distribution of the data, and the model assumes that the identified subtypes are related to a latent variable (McCutcheon, 2002). The technique postulates that there are one or more subgroups in the data, and that the identification of these subgroups might explain any heterogeneity in the data (Lanza, Tan & Bray, 2013). If the technique identifies only one subgroup, which would include the entire dataset, as the best solution, it is assumed that the identification of subtypes is unhelpful when explaining the heterogeneity in the population. As such, when using LCA as a technique to identify subtypes in the current dataset, the subtypes are considered to be latent variables that are related to the difference between cases of homicide. This means that whereas distance-based clustering techniques simply identify clusters based on their similarity, model-based techniques like LCA identify clusters based on their probability of belonging to the latent constructs. The model-based probabilistic nature of the technique also makes it possible to determine goodness of fit of the model, which is not possible with other forms of cluster analyses. Due to these reasons, LCA is often regarded as a more powerful clustering technique compared to other statistical methods, especially when using categorical data (Magidson & Vermunt, 2004). Compared to distance-based cluster analysis, LCA also has the advantage of involving fewer pre-decisions of the method, such as choice of aggregation algorithm and similarity measure (Mutz, Bornmann, & Daniel, 2013). Since the inclusion of such decisions made by the researcher affects the results, risking biasing the outcome, it is preferable to use a technique where these decisions are kept to a minimum.

LCA is not only capable of handling dataset issues such as missingness and hierarchical structures of the data, but the technique is also replicable and takes any underlying data structures into account. Model-based multilevel modelling using an EM-algorithm,[1] such as LCA, has been found superior to distance-based multilevel modelling on almost all accounts, including

---

1 For more information about the Expectation-Maximisation (EM)-algorithm, see McCutcheon (2002) and Muthén and Muthén (1998–2012).

Disaggregating homicide 97

clustering accuracy on both levels (Serban & Jiang, 2012). Even though such model-based techniques are computationally heavier compared to distance-based methods, LCA was considered the best suiting clustering technique for the current study and it was therefore decided to use LCA as a statistical method to identify subtypes in the data. This sort of technique can be modelled either on one level or on multiple levels depending on the data structure. Single-level LCA models, however, usually assume independence between cases, an assumption that many empirical datasets violate due to the fact that observations are often nested within groups (Henry & Muthén, 2010; Tabachnick & Fidell, 2013). For instance, the current study involves offenders and victims that are both nested within homicide incidents. In order to take this structure into account, it is therefore preferable for the current study to utilise a multilevel technique.

When discussing multilevel models, the lowest level is often described as the 'within' level whereas the second level with fewer cases is often referred to as the 'between' level. For instance, in a case of homicide offenders nested in homicide cases, the offenders would constitute the within level and the cases would be on the between level. Multilevel modelling permits the data to be modelled on more than one level, which is why it is an appropriate technique for clustered data such as the current dataset (Tabachnick & Fidell, 2013). This type of technique allows prediction of individual scores adjusted for group differences as well as the prediction of group scores adjusted for individual differences. Multilevel modelling takes care of these issues by permitting the intercepts as well as the slopes of the analysis to vary between different groups or units (Tabachnick & Fidell, 2013; Vermunt, 2003). This means that the relationship between dependent variables and independent variables is permitted to vary between groups.

Multilevel LCA (MLCA) is in other words a type of LCA that takes these hierarchical structures in the data into consideration. MLCA addresses this issue by allowing latent class intercepts to vary across between-level groups, thereby examining if and how these between-level groups influence the latent classes on the within level (Henry & Muthén, 2010). That is, the probability for an offender to belong to a certain class is likely to vary significantly across different homicide cases. In a two-level LCA model, the log-odds of belonging to one specific class rather than another are allowed to vary between groups (or in this case, homicide cases). By doing this, the nonindependence of observations is modelled and therefore accounted for. Although one of the downsides with MLCA modelling is the difficulty of convergence as well as long computation time (Tabachnick & Fidell, 2013), this type of modelling provided the most appropriate representation of the data in the current study and was therefore chosen as the best statistical technique.[2]

---

2 For more technical details on how single-level LCA modelling is extended to multilevel LCA, see Vermunt (2003).

98 *Different types of homicide*

Since probabilistic methods are used to identify the subtypes, any victim, offender, or incident in the current study has a different probability of belonging to each of the various classes the model identifies. A victim could, for instance, have an 80% probability of belonging to a certain class, but that means that the same victim has a 20% probability of not belonging to this class. This means that there will always be classification error in the model, as with any model that aims to disaggregate data into groups. As mentioned, it is therefore important to note that all the classes and types discussed in the current volume are meant as 'heuristic devices' (Sampson & Laub, 2005; Skardhamar, 2009), aimed to provide a more detailed description of homicide and violence and not as to represent actual or real groups of people or cases in the population.

Two model parameters were estimated using the software program Mplus: (a) individual probability (which is an estimate of every offender's probability of appearing in each class or subtype) and (b) class probability (which is an estimate for each class's average score on each of the observed classifying variables). Both of these parameters were used to describe the characteristics of the classes. The MLCA model also estimates two latent constructs: a within-level multinomial latent variable (classes of offenders) and a between-level multinomial latent variable (classes of incidents and summarised victim variables). For the sake of clarity, the between-level subtypes will be called subtypes and the within-level classes will be called classes. The classifying variables used to identify subtypes of homicide were chosen based on homicide typologies identified in previous research, which had examined all three aspects of a homicide case: the victim, the offender, and the incident itself. As such, the variables were chosen because they are theoretically assumed to disaggregate homicide etiologically. The variables, listed in Table 6.3, were all prevalent in previous research. As can be seen from Table 6.3, however, some variables had a very high level of missingness. Even though great efforts were made in order to decrease missing data, including extensive discussions with Police Scotland, recoding of the variables, and manual searches through the synopses of cases, a cut-off point of 60% missing data (which constitutes the majority) was implemented. This meant that certain variables, such as the level of intoxication among offenders, were excluded from analysis. While the missingness remains an important caveat to the study, additional analysis of the missing data indicated that the missingness had limited effect on the classes identified.

Overall, this resulted in a model with six classifying variables relating to the offender, which were introduced on the within level of the model; six classifying variables relating to the victim; and six variables relating to the incident, which were introduced in the between-part of the model (Skott, 2019). As in the previous chapter, time was divided into four year groups (2000–2003; 2004–2007; 2008–2011; 2012–2015), which were added as covariates in the between model, using the first year-group as the reference category. In order to explore how homicide had changed over time, two different measures were used; absolute and relative change over time.

Table 6.3 Classifying variables used in the homicide dataset

Victim variables (% missing)	Offender variables (% missing)	Incident variables (% missing)
Age at time of crime (0.0%)	Age at time of crime (0.6%)	Method of killing (0.0%)
Gender (0.0%)	Gender (0.0%)	Relationship between offender and victim (39.4%)
Employment status (47.8%)	Employment status (46.1%)	Motive (11.8%)
Ethnicity (0.0%)	Ethnicity (0.8%)	Public or private location (39.1%)
Influenced by alcohol or drugs (55.7%)	*Influenced by alcohol or drugs (72.9%)*	Inside or outside location (33.8%)
Residential status (25.0%)	Residential status (29.0%)	Weapon selection (47.8%)
	Suicide of the offender (0.0%)	

Note 1: Base: $n = 1978$.
Note 2: Percentage missing was calculated based on the number of homicide offenders.
Note 3: Offender influence status is in italics since this variable was excluded from the modelling due to high missingness.

Source: SHD.

Absolute change over time was measured by using an estimated number of offenders per year group while relative change over time was measured using the average probability for each between class per year group. The mean probabilities per year group were calculated in several steps. First, the individual probabilities for each offender was saved. That meant that every offender had a probability score for each of the different possible homicide subtypes (combination of within and between classes) that were identified in the model. Second, the probabilities of each between class were summed for each individual, which meant that every person had a summed probability for each between-level class. Third, these summed probabilities were subsequently averaged per each year group by calculating the mean of this summed probability over each year group. This resulted in an estimate measuring how likely each between class was in any year group compared to any other year group, and whether there had been a relative change over time. The average probability of belonging to each class per year group was then plotted over time. This provided a measure of the relative change of the homicide subtypes over time.

In order to compare the average probability of the classes in any given year group to the average probability of the same class in any other given year group, Mann Whitney U-tests were conducted in order to determine if the change in average probability was statistically significant. Mann Whitney U-tests were chosen instead of t-tests due to the assumed non-normality of the data, as well as the low number of data points. Bonferroni correction of the p-values, usually applied to reduce Type I error (Tabachnik & Fidell,

100 *Different types of homicide*

2013), was not implemented since this method has been criticised for reducing statistical power of the analysis as well increasing Type II error to unacceptable levels (Nakagawa, 2004; Perneger, 1998). Instead, effect size was reported using an approximate value of r^3 (Pallant, 2010).

In order to measure absolute change of the homicide subtypes over time, the estimated number of offenders per year group was calculated. This was done by multiplying the average probability of each year group by the total number of offenders in each year. That resulted in an estimate of the number of offenders per homicide type per year group. This allowed for the absolute change in homicide types to be explored over time. Since this was a summary measure (estimating the number of offenders by summing the individual class probabilities of each class per year group), no significance tests were conducted to examine the difference between year groups. Both of these measures were calculated in order to examine the absolute and relative change in homicide types over time. Even though the homicide types might be decreasing in absolute terms, there might be a relative increase in some types, and both these measures were therefore deemed important.

In order to estimate goodness of fit of the MLCA model, three statistical criteria were used alongside the substantive interpretation of the classes: the Akaike information criteria (AIC), the Bayesian information criteria (BIC), and the sample size–Adjusted Bayesian Information Criteria (ABIC; McCutcheon, 2002; Nylund, Asparouhov, & Muthén, 2007). In addition to these values, the entropy value was also compared. The entropy statistic is a measure of certainty of class membership, and the closer the entropy value is to one, the more distinct and clearly defined are the classes (McCutcheon, 2002; Vermunt & Magidson, 2002). Although entropy is not a pure fit statistic, it does provide a measure of how clearly defined the classes are (McCutcheon, 2002) and can therefore be considered relevant when deciding on the number of classes. These different values were examined and compared for different model solutions in order to identify the best fitting model. As can be seen in Table 6.4, MLCA models were run with up to four subtypes on the between level and four classes on the within level. Examining the fit criteria, where the lowest values are the most advantageous, the 4–3 model had the best BIC and ABIC while the 4–4 model had the best AIC. When the 4–3 model was compared to the 4–4 model, it was found that the additional offender class of the 4–4 model did not help distinguish between the classes. The additional class created in this model appeared to separate the female offenders which, although interesting, meant that all other traits were very similar across the four classes. The 4–3 model appeared more distinct as well as substantively interesting, so it was selected as the best fitting homicide model. The names of the classes were decided based on the most common, or in some cases, most unique traits of the subtypes or classes. The following section will now move on to explore the actual subtypes of homicides in the 4–3 model.

---

3 Calculated as: $r = z$/square root of N (Pallant, 2010).

Table 6.4 Class selection statistics of two-level LCA Homicide model (2000–2015)

No. of classes (between-within)	Loglikeli-hood value	AIC	BIC	Percentage change in BIC	ABIC	Entropy
1–2	-24148.83	48445.67	48859.31	N/A	48624.21	0.491
2–1	-20936.46	42088.92	42692.62	-12.62	42349.50	0.915
2–2	-20786.64	41813.30	42484.10	-0.49	42102.80	**0.907**
2–3	-20178.95	40701.91	41663.36	-1.93	41116.91	0.899
2–4	-20740.42	41768.84	42573.77	2.19	42116.28	0.777
3–2	-20178.95	40701.91	41663.36	-2.14	41116.91	0.899
3–3	-20145.39	40660.78	41694.90	0.08	41107.14	0.853
3–4	-20127.48	40650.95	41757.74	0.15	41128.69	0.818
4–2	-19712.34	39872.69	41124.81	-1.52	40413.16	0.837
4–3	-19650.39	39776.80	**41107.20**	-0.04	**40351.02**	0.763
4–4	-19623.95	**39751.90**	41160.50	0.13	40359.90	0.75

Note 1: Base: $n = 1978$.
Note 2: Best values indicated in bold.
Source: SHD.

Subtypes of homicide

Since the data was hierarchical, meaning it existed on two levels (the offender level nested in the incident-level, with victim variables summarised), the modelling was done on an offender-based dataset. This means that the within-level of the homicide model consisted of the offender variables, and the between-level consisted of the victim and incident variables. The two-level LCA modelling was conducted on all cases, including the missing data.

Between (incident and victim) subtypes

As mentioned, the best fitting model of homicide was a 4–3 model, meaning that there were four subtypes of homicide based on a combination of the characteristics of the incident and the victim and, within these types, there were three classes of offenders. When the four between subtypes of the 4–3 model were examined, it was revealed that the model had identified four medium-sized subtypes (see Table 6.5).

Stabbing type

The first and largest type, labelled the *Stabbing* type (31.9%, $n = 630$), consisted of homicides committed with the use of a sharp weapon (see Figure 6.1). Most of these weapons were improvised at the scene of the crime by the offender, meaning that they grabbed what was at hand (see Figure 6.2). The vast majority of the offenders and victims were friends, acquaintances or by some

102 *Different types of homicide*

Table 6.5 Identified subtypes of homicide

Type	N	Percentage of between group	Percentage of all cases
1. Stabbing subtypes (31.9%, *n* = 630)			
a. Young Unemployed Offender Stabbing	186	29.5%	9.4%
b. Mixed Unemployed Offender Stabbing	433	68.8%	21.9%
c. Employed Offender Stabbing	11	1.7%	0.5%
2. No Weapon–Bludgeoning subtypes (27.2%, *n* = 540)			
a. Young Unemployed Offender No Weapon–Bludgeoning	267	49.4%	13.5%
b. Mixed Unemployed Offender No Weapon–Bludgeoning	231	42.7%	11.7%
c. Employed Offender No Weapon–Bludgeoning	42	7.9%	2.1%
3. Rivalry subtypes (24.9%, *n* = 492)			
a. Young Unemployed Offender Rivalry	450	91.5%	22.7%
b. Mixed Unemployed Offender Rivalry	0	0.0%	0.0%
c. Employed Offender Rivalry	42	8.5%	2.1%
4. Femicide subtypes (16.0%, *n* = 316)			
a. Young Unemployed Offender Femicide	0	0.0%	0.0%
b. Mixed Unemployed Offender Femicide	189	59.9%	9.6%
c. Employed Offender Femicide	127	40.1%	6.4%

Note 1: Base: *n* = 1978.

Source: SHD.

means known to each other (see Figure 6.3) and the most common motive for the *Stabbing* homicides were some sort of fight or argument (see Figure 6.4). Most of the *Stabbing* homicides occurred in a private location indoors (see Figures 6.5–6.6). The victims of this subtype was most commonly male and were commonly under the influence of either alcohol or drugs at the time of the murder (see Figures 6.7 to 6.8). The victims were furthermore often unemployed, but very few were homeless. The majority were of white ethnicity and the most common age of the *Stabbing* subtypes victims was 31–45 years old (41%), while approximately a third were 16–30 years old (see Figure 6.9).

No Weapon–Bludgeoning *type*

The second between-level subtype was labelled the *No Weapon–Bludgeoning* type (27.3%, *n* = 540) since the most common method of killing was by physical assault, and in three fifths of the cases no weapon was used at all (see Figure 6.1). A blunt instrument was used in about a third of the cases. Similarly to the *Stabbing* subtype, the weapon used in this type of homicide were usually improvised at the scene (see Figure 6.2). Overall, the *No Weapon–Bludgeoning* type was very similar to the *Stabbing* type with the

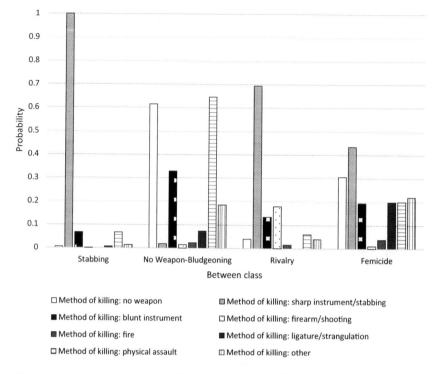

Figure 6.1 Class response probabilities of method of killing
Note 1: Base: $n = 1978$
Source: SHD

exception of method of killing. The most common motive was some sort of argument or fight (see Figure 6.4) and most of the cases were committed in a private location inside (see Figures 6.5 to 6.6). The most common relationship between the offender and victim for the *No Weapon–Bludgeoning* subtype was someone known, like a friend or acquaintance, although around a quarter of cases involved relatives (see Figure 6.3). Around 16% of the *No Weapon–Bludgeoning* cases were committed between strangers, which was higher than for the *Stabbing* type.

When the victim characteristics of the *No Weapon–Bludgeoning* type were examined, it was revealed that most of the victims were male, and, similarly to the victims of the *Stabbing* subtype, under the influence of alcohol or drugs (see Figures 6.7 to 6.8). The victims of the *No Weapon–Bludgeoning* type were also commonly unemployed, had a recorded home address and were of white ethnicity. These victims, however, tended to be older than the *Stabbing* victims; the most common age of the *No Weapon–Bludgeoning* type was 46–60 years old, with almost as many victims being 31–45 years old (see Figure 6.9).

104 Different types of homicide

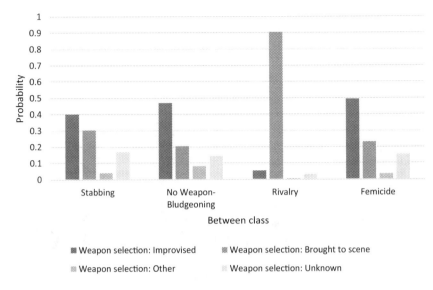

Figure 6.2 Class response probabilities for weapon selection
Note 1: Base: $n = 1978$
Source: SHD

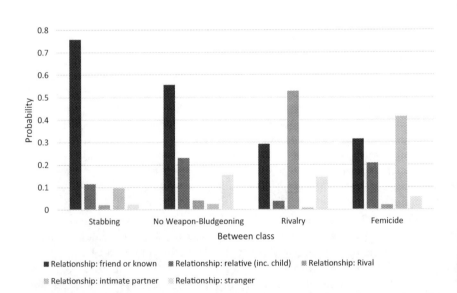

Figure 6.3 Class response probabilities of relationship between offender and victim
Note 1: Base: $n = 1978$
Source: SHD

Disaggregating homicide 105

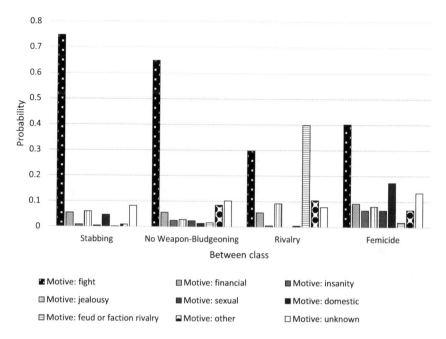

Figure 6.4 Class response probabilities of motive
Note 1: Base: *n* = 1978
Source: SHD

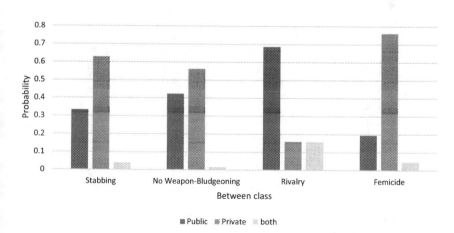

Figure 6.5 Class response probabilities of public or private location
Note 1: Base: *n* = 1978
Source: SHD

106 *Different types of homicide*

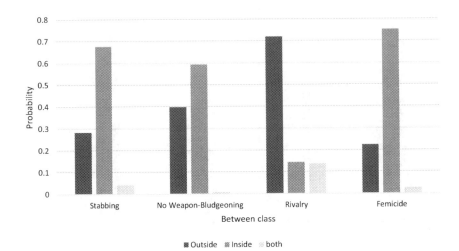

Figure 6.6 Class response probabilities of outside or inside location
Note 1: Base: $n = 1978$
Source: SHD

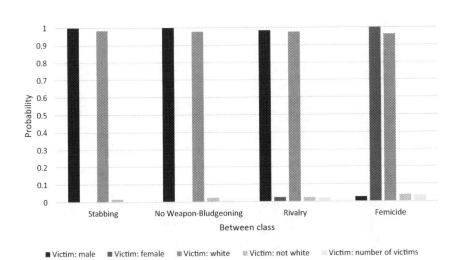

Figure 6.7 Class response probabilities of victim gender, ethnicity, and victim number
Note 1: Base: $n = 1978$
Source: SHD

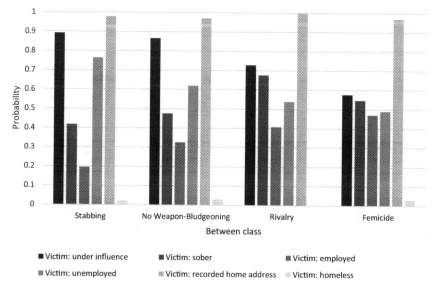

Figure 6.8 Class response probabilities for victim influence, employment status, and home address
Note 1: Base: $n = 1978$
Source: SHD

Rivalry *type*

The third between-level subtype was named the *Rivalry* type (24.8%, $n = 492$) because the most common relationship between the offender and victim was some sort of rival (see Figure 6.3) and the most common motive was feud or faction rivalry (see Figure 6.4). Most of the victims in the *Rivalry* homicides were killed by the use of a sharp instrument, although 18% of the cases involved shooting as cause of death, which was the highest of all the types (see Figure 6.1). The offender furthermore most commonly brought the weapon to the scene of the murder, which could indicate a level of planning to the crime (see Figure 6.2). The *Rivalry* homicides were also the only subtype in which the majority of the homicides took place in a public, outside location (see Figures 6.5 to 6.6). Similarly to the both previous subtypes, the victims were most commonly male, white, and unemployed, and although most victims were under the influence of drugs or alcohol at the time of murder, a high proportion of the victims were not (see Figures 6.7 to 6.8). The majority of the victims were aged 16–30 years old, making the *Rivalry* homicide the type with the youngest victims overall.

108 *Different types of homicide*

Femicide *type*

The fourth and smallest of the between-level subtypes was called the *Femicide* subtype (16.0%, *n* = 316) since all of the victims of this homicide type were female (see Figure 6.7). While stabbing was the most common cause of death, the method of killing was quite diverse in this subtype of homicide compared to the other types (see Figure 6.1). About 30% of the homicides did not involve the use of a weapon and a fifth of the victims were killed by strangulation or by the use of a ligature, which was the highest level of this method of killing compared to all the other types. In the cases where a weapon was used, this weapon was most commonly improvised at the scene, meaning the offender most commonly grabbed what was available (see Figure 6.2). The victim was most commonly an intimate partner of the offender (41%). In a fifth of the cases, the victim was, however, a relative, including children of the offender (see Figure 6.3). Although the most common motive was some sort of fight or argument, another 17% of the *Femicides* were motivated by a domestic dispute and 7% of the cases were sexually motivated, which was the highest percentage of all the types (see Figure 6.4). The majority of homicides in the *Femicide* subtype took place in private, indoor settings, such as in a home (see Figures 6.5 to 6.6).

As mentioned, most of the victims of this type were women, and although the vast majority of the victims were white, the *Femicide* type included the highest number of nonwhite victims (4%) (see Figure 6.7). While it was still much more common for a case to only include one victim, this subtype also included the highest number of multiple victims (4%). About as many of the *Femicide* victims were under the influence of drugs or alcohol as were sober, and about half of the victims were unemployed (see Figure 6.8). This would indicate a more stable victim profile compared to the previous subtypes, which showed higher levels of unemployment and use of drugs or alcohol. The age distribution was quite evenly spread for the *Femicide* victims, with the most common age bracket being 31–45 years old (see Figure 6.9).

Within (offender) classes

As mentioned, there were three within classes of offenders in the 4–3 model; two large classes (the *Young Unemployed Offenders* and the *Mixed Unemployed Offenders*), and one medium-sized class (the *Employed Offenders*) (see Table 6.5). As with the between-level subtypes, names for the classes were given based on their profile of classifying variables, which mainly distinguished classes on the basis of age and employment status. The vast majority of the offenders in every class was white and had a recorded home address (see Figure 6.10).

Young Unemployed Offender *class*

The first offender class was called the *Young Unemployed Offenders* (45.6%, *n* = 902). This class was constituted of mostly unemployed men who had a

Disaggregating homicide 109

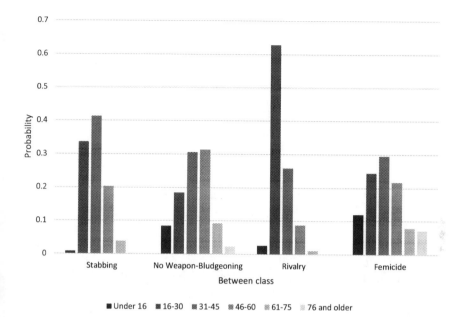

Figure 6.9 Class response probabilities for victim age
Note 1: Base: $n = 1978$.
Source: SHD

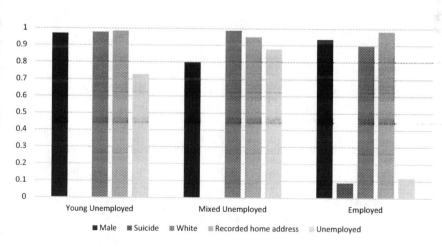

Figure 6.10 Class response probabilities for binary offender variables
Note 1: Base: $n = 1978$
Source: SHD

110 *Different types of homicide*

most common age of 16–30 years old (see Figures 6.10 to 6.11). This was overall the largest offender class with more than two fifths of the sample belonging to this class. When looking at the distribution of within-classes in the between-level subtypes (see Table 6.5), this class was the most prevalent class of offenders in both the *No Weapon–Bludgeoning* and the *Rivalry* homicides. In fact, 92% of the offenders in the *Rivalry* subtype belonged to this class. While about a third of the *Young Unemployed Offenders* belonged in the *Stabbing* subtype, none of the *Young Unemployed Offenders* were present in the *Femicide* subtype.

Mixed Unemployed Offender *class*

The second class was called the *Mixed Unemployed Offenders* (43.2%, $n = 854$). Since the majority of the *Mixed Unemployed Offenders* were unemployed, this class was very similar to the *Young Unemployed Offenders*; however, unlike in the previous class, the age distribution was more even in this class (see Figures 6.10 to 6.11). Although 16–30 years old still remained the most common age, about two fifths of the *Mixed Unemployed Offenders* were 31–45 years old, and approximately another 15% were older than 45 years old. Additionally, although all of the offender classes were mostly male, the *Mixed Unemployed Offender* class had the highest number of female offenders with one fifth of the offenders being female (see Figure 6.10). This class of offender was most prevalent in the *Stabbing* subtype, constituting 69% of the offenders in that type, as well as in the *Femicide* subtype, where they constituted 60% of

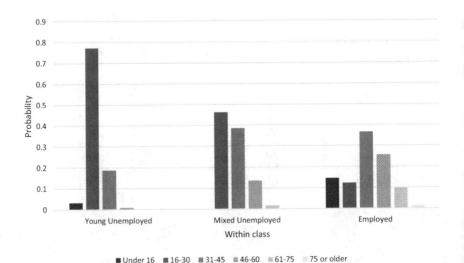

Figure 6.11 Class response probabilities for offender age
Note 1: Base: $n = 1978$
Source: SHD

Disaggregating homicide 111

the offenders (see Table 6.5). While none of the *Mixed Unemployed Offenders* were present in the *Rivalry* homicides, approximately two thirds of the *No Weapon–Bludgeoning* homicides consisted of this offender class.

Employed Offender *class*

The third and final class of offenders was also the smallest (11.2%, $n = 222$), and unlike the two previous classes, the majority of the offenders in this class were employed (see Figure 6.10). There was furthermore a higher than average percentage of nonwhite *Employed Offenders*, with approximately one in ten of the offenders belonging to an ethnicity other than white. The *Employed Offenders* was furthermore the only class where the offender committed suicide after the homicide was committed; approximately one in ten of the offenders took their own life after having taken the life of their victim. This class tended to include offenders slightly older than in the two previous classes with a most common age of 31–45 years old, and approximately another third of the offenders being older than 45 years old (see Figure 6.11). While this offender class did not constitute the majority of offenders in any of the between-level subtypes, the *Femicides* included the highest prevalence of this type of offender. More than 40% of the offenders in the *Femicide* subtype belonged to the *Employed Offender Class*.

When all of these subtypes and classes are examined, a new image of homicide in Scotland emerges. Overall, the *Stabbing* homicides mostly occurred between slightly older men who knew each other and who were unemployed. Intoxication was common among the victims, which could indicate that the overall picture of the individuals who were victims in these homicides is one of vulnerability. Although a sharp instrument was most commonly used in the homicide, this weapon was most commonly improvised at the time of murder, which also would indicate that these homicides were rarely planned and probably erupted as a result of a fight or argument that got out of hand in an inside, private location.

The *No Weapon–Bludgeoning* homicides were most commonly committed by either younger men or slightly older men against slightly older men who were either known to them, or related to them. Like the *Stabbing* homicides, both the victims and offenders may have been in a vulnerable life situation, with most of them being unemployed and the victim mostly being under the influence of either drugs or alcohol. As with the *Stabbing* homicides, most of the *No Weapon–Bludgeoning* homicides also occurred indoors in a private setting. The *Rivalry* subtypes on the other hand were very much characterised by young, quite vulnerable offenders and victims, who killed each other in the context of feuding in public, outdoor settings. This type of encounter typically reflects a premeditated street fight between competing youths in gangs or street factions. Finally, the *Femicide* subtypes were homicides most commonly committed by men against their female partners in private indoors locations and could be considered domestic in nature. Before exploring how

112 *Different types of homicide*

these subtypes have changed over time, the following section will compare the subtypes identified here to the subtypes identified in previous research in order to place these Scottish subtypes in international context.

Placing the homicide subtypes in international context

As mentioned previously, research and statistics have shown that homicide in Scotland is in decline, and has been decreasing for some time (see Chapter 2). Despite this, no research had previously examined whether there were different types of homicide based on victim, offender, and incident characteristics in Scotland, and little was known about whether different types of homicide had decreased in a similar manner. This chapter has demonstrated that there indeed are different types of homicide in Scotland based on these variables. Overall, four major types of homicide were identified based on victim, offender, and incident characteristics (*Stabbing, No Weapon–Bludgeoning, Rivalry*, and *Femicide*), representing latent patterns in the homicide data, with three separate classes of offenders in each (*Young Unemployed Offenders, Mixed Unemployed Offenders*, and *Employed Offenders*). While this typology may not be exhaustive, meaning there might be other types that are yet to be identified, this constitutes an initial step towards the identification of a homicide typology in Scotland, which is turn has provided a deeper understanding for this crime.

When comparing the subtypes identified here with the subtypes identified in previous research, there were some apparent similarities as well as differences. Both the *Stabbing* homicides and the *No Weapon–Bludgeoning* homicides bear some resemblance to the *Interpersonal Dispute* type identified by Pizarro (2008). Motivated by some sort of fight or argument, the *Interpersonal Dispute* type often included intoxicated victims and offenders and commonly occurred between friends or acquaintances (Pizarro, 2008). Although the *Interpersonal Dispute* homicides most often were committed in a public, outdoors setting which was not true for either the *Stabbing* or the *No Weapon–Bludgeoning* types, there are some strong similarities between Pizarro's *Interpersonal Dispute* type and the two types in the current study. Set in an American setting, Pizarro (2008), however, only included a binary variable measuring the use of a gun as the method of killing, so it is impossible to know how prevalent the use of a sharp instrument was in the *Interpersonal Dispute* homicides.

Sharp instruments as weapon of killing was, however, included in the study by Pridemore and Eckhardt (2008), and two of the types identified in their study, the *Victim Drinking* homicides and the *Both Drinking* homicides, were quite similar to the *Stabbing* homicides in the current study. The two types in Pridemore and Eckhardt's study predominantly involved men who were friends or acquaintances, where either both or just the victim were under the influence of alcohol and where a knife was used to kill the victim. The homicides furthermore most commonly took place in the home, which was very similar to the *Stabbing* homicides identified in the current study. As discussed, the variable measuring whether the offender was under the influence of alcohol or drugs was, however, excluded in the current study due the high levels of missingness in this variable. The levels of *offender drinking* can therefore not be compared with the study by Pridemore and Eckhardt (2008).

Both the *Stabbing* and the *No Weapon–Bludgeoning* types of homicide were furthermore similar to the *Confrontational* homicides and the *Conflict Resolution* homicides identified by Polk (1994). While the data in the current study did not allow for a more detailed analysis of the mechanisms of the motives, an argument or some sort of conflict was the most common motive for both the *Stabbing* and the *No Weapon–Bludgeoning* types and these two types furthermore share many similarities to the masculine homicides analysed by Polk (1994). Most of the offenders and victims were furthermore male, and most of the offenders knew their victims before the homicide was committed. While this means that the *Stabbing* and *No Weapon–Bludgeoning* types had characteristics in common with both the *Conflict Resolution* homicides and the *Confrontational* homicides described by Polk (1994), the fact that both types identified in the current study most commonly were committed inside in private setting makes them more similar to the *Conflict Resolution* homicides. This, since the *Confrontational* homicides involved the presence of a social audience, which is more unlikely to be present when the murder takes place in private settings.

However, the *No Weapon–Bludgeoning* homicide type does not appear to have a distinct counterpart in previous studies. There might be a few reasons for this. First, this might be due to contextual differences between the typology developed in this study compared to types in previous research. As many of the homicide typologies identified in previous research were developed in the US, gun-related homicides are much more prevalent in such datasets compared to the UK (Richardson & Hemenway, 2011). Conversely, homicides perpetrated with blunt instruments, or without the use of any weapon at all are less common in a US context, and may therefore not have been identified in previous typologies. Some typology studies furthermore only include the presence of a firearm as a binary variable to measure weapon, such as in the study by Pizarro (2008), meaning that other methods of killing are not even measured. As such, the *No Weapon–Bludgeoning* homicides might therefore be more of a culture-specific finding, prevalent either in countries where firearms are less common or in cultures with a more traditional form of machismo, where knives and fists are favoured, such as in Scotland (Carnochan, 2015). This furthermore highlights the contextual sensitivity of typologies; while some subtypes identified in the current research may be generalisable to other countries with similar cultures, other aspects might be strongly related to the Scottish context where they were developed. It is therefore important to keep in mind that some aspects of the homicide typology explored in the current volume will be different from other typologies that were developed in other contexts.

114 *Different types of homicide*

Second, there might be methodological reasons for why the *No Weapon–Bludgeoning* homicides have not been identified in previous typology studies. As previously discussed, many typology studies (see, for instance, Pizarro, 2008; Pridemore & Eckhardt, 2008) disaggregate homicide based on one single variable, such as motive, and not by the use of a statistical technique. This means that some subtypes that were disaggregated into distinct types in the current study might have been merged together in other studies. For instance, both the *Stabbing* homicides and the *No Weapon–Bludgeoning* homicides have the same most common motive: fight, rage, or quarrel. If the homicide subtypes in the current study had been disaggregated based purely on motive, it would have meant that both these types, along with the *Femicide* subtype, would have been merged into one single type, despite the fact that these types differ on many different variables. This further illustrates the differences between using an exploratory approach and identifying homicide subtypes *a priori*. While the *a priori* approach has the advantage of allowing to test different subtypes, the exploratory approach provides the opportunity to identify new subtypes which would otherwise have remained hidden in the data. As demonstrated, the current study identified the *Stabbing* homicides, the *No Weapon–Bludgeoning* homicides and the *Femicides* as distinct types of homicide, despite their shared most common motive. The exploratory data-informed method of the current study might also be an explanation for why the *No Weapon Bludgeoning* types have not been identified in any previous study.

While an equivalent to the *Rivalry* subtype has not been identified in previous research either, this type of homicide appear to typify the knife-related youth violence that has previously been discussed in the Scottish literature (Carnochan, 2015; Damer, 1990; Fraser, 2015). After a dramatic, decades-long increase in this type of violence among young people (Leyland, 2006), initiatives such as the Violence Reduction Unit (Scottish Government, 2012; VRU, 2016) and the No Knives Better Lives program (NKBL, 2014) were introduced in Scotland by the mid-2000s to work towards reducing knife crime on a local level. Knife crime, along with youth violence, was also given specific attention in the general violence policy in Scotland (Scottish Government, 2017c). Due to the similarities, the *Rivalry* homicides could be considered to constitute the extreme end of this violence, where young men kill each other with the use of sharp instruments in public places, motivated by some sort of feud. Many of the victims and offenders of this homicide type were also unemployed and under the influence of drugs and alcohol when the crime was committed, indicating that the people involved in this crime are quite vulnerable. The *Rivalry* subtype also includes a smaller group of homicides committed by an older man against a younger man (the *Employed Offender Rivalry* subtype), which could indicate homicides committed in feuds involving several generations of offenders.

The *Femicides*, which could be described as domestic in nature, bear resemblance to many of the homicide types labelled as 'Domestic' identified in previous research. For instance, the *Femicides* are similar to the *Domestic* homicide type identified by Pizarro (2008), the 'Homicides in the context of sexual intimacy' by Polk (1994), and the *Spousal Revenge* type identified by Liem and Reichelmann (2014). There are furthermore some similarities between the *Femicide* homicides and the typology of homicide–suicides developed by Morton et al. (1998), the *Extended Parricide* type identified by Liem and Reichelmann (2014), and the *Intimate-Partner Domestic Lethal Violence–Suicide* type identified by Wood Harper and Voigt (2007). As the findings of the current study has shown, about one in ten of the *Employed Offender* class included an offender who died by suicide after the homicide. As previous research has demonstrated, it is not uncommon for some men to take their own life after they have taken the life of their partner (Wood Harper & Voigt, 2007; Liem & Reichelmann, 2014). It is therefore likely that these cases belong to the *Employed Offender Femicides*, and that the *Femicide* sub-type includes a smaller subset of homicide–suicides. The highest level of multiple victims out of all the between-level classes was also found in the *Femicide* type, and about a fifth of these victims were related to the offender (other than intimate partner), including their child. The *Femicides* might therefore also include a subset of familicides where more than one family member was murdered.

Overall, these findings would indicate that there is some overlap between the homicide subtypes identified in the current study and types of homicide found in previous research. However, due to the wide range of variables and characteristics used to identify the types of homicide in the current study, these subtypes may be considered more comprehensive compared to previous typologies. Homicide typologies in previous research have tended to focus on very specific forms of lethal violence, such as homicide–suicides (Liem & Reichelmann, 2014; Morton et al., 1998; Wood Harper & Voigt, 2007), or the influence of certain variables on different types of homicides, such as alcohol (Pridemore & Eckhardt, 2008) or motive (Pizarro, 2008). While these studies included variables relating to the victims, the offenders and the incidents of homicide, the subtypes in the current study were still more inclusive due to the wider focus of homicide. The four main types of homicides identified in the current research demonstrate the importance of identifying distinct patterns in regards to the victims, offender, and incident-level variables in order to gain a full understanding of the dynamics of homicide. This is important for policy as well as theory, and also relevant when attempting to identify differing patterns of homicide over time. It is to the change of these homicides over time that we shall turn to next.

Change over time

In order to examine the change in the homicide types over time, the year in which the homicide was committed was introduced on the between level of the model as a series of binary covariates. Due to the small number of cases in

116 *Different types of homicide*

some years, the years were combined into four-year time periods from 2000 to 2015. The change in homicide subtypes was explored by examining both the absolute and relative change in homicide over time.

Absolute change in homicide over time

The absolute change in homicide subtypes over time is illustrated in Figure 6.12, where the estimated number of offenders in each subtype in each time period is indexed at the first year group (2000–2003). As can be seen from Figure 6.12, all subtypes of homicide demonstrated an absolute decrease over time. While the *Stabbing* homicides demonstrated a 36% decrease in 2012–2015 compared to 2000–2003, the *No Weapon–Bludgeoning* homicides had almost halved during the same time period. Meanwhile, the *Rivalry* homicides demonstrated a sharp increase of 142% between 2000–2003 and 2004–2007, before this subtype of homicide demonstrated an equally dramatic decrease from 2004–2007 and onward. Ultimately, this subtype of homicide had decreased by 54% in 2012–2015 compared to the first time period. The *Femicide* subtype initially demonstrated an increase in 2008–2011. This subtype also decreased by the final time period, demonstrating an overall decrease of 29% compared to 2000–2003. Overall, the *Rivalry* homicides had demonstrated the largest absolute decrease over time while the *Femicides* had the smallest absolute decrease over time.

This consequently means that all types of homicide have demonstrated a decrease in absolute terms over time. However, this is not the whole story. Even though all types have demonstrated an absolute decrease when the

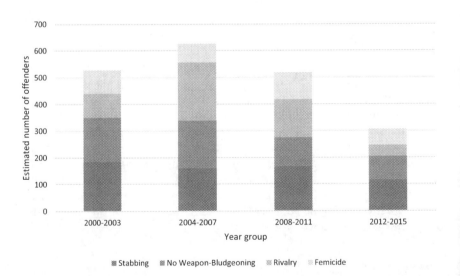

Figure 6.12 Absolute change in homicide types over time
Note 1: Base: *n* = 1978
Source: SHD

Disaggregating homicide 117

estimated number of offenders per year was examined, this does not provide any information about how the types have changed in relation to each other. Have all types decreased equally over time, or are some types changing differently in comparison to the other types?

Relative change in homicide over time

In order to examine the relative change of the homicide types over time, the average probability for each type per year-group was calculated and plotted out against time (see Figure 6.13 and Table 6.6). This reveals the proportion of all homicides made up by each type and how this proportion has changed over time. The mean probabilities were subsequently indexed at the first year in order to examine the change in each type of homicide relative to the other types over time. Mann Whitney U-tests for each subtype were subsequently performed in order to examine whether this change over time was statistically significant (see Table 6.6).

Exploring the relative change in homicide over time, the findings show that the subtypes had changed differently (see Figure 6.13). Out of the four subtypes, *Stabbing* homicides and *No Weapon–Bludgeoning* homicides remained relatively stable over time. While both these subtypes demonstrated some statistically significant changes over time (see Figure 6.13 and Table 6.6), both subtypes returned to levels similar to their original level in 2000–2003, and are arguably therefore demonstrating a stable trend over time. The *Stabbing* and *No Weapon–Bludgeoning* homicides furthermore remained the two most common subtypes of homicide. Taken together, despite absolute decreases in

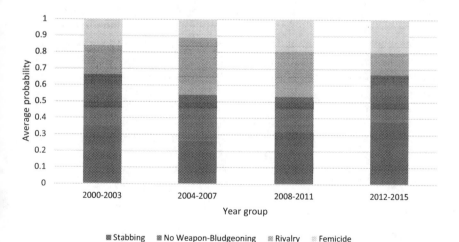

Figure 6.13 Relative change of homicide types over time
Note 1: Base: $n = 1978$
Source: SHD

118   *Different types of homicide*

Table 6.6 P-values of Mann Whitney U-tests of relative change in homicide types over time

Type of homicide	2000– 2003 vs 2004– 2007	2000– 2003 vs 2008– 2011	2000– 2003 vs 2012– 2015	2004– 2007 vs 2008– 2011	2004– 2007 vs 2012– 2015	2008– 2011 vs 2012– 2015
Stabbing	(-) **0.014**	0.513	0.285	0.128	(+) **0.002**	0.142
No weapon– bludgeoning	0.053	(-) **0.001**	0.904	(-) **0.001**	0.133	(+) **0.001**
Rivalry	(+) **0.001**	(+) **0.026**	(-) **0.001**	(-) **0.001**	(-) **0.001**	(-) **0.001**
Femicide	(-) **0.009**	0.106	0.213	(+) **0.001**	(+) **0.001**	0.883

Note 1: Base: $n = 1978$.
Note 2: p-values in bold indicates significance.

Source: SHD.

these two subtypes, the *Stabbing* homicides and the *No Weapon–Bludgeoning* homicides therefore remained relatively stable over time.

By contrast, the change in both the *Rivalry* homicides and the *Femicides* was considerably less stable. Relative to the other subtypes, the *Rivalry* subtype of homicide first demonstrated a marked, significant increase between 2000–2003 and 2004–2007 (see Figure 6.13). As Figure 6.13 demonstrates, the mean probability of belonging to this subtype increased by 104% between 2000–2003 and 2004–2007. After this dramatic increase, the *Rivalry* homicides, however, demonstrated an equally sharp decrease in relation to the other subtypes. In 2012–2015, this subtype of homicide had decreased by 21% compared to 2000–2003, making it the least common subtype of homicide in this time period compared with the other subtypes. This decrease also proved to be statistically significant (see Table 6.5). When exploring the relative change in the *Femicide* subtype, a slightly more complex trend, however, emerges. Similarly to the *Stabbing* homicides, the *Femicides* demonstrated a significant decrease by 32% between 2000–2003 and 2004–2007 relative to the other subtypes. This decrease was followed by a significant relative increase between 2004–2007 and 2008–2012, as well as a significant relative increase between 2004–2007 and 2012–2015 (see Figure 6.13 and Table 6.5). Overall, the *Femicides* had demonstrated a relative increase of 21% in 2012–2015 compared to the first time period, becoming more common in 2012–2015 than the *Rivalry* homicides.

Conclusions

This chapter has set out to disaggregate homicide using an exploratory, inductive approach in order to identify subtypes of homicide in Scotland. The results identified four main subtypes of homicide: *Stabbing, No Weapon–Bludgeoning, Rivalry,* and *Femicides*. These subtypes are distinct and have changed differently over time. Although the *Rivalry* homicides have decreased significantly over the examined time periods, *Femicides* have demonstrated a relative increase. This demonstrate the value of using an inductive, data-driven approach when disaggregating homicide, as well as the advantages of using MLCA. As a statistical technique, MLCA models the structures of the underlying data and has been found superior to distance-based multilevel modelling on almost all accounts, including clustering accuracy on both the between and within level. Allowing for more robust disaggregation in comparison to other classification techniques, there are obvious advantages to the use of this method, which should be considered further in future typology research.

When the identified homicide typologies were examined over time, the findings suggested that although there has been an absolute decrease in homicide, some homicide subtypes have reduced more than others. While both *Stabbing* and *No Weapon–Bludgeoning* homicides have remained stable over time, *Rivalry* homicides have decreased significantly over time, suggesting that this subtype contributes the greatest to the overall drop in Scottish homicides. Additionally, the *Femicides*, which had the smallest absolute decrease over time, demonstrated a relative significant increase. While increases in domestic violence previously has been explained by increases in reporting of this crime (Tonry, 2014), domestic homicide already has a very low dark figure (Brookman, 2005), making this explanation unlikely. As such, the relative increase of domestic forms of homicide evident here is likely an effect of a greater decrease in other types of homicides compared to the *Femicides*. As such, the findings suggest that the overall decrease in homicide evident in the current study has mainly been driven by a decrease in public, feud-motivated homicides involving young men and sharp instruments, whereas domestic homicides have not decreased by nearly as much. These findings, while relevant in their own right, also have important implications for understanding the crime drop (i.e. Aebi & Linde, 2010; Farrell et al., 2010; Tonry, 2014). This study has demonstrated that homicide needs to be disaggregated and the heterogeneous nature of this crime needs to be taken into account if the change in homicide is to be explained or understood. Further theoretical implications of these findings, as well as implications for policy and practice, will be discussed in Chapter 9.

The next chapter however, will, provide an in-depth examination of another, very rare type of homicide that still holds a high degree of fascination by the public, namely sexual homicide. This type of homicide will be disaggregated using both the simple approach taken in the previous chapter and using the MLCA that were used in the current chapter. The stark differences between sexual and nonsexual homicides demonstrated by previous research has led researchers to urge for isolated examination of this particular type of homicide (Skott, 2019; Skott et al., 2021; Skott et al., 2021; Skott et al., 2019). The next chapter will therefore explore various forms of sexually motivated homicides.

7 Sexual homicide

Case study

John committed the rape and subsequent murder of a 24-year-old woman, Mary. John's childhood and youth was marked by petty crime such as burglary and fraud, and he tended to move around a lot. John and Mary did not know each other prior to the murder, but they worked at the same charity shop where Mary worked the till and John was hired as a handyman to conduct some repairs. As they were both leaving work one evening, Mary was attacked by John. Mary was beaten, raped, and then stabbed 16 times in the chest. Attempting to dispose of Mary's body, John wrapped her body in garbage bags and hid her body in the basement of the charity shop, used mainly as a storage room. The forensic evidence would later suggest that Mary was still alive when her body was placed in the basement. John had previously been convicted of several serious instances of rape and attempted murder. He was able to avoid detection of the police due to his mobility and the use of several aliases. After having been missing for four days, Mary's body was found in the charity shop basement and the forensic evidence on the scene, including DNA evidence, led the police to John and he was apprehended and charged. The police were later able to link two additional previously committed unsolved murders to John with the help of forensic evidence.

Introduction

Sexual homicide is a very rare type of homicide, estimated to constitute between 1% and 4% of all homicides committed (Chan & Heide, 2008; Roberts & Grossman, 1993; Skott, Beauregard, & Darjee, 2021). Despite their rarity, however, sexual homicides often receive a lot of media attention when they occur, often rousing great public fear. The high prevalence of sexual homicide in popular culture, such as television shows and films, also leads the public to believe this crime to be much more common than it actually is. Due to the great impact this crime has on community safety and fear of crime, it is therefore important to explore this crime further, despite its low frequency.

DOI: 10.4324/9781003105282-9

Sexual homicide 121

So what constitutes a sexual homicide? A homicide is usually considered to be sexual when there is some form of sexual motive to the crime. This involves cases where there has been sexual arousal or some sort of sexual behaviour before, during, or after killing the victim. There is no legal category of sexual homicide, meaning there is no judicial difference between 'murder' or 'sexual murder' in the context of the law. This also means that the definition of sexual homicide may differ between countries but also in the context of research. While some researchers only consider murders sexual where the actual killing of the victim is itself sexually gratifying, others also include homicides where a victim was raped and the murder occurred as a way to avoid detection or apprehension. This distinction between 'lust murders' and 'rape murders' has led to some disparity in the research field, where some scholars argue there is a form of 'true sexual homicide' different from other types of sexual homicides or rape murders (Stefanska, Higgs, Carter, & Beech, 2017).

In light of this disparity, most studies in sexual homicide have, however, used the definition developed by the Federal Bureau of Investigation (FBI). When the FBI initiated their behavioural science unit in the 1970s, sexual homicide was at centre of the violence studied, leading up to the practical definition developed by Ressler, Burgess, and Douglas (1988). According to this definition, a sexual homicide case had to include at least one of the following: (a) victim's attire or lack of attire, (b) exposure of the sexual parts of the victim's body, (c) sexual positioning of the victim's body, (d) insertion of foreign objects into the victim's body cavities, (e) evidence of sexual intercourse, or (f) evidence of substitute sexual activity, interest, or sadistic fantasy (Ressler, Burgess, & Douglas, 1988). While this definition is the most common in sexual homicide research, it also has the advantage of being focused on the incident and victim variables rather than the offender. While this may seem inconsequential, most datasets used in this type of research are collected from police data, meaning that while there may be information pertaining to the offender, most of the variables are concerned with the incident and the victim of the crime. There may also be cases where the offender was never identified or apprehended, or where the offender simply did not divulge their motive behind their crime. In these cases, it would be difficult if not impossible to discern the offender's motivation. Using a definition of sexual homicide that does not rely on this information may therefore be preferable in these situations. The definition constructed by Ressler et al. (1988) furthermore does not make a distinction between 'lust murders' or 'rape murders'; such cases are all included as long as they fulfil the criteria mentioned above.

This chapter will provide an in-depth analysis of sexual homicide, exploring subtypes of homicide in a similar way to how we explored nonsexual homicide in the previous chapter. Each section will be based on a previously conducted study. The first section will explore how sexual homicide differs from nonsexual homicide, delineating the characteristics of this crime (Skott, Beauregard, & Darjee, 2021). The second section will explore sexual

122 *Different types of homicide*

homicides committed by female offenders, comparing them to female non-sexual homicide offenders as well as male sexual homicide offenders (Skott, Beauregard, & Darjee, 2019). The third section will explore sexual homicide committed against child victims, comparing this type of homicide to non-sexual homicides committed against children and adult sexual homicide (Skott, 2019). The fourth section will explore subtypes of homicide in both Scotland and Canada using the same explorative approach described in the previous chapter: Latent Class Analysis (LCA) (Skott, Beauregard, Darjee & Martineau, 2021). With this inductive, data-driven approach, subtypes in both Canada and Scotland will be identified and compared. The final section of this chapter will subsequently explore different theoretical perspectives attempting to explain why some individuals commit sexual homicide. But first, we will explore the difference between sexual and nonsexual homicides committed by male offenders.

Sexual homicide compared to nonsexual homicides

While most studies examining sexual homicide tend to compare sexual homicide with nonlethal sexual violence, such as rape, there are fewer studies that explore the difference between sexual and nonsexual lethal violence. This is, however, important to examine in order to explore whether homicide offenders are comparable across sexual and nonsexual crimes, and what effects this might have on policy and intervention programmes. The few previous studies that have explored the similarities and differences between sexual and nonsexual homicide offenders have found sexual homicide offenders to be more sexually sadistic, antisocial, and to exhibit a higher degree of psychopathic traits in comparison to nonsexual homicide offenders (Häkkänen-Nyholm, Repo-Tiihonen, Lindberg, Salenius, & Weizmann-Henelius, 2009; Langevin, Ben-Aron, Wright, Marchese, & Handy, 1988; Yarvis, 1990, 1995). Such studies have also found that sexual homicide offenders differ from nonsexual homicides in regards to who they attack (strangers more often than acquaintances), method of killing (strangulation rather than other methods) and crime scene-related behaviour (often move the body after the homicide) (Häkkänen-Nyholm et al., 2009; Langevin et al., 1988).

In light of these differences, and since it is of important substantive relevance, this section will explore the differences between homicide and non-sexual homicides in Scotland. While previous studies tend to mainly focus on offender and incident variables when comparing these crimes, research has shown that victim variables may be equally important (Langevin et al., 1988). For instance, victim gender as well as whether or not the victim is engaged in prostitution have been found to be important variables when comparing sexual and nonsexual homicide (Langevin et al., 1988; Quinet, 2011; Salfati, James, & Ferguson, 2008). As such, this section will explore whether sexual homicide offenders differ from nonsexual homicide offenders in Scotland regarding characteristics of the offender, the victim, and the incident itself,

Table 7.1 Chi-square analyses between offender characteristics and the type of homicide

Offender variables		Sexual cases	Nonsexual cases	Cohen's d
Ethnicity	White	67 (75.3%)	262 (85.6%)	0.23*
Employment status	Employed	15 (16.9%)	27 (8.8%)	0.21*
Suicide	Suicide	1 (1.1%)	16 (5.2%)	0.17
Accomplice	Yes	20 (22.5%)	50 (16.3%)	0.13
Age	Under 16 years old	4 (4.5%)	6 (2.0%)	0.14
	16–30 years old	43 (48.3%)	111 (36.3%)	0.21*
	31–45 years old	30 (33.6%)	119 (38.9%)	0.09
	46 years or older	12 (13.5%)	70 (22.9%)	0.19

* $p < 0.05$ ** $p < 0.01$ *** $p < 0.001$

only examining cases where male offenders have killed females. Only male homicide offenders targeting female victims were included since previous research on sexual homicide against male victims (Beauregard & Proulx, 2007) has shown that this crime differs substantially and should therefore not be compared together. This is also true for female-perpetrated sexual homicide (Chan, Heide & Beuaregard, 2019).

Method

The data was taken from the Scottish Homicide Database as in previous chapters, and included cases from 1990 to 2015. Although there was much missingness in the data before the year 2000, special measures were taken to remedy the missingness in the sexual homicide cases, and data from a longer time period could therefore be used. As the data was hierarchical, meaning that any one case could include multiple offenders and victims, the dataset was based on the offender, with victim variables summarised at the incident level. The dataset included 78 cases of sexual homicides, involving 89 offenders and 289 nonsexual homicide cases, including 306 offenders. The analysis was conducted using chi-square tests and sequential logistic regression.

Findings

Sexual homicide offenders were most commonly of white ethnicity, unemployed, and the most common age was between 16 and 30 years old. Compared to the nonsexual homicides however, the sexual homicide offenders were more often employed and of another ethnicity than white (see Table 7.1). Sexual homicide offenders also tended to be younger than the nonsexual offenders; while the most common age for sexual offenders was 16–30 years old, the most common age for nonsexual offenders was 31–45 years old.

124 *Different types of homicide*

Table 7.2 Chi-square analyses between victim characteristics and the type of homicide

Victim variables[a]		Sexual cases	Nonsexual cases	Cohen's d
Ethnicity	White	66 (74.2%)	236 (77.1%)	0.06
Employment status	Employed	9 (9.0%)	16 (5.2%)	0.13
Victim engaged in prostitution	Yes	6 (6.7%)	4 (1.3%)	0.29**
Age	Under 16 years old	6 (6.7%)	33 (10.8%)	0.11
	16–30 years old	40 (44.9%)	80 (26.1%)	0.35***
	31–45 years old	20 (22.5%)	91 (29.7%)	0.14
	46 years or older	25 (28.1%)	110 (35.9%)	0.14

* $p < 0.05$ ** $p < 0.01$ *** $p < 0.001$
[a] These percentages do not add up to 100% due to the possibility of multiple responses.

When the victim variables were explored, the victims of sexual homicides were most commonly white, unemployed, and between 16 and 30 years old, very similar to the offenders of sexual homicide (see Table 7.2). Compared with the victims of nonsexual homicide, the sexual homicide victims were significantly younger, and were significantly more likely to be engaged in prostitution.

Examining the incident variables, the sexual homicides were most commonly committed by someone known, like an acquaintance or a friend, and the victims were most commonly killed by strangulation or asphyxiation (see Table 7.3). In the cases where a weapon was used, this weapon was most commonly improvised at the crime scene. Besides being sexually motivated, the most common motive of sexual homicides was some sort of fight or argument. The majority of sexual homicides took place in urban, public places outdoors, and in approximately 7% of the cases, the homicide involved multiple crime scenes. In about 15% of the cases, the offender destroyed evidence after the homicide.[1] Compared with nonsexual homicides, sexual homicides were significantly more likely to involve strangulation as a method of killing. While strangulation with or without the use of a ligature was the most common method of killing among sexually motivated homicides, the victims of nonsexual homicides were most commonly killed with the use of a sharp instrument, such as a knife. While sexual homicides most commonly were committed against someone known, it was a significantly more common for sexual homicides to target strangers compared to nonsexual homicides. Meanwhile, it was significantly more likely for nonsexual homicides to be committed against intimate partners compared to sexual homicides (see Table 7.3). Intimate partner was also the most common relationship for

1 As mentioned in Chapter 5, this involved cases where the body had been moved, where the body had been covered or buried, where the body had been burned, or where the body had been dismembered.

Sexual homicide   125

nonsexual homicides, and the most common motive for nonsexual homicides was some sort of domestic dispute. Overall, this would indicate that while a significant number of nonsexual homicides are committed against an intimate partner, this is very uncommon in cases of sexual homicide.

Nonsexual homicides were furthermore significantly more likely to occur inside private locations compared with sexual homicides. While most sexual homicides occurred in urban locations, it was, however, significantly more common that sexual homicides were committed in rural areas compared to nonsexual homicides. Finally, it was also significantly more common for sexual homicides to involve evidence destruction compared to homicides that were not sexually motivated. When all variables were examined in the multivariate analysis, the sequential logistic regression revealed that the most important variables for distinguishing sexual and nonsexual homicides were the relationship between victim and offender, method of killing, and evidence destruction.

Discussion

Overall, this study has demonstrated that there are important differences between sexually motivated homicides and nonsexual homicides. While the victims and offenders appeared quite similar across the two homicide types, sexual homicides tended to involve younger offenders and victims compared to nonsexual homicides. It was furthermore more common for victims of sexual homicides to be engaged in prostitution. This study has also showed that sexual homicides more often involve strangulation or asphyxiation as the method of killing, are more commonly committed against strangers, and more often involve offenders who attempt to destroy evidence after the homicide was committed. These findings are furthermore congruent with previous research on sexual homicide (Häkkänen-Nyholm et al., 2009; Langevin et al., 1988). This study also showed that it was not very common for sexual homicides to involve a secondary motive. This contrasts with previous research, which has suggested that sexual homicides were seldom motivated by sexual desire but were more commonly fuelled by other motives such as arguments or jealousy (Hääkänen-Nyholm et al., 2009). Instead, the findings of the current study suggest that sexual motivation is very prevalent in Scotland.

As mentioned, this study also found that sexual homicides, unlike nonsexual homicides, very rarely were committed in the context of an intimate relationship. While this means that very few sexual homicides in the current study were committed between intimate partners, this also raises questions in regards to the definition of sexual homicide. The current study did not consider a homicide to be sexual simply because the offender and victims were in a sexual relationship. If a case, however, were to be considered sexual because of the sexual relationship between offender and victim, nonsexual intimate partner homicide and sexual homicides essentially become conflated. As this study has demonstrated that there are distinct differences between sexual and nonsexual homicides, this would be problematic. Not only since

126 *Different types of homicide*

Table 7.3 Chi-square analyses between incident characteristics and the type of homicide

Incident variables		Sexual cases	Nonsexual cases	Cohen's d
Method of killing	Sharp instrument	25 (28.1%)	120 (39.2%)	0.19
	Blunt instrument	26 (29.3%)	66 (21.6%)	0.15
	Shooting or firearm	0 (0.0%)	0 (2.9%)	0.17
	No weapon used	25 (28.1%)	79 (25.8%)	0.04
	Strangulation or asphyxiation	36 (40.4%)	65 (21.2%)	0.37***
	Physical assault	23 (25.8%)	60 (19.6%)	0.13
	Other	29 (32.6%)	73 (23.9%)	0.17
Relationship between offender and victim	Known or acquaintance	18 (20.2%)	50 (16.3%)	0.09
	Intimate partner	4 (4.5%)	89 (29.1%)	0.50***
	Stranger	13 (14.6%)	5 (1.6%)	0.54***
Motive	Fight, rage, or quarrel	13 (14.6%)	124 (40.5%)	0.47***
	Financial (including theft)	3 (3.4%)	28 (9.2%)	0.18
	Insanity	1 (1.1%)	23 (7.5%)	0.23*
	Domestic	3 (3.4%)	53 (17.3%)	0.34***
Rural or urban location	Rural	5 (5.6%)	4 (1.3%)	0.24*
Public or private location	Private	38 (42.7%)	172 (56.2%)	0.23*
Inside or outside location	Inside	40 (44.9%)	176 (57.5%)	0.21*
Evidence destruction	Evidence destroyed	15 (14.7%)	13 (4.2%)	0.39***
Selection of Weapon	Improvised	15 (16.9%)	57 (18.6%)	0.04
	Brought to scene	7 (7.9%)	42 (13.7%)	0.15
Multiple location	Yes	6 (6.7%)	12 (3.9%)	0.11

* $p < 0.05$ ** $p < 0.01$ *** $p < 0.001$

previous studies of intimate partner homicide have found risk factors specific to this crime that have not been explored in relation to sexual homicide (see, for instance, Campbell, 2003), but also since conflating sexual and intimate partner homicide risks obscuring important differences in both crimes that could prevent detection or even muddle research. Having explored sexual homicide committed by men, the next section will explore sexual homicides committed by female offenders.

Sexual homicides committed by female offenders

Most studies on sexual homicide tend to focus on male offenders, as indeed the previous section of this chapter has done. While male offenders of sexual homicide are much more common, research of female-perpetrated homicides

Sexual homicide 127

is equally important in order to get a full understanding of the characteristics of different forms of sexual homicide. Previous studies that have examined sexual homicide perpetrated by female offenders have found that female sexual homicide offenders were more likely to use firearms and other less physically demanding weapon compared with male offenders (Chan, Heide, & Beuaregard 2019). Studies have also found that female sexual homicide offenders were more likely to kill men rather than women, kill adult victims rather than children, and to kill someone who was known to them, like a friend or acquaintance (Chan, Heide, & Beauregard, 2019; Chan & Frei, 2013). While it appears that women commit less sexual abuse compared to men, the estimated figure of female sexual homicide is 5% of all sexual homicide (Chan, 2017; Chan & Heide, 2009, 2016; James & Proulx, 2014), there is also an issue with underreporting of female-perpetrated abuse (Cortoni, Babchishin & Rat, 2017). This may also be related to ideas of gender; women are often viewed as less capable of sexual aggression since this contradicts traditional constructs of femininity (Denov, 2003; Denov 2004; Johansson-Love & Fremouw, 2006).

As research on female sexual homicide offenders remains scarce, the aim of this study was to examine the characteristics of female-perpetrated sexual homicide in Scotland. Sexual homicides committed by female offenders will here be compared with two comparison groups: male offenders who committed sexual homicide and female offenders who committed nonsexual homicides.

Method

As in the previous study, this study used data from the Scottish Homicide Database, exploring homicides committed between 1990 and 2015. Similarly to the previous studies, the dataset was hierarchical, where any one case could involve more than one offender. In total, there were seven female sexual homicides committed over this time, involving as many offenders. This small sample was compared to a random sample of 106 female nonsexual homicide offenders over 102 cases and 89 male sexual homicide offenders over 78 cases. These three groups were compared on variables relating to the victim, the offender, and the incident itself using Fisher's exact tests.

Findings

When the offender variables were examined, the data revealed that all of the female sexual homicide offenders were of white ethnicity and the most common age was between 31 and 45 years old (see Table 7.4). While all of the female sexual homicide offenders were unemployed, only one offender was homeless at the time of the crime. None of the female sexual homicide offenders killed themselves after the murder. Interestingly, the majority of the female sexual homicides (71%) also included an accomplice. This was also true for the nonsexual homicides committed by female offenders where nearly

128 *Different types of homicide*

Table 7.4 Fisher's exact tests between offender characteristics and type of homicide

Offender variables		Female sexual homicide	Female nonsexual homicide	Cohen's d	Male Sexual homicide	Cohen's d
Ethnicity	White	7 (100.0%)	75 (70.8%)	0.32[+]	67 (75.3%)	0.31
Employment status	Employed	0 (100.0%)	9 (8.5%)	0.15	15 (16.9%)	0.24
Residential status	Homeless	1 (14.3%)	1 (0.9%)	0.50	3 (3.4%)	0.29
Suicide	Yes	0 (0.0%)	0 (0.0%)	–	1 (1.1%)	0.06
Accomplice	Yes	5 (71.4%)	49 (46.2%)	0.25	20 (22.5%)	0.61*
Age	Under 16 years old	0 (0.0%)	1 (0.9%)	0.05	4 (4.5%)	0.12
	16–30 years old	2 (28.6%)	53 (50.0%)	0.21	43 (48.3%)	0.21
	31–45 years old	3 (42.9%)	34 (32.1%)	0.11	30 (33.6%)	0.10
	46 years or older	2 (28.6%)	18 (17.0%)	0.15	12 (13.5%)	0.22

* $p < 0.05$ ** $p < 0.01$ *** $p < 0.001$ [+] $p < 0.1$

half of the offenders had an accomplice. This differed from the male sexual homicide offenders, however, where the vast majority of homicides were committed alone. While there were some other minor differences between the offenders of female sexual homicide and the two comparison groups, such as, for instance, that the offenders tended to be slightly older, none of these differences were significant.

When examining the victim characteristics, the research showed that the majority of the victims of female-perpetrated sexual homicide were male (57%) (see Table 7.5). All of the victims were white and the majority of the victims were 46 years or older. As with the offenders, the victims of female-perpetrated sexual homicide were mostly unemployed, and none of the victims was homeless or engaged in prostitution. While victim prostitution was slightly more common among the male-perpetrated sexual homicides, there were no significant differences between the female-perpetrated sexual homicides and the two comparison groups in regards to the victim variables. This would also suggest that victim prostitution, which usually is considered an important variable in relation to male-perpetrated sexual homicide (Chan & Heide, 2009), is not very relevant for female sexual homicide.

Exploring the incident variables, it was most common that the victims of the female-perpetrated sexual homicides were killed by the use of physical assault, such as kicking or punching (see Table 7.6). It was also quite common that the victims were killed with the use of either a sharp or a blunt weapon. In the cases where a weapon was used, this was most commonly

Sexual homicide 129

Table 7.5 Fisher's exact tests between victim characteristics and type of homicide

Victim variables		Female sexual homicide	Female nonsexual homicide	Cohen's d	Male Sexual homicide	Cohen's d
Gender	Male	4 (57.1%)	79 (74.5%)	0.19	26 (29.2%)	0.32
Ethnicity	White	7 (100.0%)	70 (66.0%)	0.36[†]	236 (77.1%)	0.32
Employment status	Employed	0 (0.0%)	9 (8.5%)	0.15	16 (5.2%)	0.17
Residential status	Homeless	0 (0.0%)	0 (0.0%)	–	5 (5.6%)	0.13
Victim engaged in prostitution	Yes	0 (0.0%)	0 (0.0%)	–	4 (1.3%)	0.13
Age	Under 16 years old	1 (14.3%)	19 (17.9%)	0.05	33 (10.8%)	0.15
	16–30 years old	1 (14.3%)	19 (17.9%)	0.05	80 (26.1%)	0.33
	31–45 years old	2 (28.6%)	32 (30.2%)	0.05	91 (29.7%)	0.08
	46 years or older	3 (42.9%)	36 (34.0%)	0.09	110 (35.9%)	0.17

$* p < 0.05 ** p < 0.01 *** p < 0.001 † p < 0.1$

Note: The percentages in this table do not add up to 100% due to the possibility of multiple responses.

brought to the scene by the offender. The most common relationship between victim and offender was someone known, like a friend or an acquaintance (43%), followed by a family member. None of the female-perpetrated sexual homicides were committed against an intimate partner. Other than being sexually motivated, approximately a quarter of the female-perpetrated sexual homicides were motivated by some sort of fight or quarrel. The vast majority of the cases were committed inside private settings in urban areas. In little more than a quarter of the cases, the offender destroyed evidence after the homicide was committed.

When the sexual homicides committed by female offenders were compared to nonsexual homicides committed by female offenders, the findings revealed that it was significantly more common for sexual homicides to involve physical assault as the method of killing. It was also significantly more likely for sexual homicide committed by women to be perpetrated inside, and for the offender to destroy evidence after the homicide compared with nonsexual homicides by women. In other aspects, it seemed that female sexual and nonsexual homicides were quite similar. Furthermore, when female-perpetrated sexual homicides were compared with male-perpetrated sexual homicides, the data showed that there were more similarities than differences. The only variable that differed significantly was the location; it was significantly more

130 *Different types of homicide*

common for female-perpetrated sexual homicides to occur in an indoors location. Despite the fact that male sexual homicides more often involved strangulation as a method of killing and more often were committed against strangers, these differences were not significant. The fact that female sexual homicide offenders more often killed family members compared with male sexual homicide offenders, however, approached significance (see Table 7.6).

Discussion

Taken together, this study has explored all female sexual homicides committed in Scotland between 1990 and 2015. As the first European study to explore this crime, this study has revealed some valuable insights in regards to female-perpetrated sexual homicides. Although generally similar to both nonsexual female homicide offenders and male sexual homicide offenders, female sexual homicide offenders differed in a number of important ways. The majority of the female-perpetrated homicides offenders had an accomplice when committing the crime. While this was somewhat similar to nonsexual female homicides, this differed significantly from male-perpetrated sexual homicide, where most acted alone. This suggests that the inclusion of accomplices may be a key variable when exploring sexual homicides committed by women. Previous research has also found that little more than a quarter of female-perpetrated homicides in the US involved multiple offenders and victims, meaning that this finding may be generalisable across countries (Chan & Frei, 2013). The tendency to include accomplices may also be a finding relating to gender, as previous studies have found that women who commit non-sexual homicides are also more likely to have a male accomplice (Becker & McCorkel, 2011; Sommers & Baskin, 1993).

While little more than half of the female sexual homicide offenders killed men, the majority of male sexual homicide offenders killed women and the majority of female nonsexual homicides offenders killed men. This places female sexual homicide offenders somewhere in between the two comparison groups when it comes to victim gender. As previous research has also found that the majority of female sexual homicide offenders targeted the opposite sex (Chan & Frei, 2013), this finding may be related to the high number of male accomplices in the current study. Since male sexual homicide offenders more commonly target female victims, and all of the accomplices in the current female sexual homicide cases were male, the male offenders may be driving the offense in these instances. More research into the co-offending dynamic of female sexual homicide offenders is, however, needed in order to determine the exact motivations and relationships.

There were consequently similarities as well as differences between female sexual homicide, male sexual homicide, and female nonsexual homicide cases. All things considered, female sexual homicide offenders should therefore be considered a distinct group of offenders with specific characteristics as well as needs. Future studies should therefore examine this subgroup of sexual

Sexual homicide   131

Table 7.6 Fisher's exact tests between incident characteristics and the type of homicide

Incident variables		Female sexual homicide	Female nonsexual homicide	Cohen's d	Male Sexual homicide	Cohen's d
Method of killing	Sharp instrument	3 (42.9%)	55 (51.9%)	0.09	25 (28.1%)	0.17
	Blunt instrument	3 (42.9%)	14 (13.2%)	0.41[†]	26 (29.3%)	0.16
	Shooting or firearm	0 (0.0%)	0 (0.0%)	–	0 (0.0%)	–
	No weapon used	2 (28.6%)	19 (17.9%)	0.13	25 (28.1%)	0.01
	Strangulation or ligature	1 (14.3%)	10 (9.4%)	0.08	36 (40.4%)	0.28
	Physical assault	4 (57.1%)	20 (18.9%)	0.46*	23 (25.8%)	0.37[†]
	Other	2 (28.6%)	13 (12.3%)	0.23	29 (32.6%)	0.04
Relationship between offender and victim	Known or Acquaintance	3 (42.9%)	19 (17.9%)	0.31	18 (20.2%)	0.29
	Family member	1 (14.3%)	20 (18.9%)	0.06	0 (0.0%)	0.79[†]
	Intimate partner	0 (0.0%)	15 (14.2%)	0.20	4 (4.5%)	0.12
	Stranger	0 (0.0%)	1 (0.9%)	0.05	13 (14.6%)	0.22
Motive	Fight, rage or quarrel	2 (28.6%)	56 (52.8%)	0.24	13 (14.6%)	0.20
	Financial (including theft)	0 (0.0%)	7 (6.6%)	0.13	3 (3.4%)	0.10
	Insanity	0 (0.0%)	2 (1.9%)	0.07	1 (1.1%)	0.06
	Domestic	0 (0.0%)	11 (10.4%)	0.17	3 (3.4%)	0.10
Rural or urban location	Rural	1 (14.3%)	3 (2.8%)	0.30	5 (5.6%)	0.19
Public or private location	Private	5 (71.4%)	41 (38.4%)	0.33[†]	38 (42.7%)	0.30
Inside or outside location	Inside	6 (85.7%)	46 (43.4%)	0.42*	40 (44.9%)	0.43*
Evidence destruction	Evidence destroyed	2 (28.6%)	1 (0.9%)	0.91**	15 (14.7%)	0.18
Selection of Weapon	Improvised	1 (14.3%)	17 (16.0%)	0.16	15 (16.9%)	0.16
	Brought to scene	2 (28.6%)	13 (12.3%)	0.03	7 (7.9%)	0.12
Multiple location	Yes	1 (14.3%)	6 (5.7%)	0.17	6 (6.7%)	0.15

* $p < 0.05$ ** $p < 0.01$ *** $p < 0.001$ [†] $p < 0.1$

132 *Different types of homicide*

homicide offenders further in order to achieve appropriate intervention and prevention strategies. The next section of this chapter will explore another rare subtype of sexual homicide: sexual homicide committed against children.

Sexual homicides committed against children

As with female-perpetrated sexual homicide, sexual homicide targeting children is exceedingly rare. While sexual homicide is estimated to constitute between 1% and 4% of all homicides (Chan & Heide, 2016; Roberts & Grossman, 1993), sexual homicides against children is considered to constitute 6% to 8% of all sexual homicides (Firestone, Bradford, Greenberg, Larose, & Curry, 1998; Somander & Rammer, 1991). As with all child homicides, the impact of sexual child homicide is, however, immense, with intense public attention and the exhaustion of investigative resources (Boudreaux, Lord, & Jarvis, 2001; Federal Bureau of Investigation [FBI], 2004; Neuilly & Zgoba, 2006). While previous research on this rare crime is scarce, the few studies that have examined this have found that the offender is often extrafamilal – someone outside of the family (Stroud & Pritchard, 2001). The offender is most commonly male, and a stranger to the victim, and the victim is most commonly female (Boudreaux, Lord, & Dutra, 1999; Spehr, Hill, Habermann, Briken, & Berner, 2010; Stroud & Pritchard, 2001). The victim is most commonly killed by strangulation or asphyxiation and the crime is often planned (Beauregard et al., 2008).

While there are some comparative studies that have explored the similarities and differences between sexual homicides against children and sexual nonlethal violence against children, no previous study has compared sexual and nonsexual homicide committed against children. The aim of this study is therefore to explore the characteristics of sexual homicides targeting children and compare this group of offenders with sexual homicides targeting adult victims and well as nonsexual homicides targeting children.

Method

As in the previous studies, the offender-based hierarchical dataset of the SHD was used. Between 1990 and 2015, there were in total eight sexual homicides targeting children. This constituted 0.3% of all homicides and 8% of all sexual homicides in Scotland during this time. These eight homicides were compared to 89 sexual homicides committed against adult victims and 176 nonsexual offenders targeting children. These cases were compared regarding the victim variables, offender variables, and incident variables using Fisher's exact tests.

Findings

Exploring the offender variables of sexual homicide targeting children, the data showed that the vast majority of the offenders were male, of white

Sexual homicide 133

Table 7.7 Significance tests between offender characteristics and type of homicide

Offender variables		Child sexual homicide	Adult sexual homicide	Cohen's d	Nonsexual child homicide	Cohen's d
Gender	Man	7 (87.5%)	83 (93.3%)	0.15	131 (74.4%)	0.13[a]
Ethnicity	White	8 (100.0%)	67 (75.3%)	0.32	106 (60.2%)	0.35[a**]
Employment status	Unemployed	3 (37.5%)	20 (22.5%)	0.22	26 (14.8%)	0.23[a]
Residential status	Homeless	0 (0.0%)	3 (3.4%)	0.04	2 (1.1%)	0.06[a]
Suicide	Yes	1 (12.5%)	0 (0.0%)	0.36[†]	1 (0.6%)	0.26[a†]
Accomplice	Yes	1 (12.5%)	24 (27.0%)	0.14	62 (35.2%)	0.20[a]
Age	Mean	26.6	31.6	0.25[b]	26.7	0.01[b]

$* p < 0.05 ** p < 0.01 *** p < 0.001 \ † p < 0.1$
[a] Fisher's exact test.
[b] Independent samples t-test.

ethnicity, and employed (see Table 7.7). None of the offenders were homeless and the mean age of the offenders was 27 years old. In one of the cases, the offender had an accomplice, and the offender committed suicide in one of the cases. Overall, this would indicate a rather stable offender profile, with high levels of employment and stable housing conditions. These offenders proved very similar to the offenders of both adult sexual homicides and the offenders of child nonsexual homicide. Only offender ethnicity differed significantly, as child nonsexual homicide offenders were more likely to be of another ethnicity than white compared to child sexual homicide.

When the victim variables were examined, the findings revealed that the victims of child sexual homicides most commonly were female (see Table 7.8). The majority of the victims were of white ethnicity and none of the victims was homeless. In half of the cases, the victim was intoxicated by drugs or alcohol at the time of the offence, and the mean victim age was 12 years old. With the exception of age, the victims of child sexual homicide were similar to the victims of adult sexual homicide. There were some significant differences between child sexual homicide and child nonsexual homicides, however. Most of the child nonsexual homicides were male, and very few of the victims were intoxicated at the time of the crime. While the age of the victim did not reach significance, the child nonsexual homicides were younger, with a mean age of five years old.

Exploring the incident variables, the most common method of killing was strangulation or asphyxiation for child sexual homicides (see Table 7.9). In the cases where a weapon was used, this was most commonly improvised at the scene. The offender was most commonly a friend or acquaintance of the victim; however, in a quarter of the cases the offender was a stranger and in another quarter of the cases, the relationship status was unknown. While most of the homicides were committed in a private location, as many homicides

134 *Different types of homicide*

Table 7.8 Fisher's exact tests between victim characteristics and type of homicide

Victim variables		*Child sexual homicide*	*Adult sexual homicide*	*Cohen's d*	*Child Nonsexual homicide*	*Cohen's d*
Gender	Male	2 (25.0%)	28 (31.5%)	0.13	122 (69.3%)	0.37*
Ethnicity	White	6 (75.0%)	68 (76.4%)	0.10	100 (56.8%)	0.17
Residential status	Homeless	0 (0.00%)	5 (5.6%)	0.09	0 (0.00%)	
Influence status	Intoxicated	4 (50.0%)	25 (28.1%)	0.27	12 (6.8%)	0.47**

* $p < 0.05$ ** $p < 0.01$ *** $p < 0.001$ † $p < 0.1$
Note: The percentages in this table do not add up to 100% due to the possibility of multiple responses.

occurred indoors as outdoors. Half the cases involved multiple crime scenes, which usually occurred if the body was moved or if the sexual act occurred in a different location than the murder. Evidence was destroyed after the homicide in half of the cases. One case involved the murder of another adult victim and a quarter of the cases remained unsolved.

Comparing the child sexual homicides with the two comparison groups, there were some interesting differences. Strangulation as method of killing was more common in child sexual homicide than in both adult sexual homicide and child nonsexual homicides. It was furthermore more common for child sexual homicides to involve evidence destruction and multiple locations compared to both comparison groups. It was more common that child sexual homicides involved someone known in comparison to child nonsexual homicide, and it was furthermore more common for child nonsexual homicides to be committed between family members compared with child sexual homicide. While homicides against children that are not sexual most commonly are committed by family members, it appears that sexual homicides against children are most commonly committed by someone outside the family.

Discussion

Overall, this study has provided some important insights regarding sexual homicides committed against child victims in Scotland. This was the first study to compare child sexual homicide with both adult sexual homicide and child nonsexual homicide, demonstrating that while there are similarities between both groups, child sexual homicides appear most similar to adult sexual homicide. This means that this group of offenders should be considered sexual offenders first, homicide offender second, suggesting a continuum of

Table 7.9 Fisher's exact tests between incident characteristics and the type of homicide

Incident variables		Child sexual homicide	Adult sexual homicide	Cohen's d	Child nonsexual homicide	Cohen's d
Method of killing	Sharp instrument	0 (0.0%)	28 (31.5%)	0.39[†]	31 (17.6%)	0.18
	Blunt instrument	1 (12.5%)	28 (31.5%)	0.24	19 (10.8%)	0.08
	Shooting or firearm	0 (0.0%)	0 (0.0%)	–	4 (2.3%)	0.03
	Physical assault/no weapon	3 (37.5%)	38 (42.7%)	0.12	81 (46.0%)	0.11
	Strangulation or ligature	6 (75.0%)	32 (36.0%)	0.43*	26 (14.8%)	0.60***
	Other	4 (50.0%)	27 (30.3%)	0.25	56 (31.8%)	0.17
Relationship between offender and victim	Known or Acquaintance	3 (37.5%)	19 (21.3%)	0.23	18 (10.2%)	0.29*
	Family member	1 (12.5%)	0 (0.0%)	0.36[†]	114 (64.8%)	0.42**
	Stranger	2 (25.0%)	11 (12.4%)	0.22	15 (8.5%)	0.21
	Unknown	2 (25.0%)	51 (57.3%)	0.36[†]	23 (13.1%)	0.15
Public or private location	Private	4 (66.7%)	37 (53.6%)	0.18[a]	55 (59.1%)	0.12[b]
Inside or outside location	Inside	3 (50.0%)	42 (60.0%)	0.17[c]	64 (64.0%)	0.17[d]
Evidence destruction	Evidence destroyed	4 (50.0%)	12 (13.5%)	0.47*	7 (4.0%)	0.60***
Selection of Weapon	Improvised	2 (25.0%)	15 (16.9%)	0.16	6 (3.4%)	0.30*
	Brought to scene	0 (0.0%)	8 (9.0%)	0.14	25 (14.2%)	0.15
Multiple location	Yes	4 (50.0%)	6 (6.7%)	0.63**	5 (2.8%)	0.50***
Additional adult victim	Yes	1 (12.5%)	2 (2.3%)	0.24	13 (7.4%)	0.11
Unresolved	Yes	2 (25.0%)	26 (29.5%)	0.11	52 (29.5%)	0.08

* $p < 0.05$ ** $p < 0.01$ *** $p < 0.001$ [†] $p < 0.1$
[a] Twenty-two unknown cases excluded.
[b] Eighty-five unknown cases excluded.
[c] Twenty-one unknown cases excluded.
[d] Seventy-eight unknown cases excluded.

136 *Different types of homicide*

sexual violence. The findings of this study also corresponded to previous research, which stated that offenders of child sexual homicides most commonly were male, that the victim most commonly was female and that strangulation was the most common method of killing (Beauregard et al., 2008; Boudreaux et al., 1999). This study did, however, not find that the offender most commonly used a weapon (Beauregard et al., 2008) or that the most common relationship between offender and victim was stranger (Boudreaux et al., 1999; Spehr et al., 2010; Stroud & Pritchard, 2001). These differences may be methodological, but they may also be related to underlying jurisdictional differences between sexual child homicide offenders in other countries compared to Scotland. Future studies should compare child sexual homicide in different countries in order to explore whether there are any contextual differences to this crime.

While child sexual homicides are most similar to adult sexual homicide, the evidenced differences between these two crimes suggest that child sexual homicide should be considered a distinct type of sexual homicide (Beauregard et al., 2008; Spehr et al., 2010). The characteristics of child sexual homicide identified here also bear resemblance to the modus operandi of sadistic offenders descried by Dietz et al. (1990). As Dietz et al. describe, it is common that sadistic offenders planned their crime, that a varied range of sexual acts was performed, that the body of the victim often was concealed, and that the most common cause of death was strangulation. This study did not include a specific variable measuring premeditation; however, the fact that child sexual homicide offenders often destroyed evidence, used multiple locations, and drugged their victims suggest a level of planning compared to the other types of homicide examined. The fact that the victims often were someone known to the offender outside the immediate family might also suggest premeditation, as previous research on sexual violence against children has found that offenders might groom or stalk the victims for some time before abusing them (Carter, Barnett, Stefanska-Hodge, & Higgs, 2014). As previous research also has linked child sexual homicide to sadism, even describing it as salient to this crime (Beauregard et al., 2008; Heide et al., 2012; Schmidt & Madea, 1999), the offenders of child sexual homicide appear to demonstrate higher levels of sadism in comparison to other types of sexual and homicidal offenders.

While the obvious small number of cases in the current study means that the conclusions drawn here should be made with caution, this study has provided some valuable insights into a very rare and extreme type of violent crime. The fact that this was a population-based study also increase the generalisability of the results. Due to the rarity of this crime, and indeed, all sexual homicides, it would be beneficial if international samples could be combined in order to pool together samples and get a higher statistical number of cases. For that to be possible however, international samples need to be compared in order to explore whether the samples are similar enough to be combined. The final section of this chapter will therefore explore sexual homicides in two different jurisdictions, Canada and Scotland, in order to examine whether the samples are compatible.

A comparison between Scotland and Canada: subtypes of sexual homicide

Very few studies have compared sexual homicide internationally. For instance, James et al. (2018) and Chopin and Beauregard (2019) both compared sexual homicides in Canada and France, finding that the samples were more similar than different across countries. A study comparing Canadian sexual homicides with sexual homicides occurring in North Korea (Sea, Beauregard & Martineau, 2019) also found striking similarities between the samples. However, the scarcity of this research means that whether homicides differ across jurisdiction, and if so how, remains unclear. Can findings regarding sexual homicide in one country be applied to another? Is it possible to pool large international samples? In order to answer these questions, sexual homicides in different countries must first be compared. If there are few differences between countries, this would indicate that the samples could be quite easily combined; however, if there are substantial differences between the samples, these differences needs to be explored further. If the differences are due to underlying crime processes, indicated, for instance, by differences in motivation, sexual functioning, or psychopathology, this might indicate more radical difference than if there are cultural differences between countries, manifested in demographical, geographical, juridical, or cultural factors, which may affect overt manifestations even though the underlying process remains the same.

This study therefore aims to expand on the small field of cross-national research by comparing sexual homicide committed in Scotland and Canada. This will be done by comparing the country samples on both the bivariate and multivariate level. Previous research in homicide has demonstrated that despite differences on the bivariate level, similar underlying patterns may be found when the samples are explored using multivariate analysis, such as the identification of subtypes (Messner & Savolainen, 2001). When homicides in the US and Finland were compared, Messner and Savolainen, for instance, found that while the ratio of male to female homicides was significantly larger in the US, similar patterns were observed when homicide was disaggregated into subtypes. The exploration of subtypes of sexual homicide may therefore reveal similar underlying patterns, which may not be observed through bivariate analysis alone.

While previous research examining sexual homicide subtypes have found a range of different types, studies tend to find between two and three main, recurring types (Chan & Heide, 2009; Higgs, Carter, Stefanska, & Glorney, 2017; Higgs, Carter, Tully, & Browne, 2017). While the types are often given varying names, many reflect similar behaviours or offender pathways. This usually falls into one organised or sadistic type, where the crime is often

138   *Different types of homicide*

planned, the victims are often strangers, and the crime is characterised by high levels of control and premeditation, and a second, disorganised or angry type, where the behaviour is impulsive, the victims are often known, and the crimes are characterised by disorganisation and anger (Beauregard & Proulx, 2007; Higgs et al., 2017; Ressler et al., 1988). Although there are similarities in typologies from different countries, no previous study has compared empirically, data-driven typologies in different international samples. The current study will therefore both explore the bivariate differences in sexual homicide in Scotland and Canada as well as identify subtypes of sexual homicide in both countries.

Method

The current study used two samples: one Scottish sample, gathered from the Scottish Homicide Database (SHD) and one Canadian sample, gathered from the national database held by the Royal Canadian Mounted Police (RCMP). The Scottish sample consisted of $n = 89$ sexual homicide offenders over 78 cases committed between 1990 and 2015 and the Canadian sample included $n = 150$ sexual homicides over as many cases between 1990 and 2015. Variables concerning the victims and the modus operandi were initially compared using chi square analysis. Then, subtypes of sexual homicides were identified using Latent Class Analysis (LCA), similarly to what was done to the homicide data in Chapter 6. While the model was initially run with all victim and incident variables included, some variables were subsequently excluded since they failed to disaggregate between the types. The excluded variables were: victim employment status; victim age 16–31; victim age 31–45; method of killing by shooting or firearm; 'other' as method of killing (i.e. *not* using a firearm, sharp implement, strangulation/asphyxiation, or blunt force trauma); inside location; and rural or urban location. Since these variables could be removed without affecting the model they were deemed redundant to the model. The best fitting model was decided based on the Bayesian Information Criteria (BIC), and the substantive interpretation of the classes (see Table 7.10). The BIC has been found to be a superior indicator of model fit (Hagenaars & McCutcheon, 2002; Yu & Park, 2014) and models with lower BIC are generally preferred.

Table 7.10 BIC and entropy for 2–5 class models of Scottish and Canadian subtypes

Number of classes	Scotland BIC	Entropy	Canada BIC	Entropy
1	1409.65		2746.41	
2	**1379.05**	1	2703.45	1
3	1403.82	0,989	**2673.52**	1
4	1437.33	0,966	2679.61	1

Note: Best fitting models indicated in bold.

Sexual homicide 139

Findings

When comparing the victim variables across the two samples, the data revealed that most of the victims were female in both Canada and Scotland, although it was significantly more common that victims were male in Scotland (see Table 7.11). While the victims were most commonly white in both samples, it was significantly more common that the victims were of another ethnicity than white in Canada. The victims were furthermore more commonly unemployed in Scotland compared to Canada. While it was slightly more common for the victim to be engaged in prostitution in Canada compared to Scotland, this difference was not significant. The most common victim age was 16–30 years old in both samples. When the incident variables were explored, the data showed that while the most common method of killing in Scotland was strangulation or asphyxiation, the most common cause of death in Canada was by physical assault, which was significantly more common in Canada. Strangulation was, however, also very prevalent in the Canadian sample, with half of the victims being killed using this method. It was also significantly more common for Canadian cases to involve firearms or guns compared to the Scottish sample and 'other' as cause of death was more common in Scotland. When a weapon was used, this was more commonly improvised at the crime scene in both countries; however, it was significantly more common that the Canadian sexual homicide offenders brought the weapon with them to the scene of the crime.

The most common relationship between victim and offender in Canada was someone known, like a friend or acquaintance, which was also significantly more common in comparison to Scotland. It was also significantly more common that sexual homicides involved family members in Canada. There was, however, a very high degree of missingness in the Scottish sample in this regard; the relationship between victim and offender was coded as unknown in more than 60% of the cases, which was significantly higher than in Canada. The relationship might be unknown if the case remains unresolved or if this information simply is unknown to the police. While it was more common that sexual homicide offenders targeted strangers in Canada, this difference did not reach statistical significance.

The two samples were very similar in regards to crime location; the majority of cases took place in urban settings, and it was slightly more common for the sexual homicides to occur in public outdoor locations than in private indoor locations in both samples. It was significantly more common that the Canadian sexual homicide offenders destroyed evidence after the homicide was committed, and it was furthermore significantly more common that the Canadian sexual homicides involved multiple locations.

In the multivariate analysis, LCA models were run on both samples separately, running models with 1–4 classes in each sample. As can be seen from Table 7.10, the BIC indicated a 2-class solution to be superior in the Scottish sample, and the 3-class model to be the best Canadian model. However, the Scottish 2-class

Table 7.11 Chi-square analyses between victim and incident characteristics and the type of homicide

Variables		Total sample	Scotland	Canada	Cohen's d
Victim gender	Male	47 (19.7%)	26 (29.2%)	21 (14.0%)	0.38**
Victim ethnicity	White	145 (60.7%)	66 (74.2%)	79 (52.7%)	0.44***
Victim employment status	Employed	73 (30.5%)	9 (9.0%)	65 (43.3%)	0.77***
Victim engaged in prostitution	Yes	23 (9.6%)	6 (6.7%)	11 (11.3%)	0.15
Victim age	Under 16 years old	28 (11.7%)	6 (6.7%)	22 (14.7%)	0.24†
	16–30 years old	112 (46.9%)	40 (44.9%)	72 (48.0%)	0.06
	31–45 years old	55 (23.0%)	20 (22.5%)	35 (23.3%)	0.02
	46 years or older	46 (19.2%)	25 (28.1%)	21 (14.0%)	0.35*
Method of killing	Sharp instrument	70 (29.3%)	25 (28.1%)	45 (30.0%)	0.04
	Shooting or firearm	7 (2.9%)	0 (0.0%)	7 (4.7%)	0.27*
	Strangulation or ligature	111 (46.4%)	36 (40.4%)	75 (50%)	0.19
	Physical assault	102 (42.7%)	23 (25.8%)	79 (52.7%)	0.54***
	Other	55 (23.0%)	29 (32.6%)	26 (17.3%)	0.36*
Relationship between offender and victim	Known or Acquaintance	87 (36.4%)	18 (20.2%)	69 (46.0%)	0.54***
	Familial	31 (13.0%)	4 (4.5%)	27 (18.0%)	0.40**
	Stranger	50 (20.9%)	13 (14.6%)	37 (24.7%)	0.24†
	Unknown	72 (30.1%)	54 (60.7%)	18 (12.0%)	0.44***
Rural or urban location	Rural	17 (7.1%)	5 (5.6%)	12 (8.0%)	0.09
Public or private location	Private	111 (46.4%)	38 (42.7%)	73 (48.7%)	0.12
Inside or outside location	Inside	109 (45.6%)	40 (44.9%)	69 (46.0%)	0.02
Evidence destruction	Evidence destroyed	95 (39.7%)	15 (14.7%)	81 (54.0%)	0.82***
Selection of weapon	Improvised	52 (21.8%)	15 (16.9%)	37 (24.7%)	0.18
	Brought to scene	39 (16.3%)	7 (7.9%)	32 (21.3%)	0.36**
Multiple location	Yes	55 (23.0%)	6 (6.7%)	49 (32.7%)	0.62***

* $p < 0.05$ ** $p < 0.01$ *** $p < 0.001$ † $p < 0.1$

model included a class with very high levels of 'unknown' variables, as well as a very diverse class, suggesting that this solution could be a statistical artefact (Skardhamar 2009). Since the 3-class solution was more interesting substantively, as well as more interpretable, this solution was chosen for both samples.

Scottish subtypes

The three classes in the Scottish sample were labelled *Controlled-Organised* (27%), *Diverse* (12%), and *Unknown* (61%). As can be seen from Figure 7.1, the vast majority of the victims of the *Controlled-Organised* type were white females. About 13% of the victims were prostitutes and only a small amount of the victims were either very young (under 16 years old) or old (over 45 years old). When the incident variables of the *Controlled-Organised* type was examined, the data showed that the most common method of killing in this type was strangulation or asphyxiation and most of the offenders in this type killed strangers (see Figure 7.2). If a weapon was used, this was brought to the crime scene in about a fifth of the cases. Most of these cases occurred in a private location, and in a fifth of the cases, multiple locations was used (see Figure 7.3). Almost 40% of the *Controlled-Organised* sexual homicides offenders attempted to destroy evidence after the homicide was committed. Overall, the *Controlled-Organised* subtype demonstrated behaviour consistent with what previous research has described as organised or controlled, such as having a higher probability to bring the weapon to the scene, using multiple locations and targeting prostitutes and strangers (Mjanes et al., 2018; Ressler et al., 1988).

The *Diverse* type was labelled as such since these offenders demonstrated a more diverse type of behaviour. More than half of the *Diverse* type of sexual homicide involved male victims, which was the highest rate of male victims of all types in Scotland (see Figure 7.1). Most of the victims were older in this type; more than 65% of the cases included a victim older than 45 years old. Similarly to the *Controlled-Organised* type, the majority of the victims were of white ethnicity. None of the *Diverse* victims were engaged in prostitution. When the incident variables were explored, the data showed that a third of the *Diverse* sexual homicides were killed using a sharp weapon and another 28% were killed using physical assault (see Figure 7.2). In the cases where a weapon was used, the offender improvised this weapon at the crime scene, which would indicate that many of these crimes were improvised. All of these offenders knew their victims, meaning none of them were strangers. Exploring the location variables, the data showed that the majority of the *Diverse* homicides were committed in private locations (see Figure 7.3). None of the cases involved multiple locations, and none of the offenders destroyed evidence after the homicide.

The third and final subtype in the Scottish sample was labelled *Unknown* due to the fact that the most common relationship between offender and victim was unknown (see Figure 7.3). This type of sexual homicide offender demonstrated, similarly to the *Diverse* type, a quite diverse behavioural pattern. While most of the sexual homicides targeted female victims, more than a third

142 *Different types of homicide*

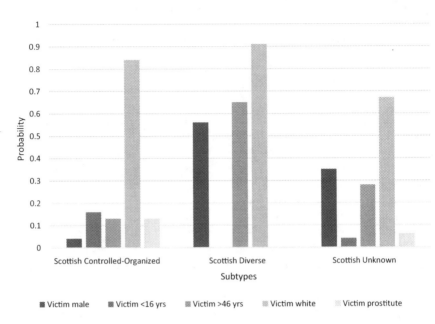

Figure 7.1 Victim variables in sexual homicide types in Scotland
Note 1: Base: *n* = 89
Source: The SHD

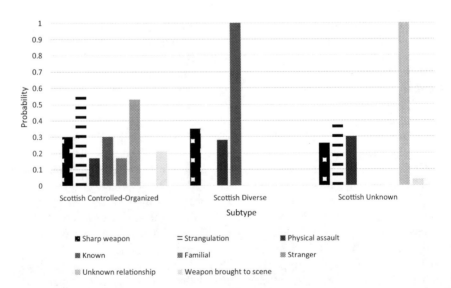

Figure 7.2 Incident variables for sexual homicide types in Scotland
Note 1: Base: *n* = 89
Source: The SHD

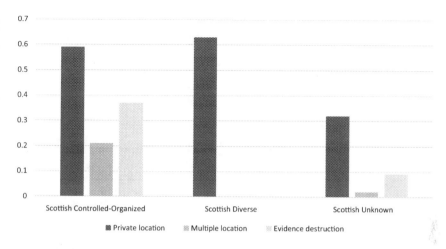

Figure 7.3 Location variables for sexual homicide types in Scotland
Note 1: Base: *n* = 89
Source: The SHD

of the victims of the *Unknown type* were male (see Figure 7.1). More than a fifth of the *Unknown* victims were older than 45 years old and while the majority of the victims were white, a third of the victims were of another ethnicity than white, which was the highest for all Scottish subtypes. When the incident variables were examined, the data showed that the method of killing was quite diverse. While the most common method of killing was strangulation, another third of the victims of the *Unknown* type was killed using physical assault and another quarter of the cases involved a sharp weapon (see Figure 7.2). The offender improvised the choice of weapon in most of the cases that involved a weapon, suggesting that most of these crimes were improvised. As mentioned, the most common relationship between victim and offender was unknown. Most of the *Unknown* sexual homicides occurred in a public location, unlike the two previous types, and while multiple locations was rare, 9% of the cases involved evidence destruction.

Canadian subtypes

Three subtypes were identified in the Canadian sample labelled; *Controlled-Organised* (25%), *Diverse* (45%), and *Familial* (30%). The majority of the victims of the *Controlled-Organised* subtype were white females (see Figure 7.4). Almost 20% of the victims were under the age of 16 years old, and in a fifth of the cases, the victim was a prostitute. The majority of the *Controlled-Organised* offenders strangled their victims, although half of the cases also involved physical assault (see Figure 7.5). In the cases where a weapon was used, the offender brought it to the crime scene in about a quarter of the cases. All

144 Different types of homicide

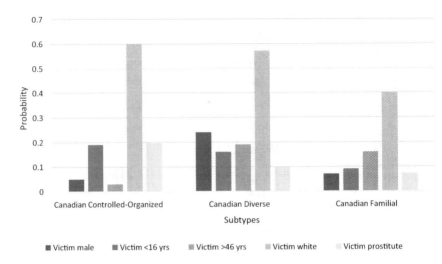

Figure 7.4 Victim variables of sexual homicide types in Canada
Note 1: Base: *n* = 150
Source: The Canadian national database on sexual homicide held by RCMP

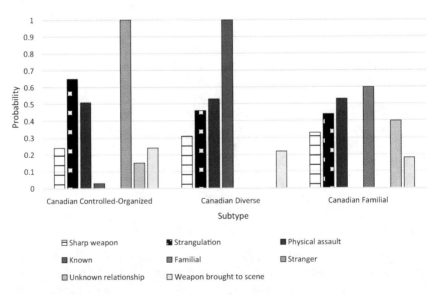

Figure 7.5 Incident variables for sexual homicide types in Canada
Note 1: Base: *n* = 150
Source: The Canadian national database on sexual homicide held by RCMP

of the *Controlled-Organised* victims were strangers. Most of the *Controlled-Organised* sexual homicides occurred in public settings, and about 45% of the cases involved multiple locations. Almost 40% of the *Controlled-Organised* offenders attempted to destroy evidence after the homicide. Overall, this type of sexual homicide was very similar to the Scottish *Controlled-Organised* type, and reflect similar organised and controlled behaviour as indicated by previous research (Mjanes et al., 2018; Ressler et al., 1988).

The second Canadian subtype was called *Diverse*, and similarly to the Scottish subtype with the same name, the behavioural pattern of this subtype was quite diverse. While most of the victims of the *Diverse* type were female, almost a quarter of the victims were male (see Figure 7.4). Little more than 15% of the victims were younger than 16 years old and almost a fifth were older than 45 years old. The majority of the victims were white, and in 10% of the cases, the victim was engaged in prostitution. All of the offenders knew the victims in the *Diverse* sexual homicides (see Figure 7.5). The method of killing was, as mentioned, quite diverse; the most common method of killing was by physical assault (53%), but in another 46% of the cases, the offender strangled the victim and in another third of the cases, the victim was killed with a sharp instrument. If a weapon was used, the offender brought the weapon with them to the crime scene in little more than a fifth of the cases. The majority of the *Diverse* cases took place in a private setting, and multiple locations were used in a third of the cases (see Figure 7.6). The majority of cases (57%) involved evidence destruction.

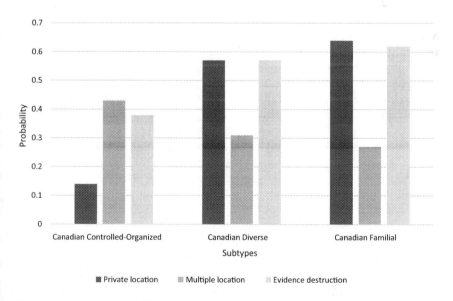

Figure 7.6 Location variables for sexual homicide types in Canada
Note 1: Base: $n = 150$
Source: The Canadian national database on sexual homicide held by RCMP

146   *Different types of homicide*

The third and final Canadian subtype was called *Familial* since most of the offenders in this type targeted family members (see Figure 7.5). The victims of this subtype were most commonly female (see Figure 7.4). In 16% of the cases, the victim was older than 45 years old and in barely a tenth of the cases the victim was younger than 16 years old. Most of the victims of this subtype were of a nonwhite ethnicity and in 7% of the cases, the victim was a prostitute. While most of the victims were related to the offenders, the relationship between offender and victim was unknown in 40% of the cases (see Figure 7.5). The method of killing was quite diverse; while more than half of the victims were killed by physical assault, another 44% were strangled and a third of the victims were killed with the use of a sharp instrument. When a weapon was used, the offenders brought the weapon with them to the crime scene in almost a fifth of the cases. The majority of the cases were committed in a private location, and in little more than a quarter of the cases, multiple locations were used (see Figure 7.6). In more than 60% of the cases, the offender destroyed evidence after the crime was committed.

Discussion

When the Canadian and Scottish sexual homicides were compared on the bivariate level, there were quite a few differences between the countries. These differences included differences in victim gender, relationship between offender and victim, method of killing and victim ethnicity. However, when multivariate analysis was conducted and subtypes in both samples were identified, there were striking similarities between the two different jurisdictions. A three-class model was the best fitting solution in both samples, and the characteristics of these subtypes suggest very similar underlying behavioural patterns in the two countries. The *Controlled-Organised* types in Scotland and Canada were both characterised by a greater probability of targeting strangers and prostitutes, of using multiple locations, and of bringing the weapon to the crime scene. The victims were predominantly female and strangulation was the most common method of killing for the *Controlled-Organised* sexual homicides. The offenders often destroyed evidence after the homicide in both jurisdictions. While there were some differences between Scottish and Canadian *Controlled-Organised* subtypes, such as the location of the crime, the overall profile of this subtype is similar in both countries. This profile, which is characterised by control and organisation, bears similarities to the organised (Ressler et al., 1988) and sadistic (Beauregard & Proulx, 2002) subtypes identified in previous research and suggest a premeditative offending behaviour. Since power and control are key aspects of sexual sadism (Mokros 2018), such behaviour may also indicate sexual sadism.

The *Diverse* types were also similar across jurisdictions. This subtype included sexual homicides most commonly committed in a private setting with the use of a sharp weapon or by the use of physical assault. While this type included the highest number of male victims, the victims were most commonly female, and they were most commonly known to the offender. Even though there were some differences between Scotland and Canada, for instance regarding victim age, the overarching pattern of these sexual homicides was characterised by impulsivity, opportunity, disorganisation, and lack of planning. This resembles the disorganised (Ressler et al., 1988) and the angry (Beauregard & Proulx, 2002) subtypes identified in previous research.

Finally, the third type identified in both jurisdictions (the Scottish *Unknown* and the Canadian *Familial*) were also similar across the two samples. As mentioned, while most of the *Familial* homicide offenders killed a family member, the relationship was unknown in 40% of the cases, similarly to the *Unknown* type. Both subtypes also demonstrated a very diverse method of killing, and both had the highest level of nonwhite victims in each country. Since the relationship between victim and offender has been found to be very important when disaggregating sexual homicide (see, for instance, Skott et al., 2021), it is possible that these *Unknown* cases represent an underlying subtype with a specific relationship, such as family members, that remains undetected. Furthermore, due to the nature of LCA as a technique, it is possible that the *Unknown* subtype in the Scottish sample may be considered something of a statistical artefact (Skardhamar, 2009) with limited practical implications. As such, while this study has identified a Scottish subtype characterised by the unknown relationship between victim and offender, this subtype may in fact represent another, yet hidden subtype that should be explored further.

The bivariate differences found in this study may thus represent general differences between the countries relating to culture, ethnicity, laws, and weapon availability rather than the underlying offending process. As such, these processes may actually be similar or the same, regardless of country or jurisdiction. For instance, Scotland has stricter firearms regulations compared to Canada (Law Library of Congress, 2015), which may affect the method by which the victims were killed, yet which doesn't change the underlying motivational or behavioural patterns of the offenders. This, along with the similarity of the subtypes identified in the current study with subtypes identified in previous research, would suggest that the number of scripts dictating offending behaviour in sexual homicide is limited (Beauregard, Proulx, Rossmo, Leclerc, & Allaire, 2007), and that this behaviour transcends jurisdiction. As such, this study has indicated that there is universality in the underlying latent pathways of sexual homicide, across a North American and a Western European jurisdiction, which furthermore could indicate that the pooling of international samples could be conducted in the future. The next section will explore different theoretical perspectives aiming to explain why some individuals commit sexual homicide.

Theories of sexual homicide

Why does anyone commit sexual homicide? While there is not any one definitive answer to this question, there are some theoretical explanations for why individuals may commit this, often gruesome, type of crime. Some of the theories outlined in Chapter 4 are applicable here as well, particularly

148 *Different types of homicide*

theories relating to gender as many of the sexual murders are characterised by misogynist sentiments and motivations. But there are also some theories specific for the perpetration of sexual homicide. One of the most prevalent explanatory factors is previous trauma in the offender's childhood (Proulx, Cusson, & Beauregard, 2007; Ressler et al., 1988). This trauma could be physical, psychological, or sexual, and often results in social isolation. Trauma and isolation in combination with problematic family relationships often lead to the development of violent sexual fantasies which slowly build within the offender, compensating for the lack of control they experience in real life. These emerging fantasises become increasingly violent and invasive over time, escalating into violent acts of sexual aggression. The trauma and the intense sexual fantasies experienced by offenders of sexual homicide may also lead to dissociation (Chan, 2018). As cognitive distortions develop as a way to cope with previous trauma, these offenders may perceive themselves in an overly favourable or narcissistic way, or may even repress the memories of their actions, being unable to recall their crimes.

Another, psychologically oriented explanation of sexual homicide is to be found in the presence of paraphilia, such as sexual sadism, fetishism, voyeurism, paedophilia, or necrophilia (Hazelwood & Warren, 1990; McKenzie, 1995; Proulx et al., 2007). Paraphilia may develop in a similar way to violent sexual fantasies, through a process of trauma, social isolation and an elaborate inner world (Chan, 2018). Individuals troubled by these abnormal, often harmful desires tend to prefer their fantasy world to the real world, and are constantly developing new fantasies aimed to increase sexual gratification, which often escalate. For instance, sadistic offenders tend to withdraw into an elaborate inner world of violent and coercive fantasies as a way to escape failed relationships. Acting out these fantasies then becomes a coping mechanism; an outlet for their inner anger, pain, and humiliation (Proulx, McKibben, & Lusignan, 1996; Proulx et al., 2007). Sadistic offenders targeting child victims may experience these failed relationships with other adults, and the triggers reinforcing the fantasies may be feelings of rejection and low self-esteem (Beauregard et al., 2008). The high level of organisation and ritualization prevalent in sadistic sexual homicides may also be indicative of serial offending (Dietz et al., 1990; Proulx, Blais, & Beauregard, 2007). As Proulx et al. (2007: 17) explains, 'voyeurism, exhibitionism, rape and sexual murder are thus simply stages of a paraphilic continuum'.

Personality disorders are also quite prevalent in offenders committing sexual homicide, particularly psychopathy (Porter & Rose, 2018), borderline personality disorder (Gacono, Meloy & Kennedy, 1994), narcissistic personality disorder (Proulx & Sauvêtre, 2007), and schizoid personality disorder (Myers & Monaco, 2000). Previous research has found that these personality disorders affect both the daily life of sexual homicide offenders as well as determining their behaviour in the sexual homicidal acts (Proulx & Sauvêtre, 2007). However, as mentioned in Chapter 4, no personality disorder alone is a sufficient condition for a recourse to violence.

Aiming to develop a criminological rather than psychological theory of sexual homicide, Chan, Heide, and Beauregard (2011) developed an integrated theoretical framework of social learning and routine activities theories. Focusing on both the environmental aspects to sexual homicide as well as the offender characteristics, this theory posits that the motivation to kill sexually is socially learned from parents, peers, or sadistic pornographic material. As this process of social learning reinforces the deviant sexual acts, sexual homicide offenders will continue to seize opportunities to attack 'suitable or attractive target in the absence of a capable guardian or an effective guardianship in the immediate surroundings' (Chan et al., 2011: 241). As such, this theory draws on both individual and situational factors to attempt to explain why individuals become motivated to commit sexual homicide, concluding this offence to be a combination of predisposition (such as abusive home environments or previous sexual victimisation) and opportunity (such as a suitable target and the absence of a capable guardian) (Chan, 2018). Chan (2015) later revised this theoretical model by including pre-crime precipitating factors, arguing to have an increased motivating effect on the offender. Such factors, usually occurring within 48 hours of the sexual homicide, may be the consumption of alcohol or drugs, viewing of pornography, indulgence in deviant sexual fantasies or conflicts in relation to interpersonal relationships. As Chan (2015) argued, these precipitating factors may function as triggers for the offender, providing further motivation for the offence.

Conclusions

This chapter has provided an in-depth examination of a rare yet impactful type of homicide: sexual homicide. Having explored different aspects of this crime, this chapter has provided answers to the questions of how sexual homicides differ from nonsexual homicides, how female sexual homicide offenders differ from male sexual homicide offenders, and how sexual homicide targeting children differ from sexual homicide targeting adults. This chapter has also put Scottish sexual homicide in international context by comparing sexual homicide in Scotland to sexual homicide in Canada, exploring this crime on both bivariate and multivariate levels. Overall, this chapter has shown that while there are some differences between different forms of sexual homicide, sexual homicide is a very distinct type of homicide that should be explored separately from other types of homicide. This chapter has also shown that although there might be differences between two countries on the bivariate level, similar underlying patterns appear to exist that seem universal across jurisdictions. This does not only open up for the possibility of combining international datasets in order to get larger samples, allowing for more sophisticated statistical analysis, but this also suggest a limited number of behavioural patterns for sexual homicide offenders, as similar subtypes have been found in different countries. This chapter concludes the second part of the book, and we will now continue to the third and final part, called theorising homicide.

Part III

Theorising homicide

The first and the second parts of the book have provided the descriptive and empirical foundations towards a deeper understanding of homicide. We have explored different types of homicide, including sexual homicide, using different methodological approaches and an argument has been made that an explorative, inductive approach is favourable when examining lethal and nonlethal violence. This final section of the book will provide an even more in-depth analysis of homicide by theorising this crime. In Chapter 8, we will first examine the relationship between homicide and nonlethal violence by comparing subtypes of nonlethal violence to the identified subtypes of homicide presented in Chapter 6. These two typologies will be compared in regards to characteristics as well as how they have changed over time in order to provide a deeper understanding for the relationship between lethal and nonlethal violence. In Chapter 9, we will subsequently explore the implications of the findings of this research, and the possible effects on policy as well as theory will be explored. Chapter 9 will also present a new, theoretical framework called *Doing Violence* to help theorise and explain homicide and nonlethal violence. Finally, Chapter 10 will provide a summary of the findings as well as the main conclusions of this book. Here, we will summarise what we have learned and what you as a reader may take away from this book. The chapter and the book will end with some concluding remarks, encapsulating how this volume has helped to provide a deeper understanding of homicide.

DOI: 10.4324/9781003105282-10

8 The relationship between homicide and violence

Introduction

While the last chapter provided an in-depth exploration of sexual homicide, this chapter will examine the relationship between homicide and other forms of nonlethal violence in Scotland. As this chapter will explain, there is a knowledge gap relating to the relationship between lethal and nonlethal violence, and it is unclear whether trends of homicide and violence are following a similar trend over time, or indeed if homicide can even be regarded as the extreme end of a violence spectrum. This chapter will provide some answers to these questions relating to this relationship by comparing subtypes of homicide (which were identified in Chapter 6) to subtypes of nonlethal violence. These violence subtypes will be identified in the current chapter using the same explorative, data-driven approach used to identify homicide subtypes – Multilevel Latent Class Analysis (MLCA). By comparing subtypes of these two crimes, we will not only be able to explore whether the characteristics of these crimes are similar, but also whether the trends in these crimes are following a similar pattern over time. As will be explained, whether or not homicide and violence are declining or increasing in tandem has important implications for both theory and practice. This chapter will, however, begin with a brief examination of the previous research (and the lack thereof) in relation to the relationship between homicide and nonlethal violence.

A gap in our knowledge: the lack of previous research

As the most serious of violent crimes, homicide has devastating consequences for the victim as well as for the victim's family, friends, and the community as a whole. Yet, there is a gap in the understanding of how homicide relates to wider violence. Harries (1989) identified this gap in the violence literature regarding the relationship between homicide and violence more than 30 years ago. Harries argued that knowledge was lacking in two aspects of this relationship: qualitative aspects, such as information about the similarities in characteristics of homicide and violence; and quantitative aspects, such as information about the similarities in the temporal patterns of these

DOI: 10.4324/9781003105282-11

154   *Theorising homicide*

two crimes. This lack of knowledge meant that it had not yet been established whether homicide and wider violence could be viewed as similar behaviours only differentiated by the outcome (Harries, 1989).

This lack of understanding is problematic for a number of reasons. Not only would intervention strategies and policies designed to prevent violence and homicide be more efficient with this knowledge, but theoretical insights could also be gained through a deeper understanding of how homicide relates to wider violence. Very few studies have examined the two aspects of the relationship between homicide and violence outlined by Harries (1989) since his study, however. While Harries (1989) examined the relationship between short-term temporal patterns of homicide and violence (such as seasonal similarities and differences), information about long-term temporal similarities between these two crimes is also needed. The following two sections will therefore outline previous research regarding the similarities and differences between characteristics of homicide and violence and the similarities and differences between the change over time in these two crimes. The subsequent sections will also describe the implications of this lacking knowledge and why it is important to examine these aspects further.

Characteristics of homicide and violence

Although many researchers intuitively assume a relationship between homicide and violence (Harries, 1989), very few studies have examined the similarities and differences between characteristics of homicide and violence in order to establish whether these two crimes reflect the same underlying behaviour. Harries (1989) discovered that while homicide and violence differed on certain variables, such as regarding the use of guns (which was more common in homicides) and the location of the crime (where homicides were more likely to occur in residential settings), the characteristics of homicide and violence were very similar. As such, the demographic and temporal similarities between homicide and violence suggested that these two crimes should be considered as the same underlying behaviour, differentiated in outcome rather than process (Harries, 1989).

A more complex relationship between homicide and violence has, however, been found in other studies. Comparing lethal and nonlethal partner violence, Addington and Perumean-Chaney (2014) found that while domestic homicides of male victims were very similar to nonlethal domestic violence of male victims, suggesting an underlying continuum of violence, domestic homicides of female victims were different from nonlethal domestic violence against female victims. This result indicated distinct characteristics of homicide and violence which therefore should not be interpreted along the same continuum (Addington & Perumean-Chaney, 2014).

Even though the research examining similarities between homicide and violence is scarce, many studies still make assumptions about this relationship. Studies examining the lethality of violence (see, for instance, Berg, 2019;

The relationship between homicide and violence   155

Dobash, Dobash, Cavanagh, & Medina-Ariza, 2007; Ganpat, Van Der Leun, & Nieuwbeerta, 2013; Lauritzen & Lentz, 2019) assume an underlying relationship between the two crimes since this type of analysis postulates that the characteristics of the incidents are similar enough to be comparable. Other scholars examine homicide and violence separately, with the unavoidable implication that they are two distinct crimes with different characteristics (see, for instance, Bossarte, Simon, & Barker, 2006; Breetzke, 2017). It is therefore important to examine the characteristics of homicide and violence further in order to establish whether these two crimes are related or not. The following section will examine previous research on the second aspect identified as lacking in the relationship between homicide and violence; the similarities and differences between the changes over time in these two crimes.

Trends in homicide and violence over time

While the decrease in homicide has been given quite extensive exploration in previous research (see, for instance, Aebi & Linde, 2010; 2012; Farrell et al., 2010), interpreting the trends in wider violence is not as straightforward. Violence, both measured by victimisation data and police recorded data, has decreased markedly in English-speaking countries, including the UK, Canada, Australia, and the US, while the trends have remained stable or increased elsewhere, for instance in Scandinavia (Tonry, 2014). Studies have found that violence has increased since the 1990s in Western Europe (Aebi & Linde, 2010; 2012; Farrell et al., 2010), while other research has suggested that these trends have declined (Blumstein, 2000; Tonry, 2014). Although these cross-national differences might be due to changes in reporting and recording of crime (Tonry, 2014), these contradictory trends might also indicate that homicide has followed a different trend in comparison to wider violence. This raises important questions about the relationship between the trends in homicide and violence. Can homicide be considered representative of other forms of violence within a country or does the trend in homicide follow a different pattern?

Previous studies that have compared trends in homicide and violence over time in the US have found opposite relationships between these two crimes. While Blumstein (2000) found that homicide and violence were following a similar pattern over time, Harris, Thomas, Fisher, and Hirsch (2002) found an inverse relationship between homicide and violence, where violence had demonstrated a much more dramatic increase in comparison to violence over time. Although both Blumstein (2000) and Harris et al. (2002) used statistics from the FBI's Uniform Crime Reports (UCR), which only includes police recorded crime that is submitted on a voluntary basis from law enforcement agencies (FBI, 2015), only Blumstein (2000) compared these findings to victimisation data (the National Crime Victimisation Survey). The differences between the two studies may thus be related to the fact that Harris et al. (2002) did not compare the police recorded crime to victimisation data.

156   *Theorising homicide*

When Blumstein (2000) only explored police recorded data they also found differences in the trends, which would indicate that the choice of data is highly important when examining the relationship between homicide and violence. Since victimisation data previously has been argued to be more reliable than police recorded crime when measuring violence (Tonry, 2014; Van Dijk, Van Kesteren & Smit, 2007), the vast increase in violence found by Harris et al. (2002) might be due to changes in public reporting and police recording rather than an actual underlying increase in violence.

Since the 1960s, victimisation data has become a more favourable measure of crime due to the many advantages of victimisation measures compared to police recorded data (Maguire, 2012; McAra & McVie, 2012). Victimisation data does not only include crimes that have not come to the attention of the police, but it is also less affected by changes in public reporting in comparison to police recorded crime. Additionally, victimisation data is less affected by changes in police recording and coding procedures, and it generally allows the researcher to collect more information about the characteristics of the crime (McAra & McVie, 2012). Although there are shortcomings to victimisation measures as well, such as sampling errors or respondents not accurately reporting their victimisation or their criminality, victimisation measures such as crime surveys are considered the most reliable measure of crime (Maguire, 2012; McAra & McVie, 2012).

The advantages of using victimisation data are also evident when examining violence (Tonry, 2014; Van Dijk et al., 2007). When comparing violence measured by victimisation data (National Crime Victimisation Survey) and police recorded crime (Uniform Crime Reports) in the US, Lauritzen, Rezey, and Heimer (2015) found the victimisation measures of violence to be more reliable. However, since victims of homicide cannot participate in crime surveys, police recorded crime data is the only measurement available for measuring homicide. Police recorded crime is generally regarded to have a higher 'dark figure' compared to victimisation data since most crimes does not come to the attention of the police (Brookman, 2005; Granath, 2011; McAra & McVie, 2012). Homicide, however, is usually considered an exception due to the practical difficulties of hiding the evidence compared to other crimes. Although some homicides never come to the attention of the police, this number is considered to be lower compared to other crimes, and homicide is therefore considered to be one of the most reliably measured crimes (Brookman, 2005; Granath, 2011).

As such, the choice of violence measurement appears to be highly important when examining the relationship between trends in homicide and violence. For instance, Lauritzen et al. (2016) found that victimisation measures of violence and police recorded violence demonstrated opposite trends over time. While victimisation measures of violence had decreased between the early 1970s until the mid-1980s, police recorded violence had increased during this time period (Lauritzen et al., 2016). When comparing both measures of violence to police recorded measures of homicide, Lauritzen et al., found that victimisation data was more closely related to homicide trends over time. Hence, like Blumstein (2000), Lauritzen et al. (2016) concluded that homicide and violence followed a similar trend over time when victimisation measures of violence were used but not when police recorded violence was used. This difference in violence measurements has also been found in European studies (Aebi & Linde, 2010; Van Wilsem, 2004).

The relationship between homicide and violence consequently seems to differ depending on the data chosen to measure nonlethal violence. While trends in homicide appears to follow similar trends to violence measured by victimisation data (Aebi & Linde, 2010; Blumstein, 2000; Tonry, 2014), homicide also appears to be negatively related to violence measured by police recorded data (Harris et al., 2002; Van Wilsem, 2004). This has two important implications for the current research. First, the relationship between the trends in homicide and violence can differ depending on how violence is measured (Blumstein, 2000; Lauritzen et al., 2016). Second, since victimisation measures are considered more accurate compared to police recorded crime, victimisation data (such as crime survey data) should be used.

Implications of the lack of knowledge for theory and policy

As such, there is not much known about the relationship between homicide and wider violence.

There is no consensus regarding whether the characteristics of homicide reflect the characteristics of wider violence, as well as whether the trends in homicide follow a similar pattern to trends in wider violence. This lacking understanding of the relationship between homicide and violence is problematic for a number of reasons and has important implications for both policy and theory. Homicide and violence place profound stress on emergency systems, as well as having a great impact on the health of the family and community (Harries, 1989; Harvey, Williams & Donnelly, 2012). These crimes also have unparalleled impact on the public perception of crime and fear of crime in society (Perkins & Taylor, 1996; Warr, 2000). In addition to the social costs of homicide and violence, these crimes also bring society great economic costs (Harvey et al., 2012; Waters, Hyder, Rajkoti, Basu, & Butfigure, 2005). It is therefore important to have a full understanding of the characteristics of homicide and violence as well as the change of these crimes over time if these crimes are to be reduced and prevented. Lack of such knowledge means a lacking understanding of the exact impact these crimes have on society and the people in it.

Furthermore, whether or not homicide and violence can be interpreted as incidents on the same continuum has important implications for prevention strategies. If the similarities between the characteristics of homicide and violence were such that these crimes could be considered related, the same prevention strategies could be used to tackle both crimes. Similarly, if the trends in homicide and violence follow a similar pattern over time, the changing

158 *Theorising homicide*

trends in homicide could be used to monitor the changing trends in violence. As mentioned, homicide is generally considered a more robust measurement with a lower dark figure compared to other crimes, which are not reported to or recorded by the police as often (Brookman, 2005; Granath, 2011; Haen Marshall & Summers, 2012; Tonry, 2014). This means more is generally known about homicide compared to other violent crimes that have a higher dark figure. By using trends in homicide as a barometer for the trends in wider violence, more information about the changing patterns in violence could be obtained. This would have great advantages for the police in increasing the efficiency when directing resources to prevent as well as tackle lethal and nonlethal violence.

If the characteristics or trends of homicide are unrelated to wider violence, this would, however, suggest there was something qualitatively different about the act of homicide compared to other violent crimes. This would imply that separate prevention strategies might be required for homicide. It might also suggest that the factors that affected one trend do not seem to affect the other. The violence policies in Scotland, which were described in Chapter 3, are currently included within a broader preventative and collaborative framework to tackle crime (Scottish Government, 2012; 2021). Policies aimed at reducing and preventing violence can broadly be considered to exist along two main lines in Scotland: action against violence generally, which is mainly focused on youth violence and knife crime, and action against domestic violence and violence against women, including sexual violence. As such, there is no policy aimed at reducing homicide specifically; instead, homicide is covered within the larger policy strategies targeting violence. Examining the extent to which homicide reflects the characteristics and trends of wider violence is therefore highly important in order to develop and evaluate efficient violence policies.

The examination of the relationship between homicide and violence furthermore have important implications for theory. Many researchers consider homicide an extreme end of a violence spectrum, thereby assuming that there is a relationship between homicide and violence (Brookman & Maguire, 2003; Fajnzylber et al., 2002; Harries, 1989; Harris et al., 2002; Sampson, Raudenbusch, & Earls, 1997; Van Wilsem, 2004; Zimring, 1968). As a consequence of this mindset, homicide is often used as a proxy for other forms of violence. As mentioned however, there is no empirical evidence to support such an assumption, even though homicide and violence intuitively may seem related (Harries, 1989). Other scholars have also made such unsupported assumptions when attempting to theoretically explain the homicide drop evident in Western Europe. Although various theories and hypotheses regarding the causes of the crime drop has been proposed (Hale, 1998; Eck & Maguire, 2000; Levitt, 2004), not many of them have been able to effectively explain why homicide has declined (Tonry, 2014).

Some theories assume that homicide is decreasing along with other forms of crime, including violence. These theories include the Security Hypothesis and the Debut Crime Hypothesis (Farrell et al., 2010; 2014).

The relationship between homicide and violence   159

Other theoretical frameworks, such as the 'Medical Care Hypothesis', instead assume the opposite relationship; that homicide is decreasing while homicide is increasing. Both Blumstein (2000) and Harris et al. (2002) for instance explain the increases in violence and decreases of homicide as symptomatic of improved medical care. This disparity underlines the theoretical importance of exploring the relationship between homicide and violence. As the theories mentioned build on contrasting assumptions regarding the relationship between homicide and violence, this opens up questions that necessitates answers. Can homicide be regarded as the extreme end of a violence spectrum or are the characteristics of homicide substantially different from wider violence? Do the trends in homicide reflect the trends in wider violence or do these two crimes change differently over time? In order to provide answers to these questions, we will compare subtypes of homicide to subtypes of nonlethal violence. As mentioned in Chapter 6, research has shown that homicide as well as violence are heterogeneous constructs that needs to be disaggregated in order to be fully understood. As such, the next section will describe subtypes of nonlethal violence identified in Scotland in order to be able to compare these subtypes to the homicide subtypes identified in Chapter 6.

Subtypes of nonlethal violence

In order to identify subtypes of nonlethal violence, another dataset was needed since the Scottish Homicide Database only included homicides. As previous research has found victimisation data superior to police recorded data (Maguire, 2012; McAra & McVie, 2012), and since the choice of data measurement has been proved important when comparing trends in homicide and violence (Lauritzen et al., 2016), data from the Scottish Crime and Justice Survey (SCJS) was collected. The SCJS is a repeated cross-sectional self-reported victim survey administered by the Scottish Government, aimed to measure the levels of crime and victimisation in Scotland (Scottish Government, 2016d). The survey includes measures of property crime and violent crime, including sexual crime, based on approximately 3000 to 16 000[1] face-to-face interviews with individuals aged 16 and older. A combined dataset using five sweeps from 2008–2009 to 2014–2015 was used. Due to differences in the questionnaires and the way certain variables were coded, it was not possible to include sweeps earlier than 2008–2009. In total there were 2097 violent crimes reported by 1879 victims in the survey between 2008–2009 and 2014–2015. The violence data was subsequently also weighted in order to ensure that the dataset was representative of Scotland overall. This is standard practice when dealing with survey data, and since a combined dataset with multiple sweeps was used, a specific weight was calculated for this dataset.

---

1 This figure changes from sweep to sweep.

160   *Theorising homicide*

Table 8.1 Classifying variables of the violence dataset

Variables	Missing (%)
Victim variables:	
Victim gender (male/female)	0.0%
Victim age (3 categories[a])	0.0%
Victim employment status (Unemployed/not unemployed)	14.3%
Victim ethnicity (white/not white)	0.0%
Victim residential status (social housing/not social housing)	0.9%
Offender variables:	
Offender gender (male/victim/both)	18.2%
Offender age (4 categories[b])	18.6%
Offender influence of drugs or alcohol (Under the influence/ sober)	9.7%
Offender ethnicity (white/not white)	18.4%
Incident variables:	
Motive (7 variables)	3.4%
Relationship between victim and offender (9 variables)	18.2%
Weapon (6 variables)	3.9%
Violence used (6 variables)	16.3%
Injuries sustained (5 variables)	14.4%
Location (6 variables)	2.6%
Whether the crime was a repeat offence (1 variable)	0.0%
Time of day (1 variable)	1.5%
Victim influence of drugs or alcohol (1 variable)[c]	15.9%
Sexual aspect in crime (1 variable)	16.2%

Note 1: Base: $n = 2097$.

Note 2: For definition of each variable see section 8.2, Chapter 8.

[a] Victim age was divided into three age groups: 16–24 years old; 25–39 years old and 40 or older. This was done to correspond with the offender age groups. No victims were under the age of 16 since only individuals aged 16 and older participate in the survey (Scottish Government, 2016d).

[b] Offender age was divided into four categories: Under 16 years old (school age); 16–24 years old; 25–39 years old; and 40 years or older.

[c] Since the victims were asked whether they were under the influence in relation to each violent incident, this variable is an incident-level variable and not a victim-level variable.

Source: SCJS pooled dataset.

In order to disaggregate the violence data into subtypes of nonlethal violence, 54 classifying variables were included in the model (see Table 8.1). All but two of the classifying variables (victim age and offender age) were binary variables. These classifying variables were related to the victim, offender, and the incident of violence, and they were included in order to make the violence model as similar as possible to the homicide model. This meant that, where possible, the same variables were included on each level (victim, offender, and incident) as in the homicide dataset. Some differences between the datasets, however, led to discrepancies in the modelling. Certain variables that proved relevant in the homicide dataset (such as offender employment status) did not exist in the violence dataset and could therefore not be included. Other

The relationship between homicide and violence 161

variables, such as victim residential status, did exist in the violence dataset but were coded slightly differently. Since the SCJS is a household survey, there were no homeless respondents in the violence dataset like there was in the homicide dataset. Instead, the victim residential status variable measured victims living in social housing in the violence dataset since this arguably measured a similar vulnerability to homelessness.

While other variables, such as motive or the relationship between victim and offender, measured the same construct across the two datasets, the categories were different. The violence variables were coded in order to resemble the homicide categories as much as possible; however, in some instances, the restrictions of the data made this impossible. Conversely, some variables were important to include in order to understand the violence subtypes but were not included in the homicide dataset. Examples of such variables were whether or not the violent act was a repeat incident or what time of day the crime took place. The classifying variables for the violence model were, similarly to the variables in the homicide model, included since they had been identified as important in typology research of violence (see, for instance, Bijleveld & Smit, 2006; Holtzworth-Munroe, 2000; Pizarro, 2008; Pridemore & Eckhardt, 2008; Wood Harper & Voigt, 2007).

The violence dataset was just like the homicide dataset hierarchical in nature. The hierarchical structure was, however, slightly different; while any one homicide case may involve multiple offenders and victims, any one victim of nonlethal violence in the SCJS can report more than one crime. This means that the crime incidents were nested within the victims in the violence dataset. Just as with the homicide data, the violence data was therefore subjected to multilevel modelling in order to take these structures into account. However, in contrast to the homicide dataset, the within-level in the violence data was constituted by the incidents and summarised offender variables, whereas the between-level was constituted by the victim variables.

Overall, this resulted in a model with five victim variables, which were introduced on the between-level of the model, six offender variables and ten incident variables which were both introduced on the within-level of the model (Skott, 2021). Time was divided into dummy variables representing each sweep (2008–2009; 2009–2010; 2010–2011; 2012–2013; and 2014–2015), where the first sweep was the reference category. In order to explore how nonlethal violence had changed over time, two different measures were used: absolute and relative change over time. These measures were calculated in exactly the same way as with the homicide data (see Chapter 6).

Just as with the homicide model, three statistical criteria were used alongside the substantive interpretation of the classes in order to measure goodness of fit: the Akaike information criteria (AIC), the Bayesian information criteria (BIC), and the sample size – Adjusted Bayesian Information Criteria (ABIC; McCutcheon, 2002; Nylund, Asparouhov, & Muthén, 2007). When these were examined and compared in order to identify the best fitting model (see Table 8.2), two models had the best fit statistics and entropy: the

162 *Theorising homicide*

Table 8.2 Class selection statistics of two-level LCA violence model

No. of classes (within-between)	Loglike-li-hood value	AIC	BIC	Percentage change in BIC	ABIC	Entropy
1–2	–44878.38	89908.75	90338.02	N/A	90096.56	1.000
2–1	–45756.44	91738.89	92377.14	2.26	92018.13	0.944
2–2	–44207.10	88656.20	89339.64	–3.29	88955.21	0.892
2–3	–43409.58	**87077.16**	**87805.78**	–1.72	**87395.94**	0.915
2–4	*–42858.40*	*85990.81*	*86764.62*	*–1.19*	*86329.36*	*0.927*
3–2	–47696.49	95748.99	96754.38	11.51	96188.86	0.927
3–3	–46114.25	92602.50	93658.72	–3.20	93064.60	0.939
3–4	*–45057.35*	*90506.71*	*91613.77*	*–2.18*	*90991.06*	*0.973*
4–2	–51393.69	103257.38	104584.73	14.16	103838.12	**0.963**
4–3	–49015.91	98521.82	99905.64	–4.47	99127.25	0.953

Note 1: Base: n = 2097.
Note 2: Models in italics failed to replicate the best loglikelihood value, even with more than 400% increase in random starts compared to the 1–2 model.

Source: SCJS pooled dataset.

2–3 model and the 4–2 model. When these two models were compared, the 4–2 model was chosen since it was considered to be the most substantively interesting model since the within-level classes were deemed more informative in the 4–2 model.[2] For the sake of clarity, the within-level subtypes will be called subtypes and the between-level classes will be called classes. The names of the classes and subtypes were decided based on the most common, or in some cases, most unique traits. The following section will now move on to explore the actual subtypes of nonlethal violence in the 4–2 model.

Violence typology

The hierarchical structure of the violence dataset meant that there were four within subtypes (consisting of incident and offender variables) and two between-level classes (including victim variables) in the 4–2 model (see Table 8.3). The four within-level subtypes were of approximately the same size.

Domestic *subtype*

The first and the largest subtype was labelled *Domestic* (29.0%, n = 608). This type included nonlethal violent acts that occurred between intimate partners, motivated by some sort of previous history or argument between the offender and victim (see Figures 8.1 to 8.2). The *Domestic* subtype most commonly occurred inside or in a place adjacent to the victim's own home (see Figure 8.3). The offenders were most commonly male and between 25

---

2 For more information about the modelling, see Skott (2021).

Table 8.3 Identified subtypes of nonlethal violence

Subtype	N	Percentage of within group	Percentage of all cases
1. Domestic subtypes (29.0%, n = 608)			
a. Male Victim Domestic	225	37.0%	10.7%
b. Female Victim Domestic	383	63.0%	18.3%
2. Public No Weapon subtypes (27.8%, n = 583)			
a. Male Victim Public No Weapon	459	78.7%	21.9%
b. Female Victim Public No Weapon	124	21.3%	5.9%
3. Public Weapon subtypes (24.0%, n = 503)			
a. Male Victim Public Weapon	333	66.2%	15.9%
b. Female Victim Public Weapon	170	33.8%	8.1%
4. Work-related subtypes (19.2%, n = 403)			
a. Male Victim Work-related	204	50.6%	9.7%
b. Female Victim Work-related	199	49.4%	9.5%

Note 1: Base: *n* = 2097.

Source: SCJS pooled dataset.

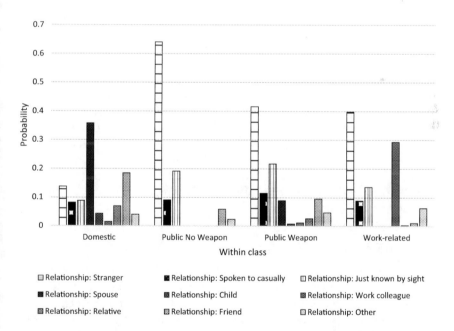

Figure 8.1 Class response probabilities of relationship between offender and victim
Note 1: Base: *n* = 2097
Source: SCJS pooled dataset

164 *Theorising homicide*

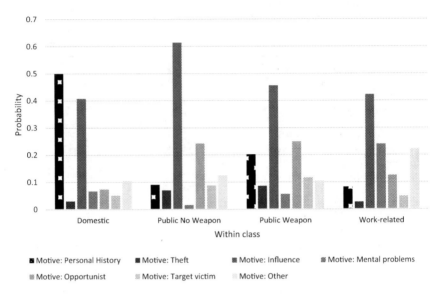

Figure 8.2 Class response probabilities of motive
Note 1: Base: *n* = 2097
Source: SCJS pooled dataset

and 39 years old, although almost a third of the offenders were older than 40 years old (see Figures 8.4 to 8.5). The vast majority of the violence in the *Domestic* subtype did not involve any weapons, and the offenders were twice as likely to be under the influence of drugs or alcohol compared to the victim (see Figures 8.4 to 8.6, and 8.9). The type of violence usually included in the *Domestic* subtype was punching and grabbing (see Figure 8.7), and the most common injuries sustained was bruising, followed by cuts (see Figure 8.8). Overall, this would indicate a subtype of domestic violence, occurring between intimate partners.

Public No Weapon *subtype*

The second largest subtype was called *Public No Weapon* (27.8%, *n* = 583) since this type most commonly involved violence in a public place that did not involve any weapons (see Figures 8.8. and 8.9). The most common relationship between victim and offender in this subtype was strangers (see Figure 8.1), and the most common motive was the offender's influence by alcohol or drugs (see Figure 8.2). The vast majority of the *Public No Weapon* offenders were white men between 16 and 24 years old (see Figures 8.4 to 8.5) and the majority of both victims and offenders were intoxicated when the crime was committed (see Figure 8.6). The most common type of violence used in the *Public No Weapon* subtype was punching, and the most common reported injury was

The relationship between homicide and violence 165

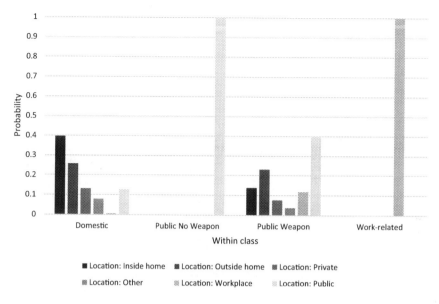

Figure 8.3 Class response probabilities of location of the crime
Note 1: Base: *n* = 2097
Source: SCJS pooled dataset

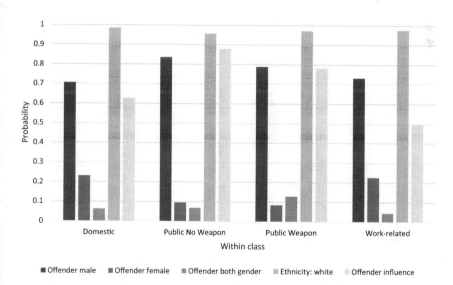

Figure 8.4 Class response probabilities of binary offender variables
Note 1: Base: *n* = 2097
Source: SCJS pooled dataset

166 *Theorising homicide*

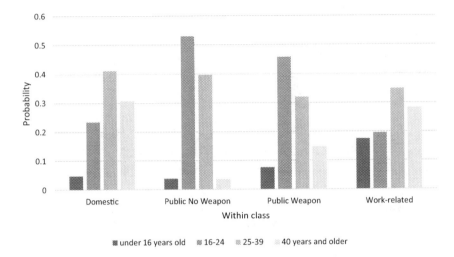

Figure 8.5 Class response probabilities of offender age
Note 1: Base: *n* = 2097
Source: SCJS pooled dataset

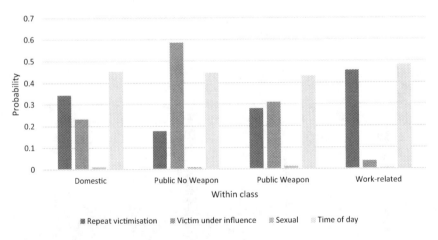

Figure 8.6 Class response probabilities of case-related variables
Note 1: Base: *n* = 2097
Source: SCJS pooled dataset

bruising (see Figures 8.7 to 8.8). Overall, this type of violence indicated public violence among young men, without the use of weapons, where both victims and offenders were intoxicated.

The relationship between homicide and violence 167

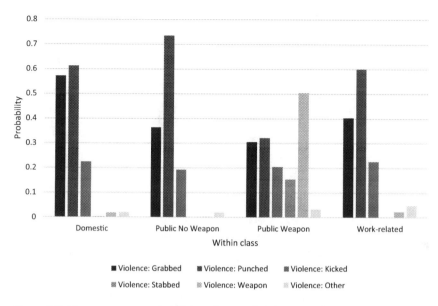

Figure 8.7 Class response probabilities of type of violence used
Note 1: Base: $n = 2097$
Source: SCJS pooled dataset

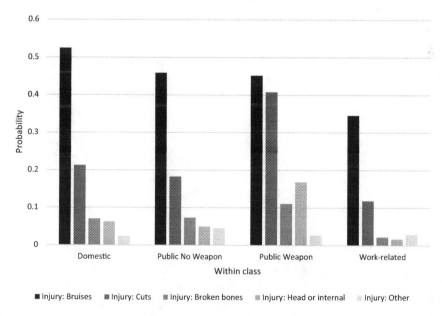

Figure 8.8 Class response probabilities of type of injury
Note 1: Base: $n = 2097$
Source: SCJS pooled dataset

168   *Theorising homicide*

Public Weapon *subtype*

The third type of nonlethal violence was labelled *Public Weapon* (24.0%, $n = 503$), and as the name would suggest, this type is very similar to the *Public No Weapon* type. While the violence in this type most commonly occurred in public places (see Figure 8.3), unlike the *Public No Weapon* type, the *Public Weapon* type, however, most commonly involved sharp weapons (see Figure 8.9). It was also not uncommon for this subtype of nonlethal violence to involve glasses or bottles as weapons and the most common reported injury was bruising, closely followed by cuts. While the most common relationship between offender and victim was stranger, another fifth of the cases involved people who knew each other by sight (see Figure 8.1). The most commonly reported motive was that the offender was under the influence of alcohol or drugs, and the majority of the offenders were intoxicated when the crime was committed (see Figures 8.2 and 8.4). Most of the offenders were male, white, and young (between 16 and 24 years old). Overall, this type of violence indicated public violence among young men involving alcohol, with the use of weapons.

Work-related *subtypes*

The final within-level subtype of nonlethal violence was called *Work-related* violence (19.2%, $n = 403$) since all of these violent acts occurred at the workplace of the victim (see Figure 8.3). While the most common relationship was stranger, almost a third of the *Work-related* violence occurred between co-workers or colleagues (see Figure 8.1). The most commonly reported motive was intoxication on behalf of the offender; however, in more than a fifth of the cases the motive was related to the offender's mental illness (see Figure 8.2). Most of the offenders were male and white and the most common offender age was 25–39 years old (see Figures 8.4 to 8.5). The victim was most commonly sober, and this subtype was the type of nonlethal violence that had the highest rate of repeat victimisation; in 45% of the cases, the victim reported that this was not a one-off crime but had happened repeatedly (see Figure 8.6). Most commonly, no weapons were used (see Figure 8.9). The most common type of violence used was punching and the most common injury sustained was bruising (see Figures 8.7 to 8.8). The following section will explore the two between-level classes of nonlethal violence.

Male Victim *class*

As mentioned, the between-level classes included the victim variables. The first between-level class was called the *Male Victim* class (58.2%, $n = 1221$) since all of the victims in this class were male (see Figure 8.10). The majority of the *Male Victims* were white and employed, and approximately a third lived in social housing. While the age distribution was quite even, the most common age bracket was 40 years or older. When the distribution of the *Male Victim*

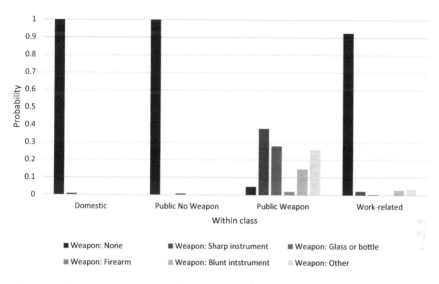

Figure 8.9 Class response probabilities of type of weapon used
Note 1: Base: $n = 2097$
Source: SCJS pooled dataset

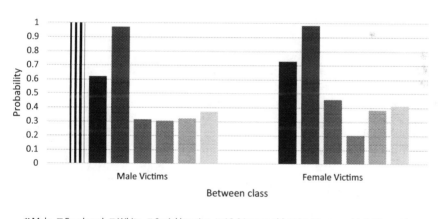

Figure 8.10 Class response probabilities for victim variables
Note 1: Base: $n = 2097$
Source: SCJS pooled dataset

class across the within-level types were examined, the *Male Victims* were more prevalent in both the *Public Weapon* type and the *Public No Weapon* type. The highest proportion of *Male Victims* were found in the *Public Weapon* type, where almost 80% of the victims were male.

170   *Theorising homicide*

Female Victim *class*

The *Female Victim* class (41.8%, $n = 876$) only consisted of female victims (see Figure 8.10). As with the *Male Victim* class, the majority of the victims in this class was employed and of white ethnicity. More than two fifths of the *Female Victim* class victims resided in social housing. A higher proportion of the victims in this class were older, with more than 40 years old being the most common age bracket. When the proportion of the *Female Victims* across the within-level types was examined, the data showed that this class was most prevalent in the *Domestic* violence subtype, where 63% of the victims were female. Half of the victims of the *Work-related* violence subtypes were male and half were female. The next section will examine how these subtypes have changed over time in Scotland before this change over time will be compared to the change in homicide trends.

Change in violence types over time

As with the homicide data, we will explore both the absolute and relative change in violence subtypes over time. For more information about how these measures were calculated, see Chapter 6.

Absolute change over time

When examining the absolute change over time in the nonlethal violence subtypes, the data showed that all types of violence demonstrated an absolute decrease over time (see Figure 8.11).

The *Public Weapon* type decreased by 70% between 2008–2009 and 2014–2015, demonstrating the largest absolute decrease over time, and the *Public No Weapon* type more than halved during the same time. The *Work-related* type and the *Domestic* type also decreased, albeit less dramatically. The *Work-related* violence type decreased by 47% and the *Domestic* violence type decreased by 44%, demonstrated the smallest absolute decrease over time.

Relative change over time

Examining the relative change over time, a slightly different pattern, however, emerges. While the absolute change over time is informative in regards to actual change in numbers, relative change over time can provide information about the proportional shifts of certain subtypes. Even though all types had decreased, certain types may have decreased unequally, meaning that some types have become more common than others over time. As can be seen from Figure 8.12, one type demonstrated no change (*Public No Weapon*), two types demonstrated an increase (*Work-related* and *Domestic*) and one type of violence demonstrated a decrease (*Public Weapon*). Even if the *Public No Weapon* type fluctuated up and down a little, the relative share of this type returned

The relationship between homicide and violence 171

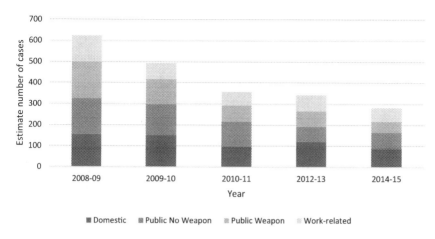

Figure 8.11 Absolute change in violence types over time
Note 1: Base: *n* = 2097
Source: SCJS pooled dataset

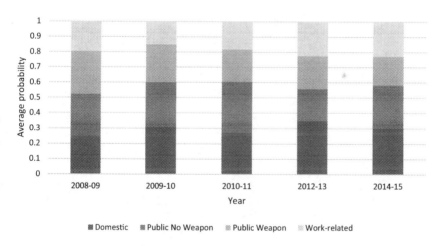

Figure 8.12 Average (mean) probability of within type over time
Note 1: Base: *n* = 2097
Source: SCJS pooled dataset

to its original level in 2014–2015, only showing a 2% increase from 2008 to 2009. As such, even if this type has decreased in absolute terms, the relative proportion of the *Public No Weapon* type has arguably therefore remained stable over time in Scotland.

The *Public Weapon* type was the only type that demonstrated a consistent relative decrease over time (see Figure 8.12 and Table 8.4). Between

172 *Theorising homicide*

Table 8.4 P-values of Mann Whitney U-tests of relative change in violence types over time

Type of violence	2008–2009 vs 2009–2010	2008–2009 vs 2010–2011	2008–2009 vs 2012–2013	2008–2009 vs 2014–2015
Domestic	0.088	**(+) 0.001**	**(+) 0.006**	**(+) 0.008**
Public No Weapon	0.363	0.264	**(−) 0.051**	0.778
Public Weapon	0.103	0.130	**(−) 0.015**	**(−) 0.001**
Work-related	**(−) 0.021**	0.196	0.526	**(+) 0.026**
	2009–10 vs 2010–11	**2009–10 vs 2012–13**	**2009–10 vs 2014–15**	-
Domestic	**(−) 0.016**	0.236	0.273	-
Public No Weapon	0.856	**(−) 0.008**	0.623	-
Public Weapon	0.955	0.369	**(−) 0.011**	-
Work-related	0.431	**(+) 0.011**	**(+) 0.001**	-
	2010–11 vs 2012–13	**2010–11 vs 2014–15**		
Domestic	0.347	0.409	-	-
Public No Weapon	**(−) 0.003**	0.370	-	-
Public Weapon	0.360	**(−) 0.010**	-	-
Work-related	0.084	**(+) 0.002**	-	-
	2012–13 vs 2014–15	-	-	-
Domestic	0.990	-	-	-
Public No Weapon	**(+) 0.043**	-	-	-
Public Weapon	0.107	-	-	-
Work-related	0.148	-	-	-

Note 1: Base: $n = 2097$.
Note 2: p-values in bold indicates significance.
Note 3: The signs before the p-values demonstrate increase (+) or decrease (−) in the trend.

Source: SCJS pooled dataset.

2008–2009 and 2014–2015, this type had decreased by 34%, becoming the least common type of violence in 2014–2015. This decline was also statistically significant (see Table 8.4). Both the *Domestic* type and the *Work-related* types demonstrated relative increases over time (see Figure 8.12 and Table 8.4). The *Work-related* type had increased by 17% in 2014–2015 compared to 2008–2009, and the *Domestic* nonlethal violence had increased by 22% during the same time period, which was the largest increase over time. Both of these increases proved to be statistically significant (see Table 8.4).

As can be seen from Figure 8.12, the *Work-related* type and the *Domestic* type had also changed their relative position in comparison to the other types over time. While the *Domestic* nonlethal violence type initially was the third most common type of violence in 2008–2009, this type had become the most common subtype of violence in 2014–2015. Similarly, while the *Work-related* violence type was the least common type of violence in the first year of measurement, this type became the second least common type in 2014–2015. As

The relationship between homicide and violence over time

While the previous section has described the subtypes of nonlethal violence identified in Scotland, as well as how these types have changed over time, this section will compare these subtypes to the homicide subtypes identified in Chapter 6. The subtypes will be compared regarding both general characteristics and how these types have changed over time in order to determine the relationship between homicide and violence. We will begin by comparing the characteristics of homicide subtypes with the characteristics of the subtypes of nonlethal violence.

Characteristics of lethal and nonlethal subtypes

When the subtypes of nonlethal violence identified in this chapter were compared to the subtypes of homicide identified in Chapter 6, we can immediately see that there are many similarities between the two typologies (see Table 8.5). Both the *Femicides* and the nonlethal *Domestic* subtypes occurred between intimate partners, were perpetrated indoors in private settings and were most commonly motivated by some sort of domestic or personal dispute. The victim was most commonly a woman in both types. While the nonlethal *Domestic* type did most commonly not involve any weapons, the most common weapon used in the *Femicides* was a sharp instrument, such as a knife. Although previous research has shown that the use of weapons, including knives, increases the risk of lethality (Felson & Messner, 1996), one fifth of the *Femicides* included death by physical assault, meaning a substantial part of the lethal acts of domestic violence did not involve the use of a weapon. Overall, the similarities between the *Femicide* homicides and the *Domestic* violence subtypes were so striking that they can be regarded as the same type of violence where one ended lethally and the other did not. As such, *Femicides* could, in other words, be argued to represent the extreme end

Table 8.5 Subtypes of the homicide and violence typologies

Homicide typology	Violence typology
Rivalry (24.8%)	*Public Weapon* (24.0%)
Femicide (16.0%)	*Domestic* (29.0%)
No Weapon–Bludgeoning (27.3%)	*Public No Weapon* (27.8%)
Stabbing (31.9%)	*Work-related* (19.2%)
Total (n): 1978	**2097**

Source: Skott (2019a; 2019b).

174 *Theorising homicide*

of a spectrum of domestic violence, where the use of a weapon is likely to increase the lethality of such an incident.

There were also strong similarities between the *Rivalry* homicides and the *Public Weapon* subtype of violence. Both of these violent acts were most commonly committed between young male offenders and victims in public settings outdoors, usually involving the use of a knife. In contrast to the *Femicides* and *Domestic* acts of violence, both the *Rivalry* and the *Public Weapon* subtypes involved the use of a sharp instrument even though only the *Rivalry* type ended with the death of the victim. This would indicate that the use of a weapon is perhaps not the most important factor when differentiating lethal acts of violence in these types. While the *Rivalry* and the *Public Weapon* types were very similar, they differed in regards to motive, where 'feud' was the most common in the *Rivalry* type and 'offender under the influence of drugs or alcohol' was the most commonly reported motive for the *Public Weapon* type. The types also differed in regards to relationship; while the *Rivalry* homicides most commonly occurred between rivals, the *Public Weapon* violence type most commonly occurred between strangers.

There were also some similarities between the *No Weapon–Bludgeoning* homicides and the *Public No Violence* subtypes. Both of these types most commonly involved male offenders and male victims who were intoxicated at the time of the crime. The violence also very rarely involved weapons. The motive was, however, slightly different between these two subtypes; while the most commonly reported motive was some sort of fight or conflict for the *No Weapon–Bludgeoning* homicides, the most common motive for the *Public No Weapon* subtype was that the offender was intoxicated. The two motivations might, however, be related. Although the motive variables were constructed differently in the two datasets, a violent act instigated by the consumption of alcohol could also have involved some sort of fight or argument, meaning that there may still be similarities between the datasets, despite the differences in coding. The *No Weapon–Bludgeoning* homicides and the *Public No Weapon* type also differed in regards to the most common relationship between offender and victim. While the *No Weapon–Bludgeoning* homicides most commonly were committed between people who knew one another, the victims of the *Public No Weapon* subtype typically did not know the offender. The *No Weapon–Bludgeoning* homicides furthermore occurred in private settings indoors more commonly, whereas most violent acts in the *Public No Weapon* subtype occurred in public. Since there are still some similarities between these two subtypes, these variables may indicate mechanisms for lethality. Violence between intoxicated men without the use of weapons may thus be more likely to end lethally if the victim and offender are known to each other and if the violence takes place in private locations indoors. These variables have also been found to be relevant for violence lethality in previous research exploring violence involving weapons (Ganpat et al., 2013); however, this study also demonstrates the importance of these variables for lethality in violence that does not involve weapons. Taken together, while there were some differences

The two final subtypes (the *Stabbing* homicides and the *Work-related* violence types) were, however, not similar across the datasets. The *Work-related* violence type was characterised by violence occurring in the course of the victim's employment, either by someone unknown to the victim or by a co-worker of the victim. While the offender most commonly was intoxicated, the victim was almost exclusively sober, and these incidents of violence rarely involved the use of a weapon. There were no corresponding homicide type that resembled the *Work-related* violence type, making this type different from the homicide typology. Homicides occurring at the workplace are, however, very rare in Scotland,[3] indicating that this type of violence could be context specific and unlikely part of a spectrum of behaviour that might lead to homicide. This is, nonetheless, a very important type of nonlethal violence that future prevention strategies should aim to address.

Overall, it was more common for all homicide types to be committed in private, indoor locations compared to nonlethal violence subtypes. Contrastingly, nonlethal violence was reported to occur more often in public, outdoor locations. This was also true for lethal and nonlethal violence involving the use of weapons (the *Public Weapon* violence type and *Stabbing* homicide type). While publicly committed violence tends to be more easily prevented due to the presence of CCTV, possible witnesses or the intervention of capable guardians such as the police (Cohen & Felson, 1979; Meier & Miethe, 1993), such prevention strategies are most commonly absent in private settings. As such, violence occurring in private locations would therefore be more likely to end lethally compared to violence occurring in public locations.

While we have highlighted a few variables relating to violence lethality, such as the location of the crime and the relationship between offender and victim, whether or not a weapon was used still seemed to be one of the most important factors when differentiating lethal and nonlethal events. All violence types, except for the *Public Weapon* type, were committed without the use of a weapon while all homicide types involved a weapon, including the *No Weapon–Bludgeoning* homicides where a third of the cases included a blunt weapon. Since the inclusion of a weapon in the context of private locations increases the risk of lethality, it is perhaps not so surprising that there were no violence subtype corresponding to the *Stabbing* homicide type, which most commonly occurred indoors using a sharp instrument, such as a knife.

Overall, it appears that the characteristics of homicide and nonlethal violence are very similar in Scotland. While there are a few exceptions, most of the identified subtypes of homicide had corresponding subtypes of nonlethal violence as well. In order to further explore the relationship between homicide and violence, we will now examine the change in these two crimes over time.

---

3 This excludes corporate homicides that have not been included in the current study.

176   *Theorising homicide*

Change in lethal and nonlethal trends over time

As described in Chapter 6, the four main subtypes of homicide had demonstrated different trends over time. While two of the homicide types had remained quite stable over time (*Stabbing* and *No Weapon–Bludgeoning*), one type had demonstrated a relative decrease over time (*Rivalry*) and one type had increased over time in relative terms (*Femicides*). As the *Rivalry* homicides became the least common homicide type in 2012–2015 compared to 2000–2003, the *Femicides* contrastingly became the most common type of homicide during this time. This change suggests that the decrease in *Rivalry* homicide type had the greatest overall impact on the decline in Scottish homicides.

Just as with the characteristics of lethal and nonlethal violence, there were substantial similarities between the trends in homicide and violence over time. Both lethal and nonlethal public acts of violence, predominantly committed by young men with the use of sharp instruments (the *Rivalry* homicides and the *Public Weapon* nonlethal violence type), had demonstrated significant relative increases over time. This is also similar to what has been found previously in regards to homicide in England and Wales (Miles & Buehler, 2020). While the *Rivalry* homicides had decreased since 2004–2007, nonlethal public violence had decreased since 2008–2009; however, the decline may also predate this time. These findings suggest that the trends in this type of violence have followed a similar pattern over time, both in regards to lethal and nonlethal violence.

There were furthermore similarities in regards to trends in domestic forms of lethal and nonlethal violence. Both the *Femicides* and the *Domestic* violence type had demonstrated relative increases, becoming more common in relation to the other subtypes over time. This means that while there has been a substantial decrease of public acts of lethal and nonlethal violence committed with sharp instruments by young men, the proportion of domestic homicide and violence has increased over time in Scotland. In regards to homicide, this relative increase has been evident since 2004–2007, and regarding nonlethal violence, domestic violence has increased in relative terms since 2010–2011.

The way in which the *No Weapon–Bludgeoning* homicides and the *Public No Weapon* violence subtype had changed were also very similar across the two datasets. While both these types of violence had fluctuated somewhat over time, they both returned to levels similar to the original year of measurement, indicating that they had both remained stable over time. This would indicate that that lethal as well as nonlethal violence among intoxicated men who did not use a weapon has remained approximately as common over time compared to other types of homicide and nonlethal violence.

The two subtypes that did not correspond to any other in respective dataset (the *Stabbing* homicides and the *Work-related* violence type), however, also demonstrated different trends. While the *Stabbing* homicides remained stable over time, similarly to the *No Weapon–Bludgeoning* homicides, the *Work-related* violence type had demonstrated a relative increase over time.

The relationship between homicide and violence 177

This increase in work-related violent incidents in Scotland was evident since 2009–2010. This means that while the *Femicides* was the only homicide type to have increased relative to other homicide types over time, there were two types of nonlethal violence that had demonstrated relative increases over time (*Domestic* and *Work-related*).

Taken together, these findings suggest that the change in nonlethal violence types reflect the change in homicide subtypes over time in Scotland. The absolute decrease evident in both homicide and nonlethal violence seems to be primarily driven by a decline in public, violent acts between young men, predominantly involving weapons, and often involving some form of conflict or feuding rivalry. During the same time, there has however, been a relative increase in the proportion of both lethal and nonlethal domestic violence taking place between intimate partners in private settings. Lethal and nonlethal acts of alcohol-fuelled violence between men without the use of weapons have remained stable in relative terms in both datasets. As such, when the trends in homicide and violence subtypes are compared over time, lethal and nonlethal violent trends appear to follow a similar pattern over time.

Conclusions

This chapter has explored the relationship between homicide and nonlethal violence by comparing trends in subtypes of homicide with trends in subtypes of violence over time. As this chapter has demonstrated, there were stark similarities between the lethal and nonlethal subtypes identified. Both typologies identified lethal and nonlethal public acts of violence between young, often intoxicated men using sharp instruments (*Rivalry* homicides and *Public Weapon* violence type) and domestic violence between intimate partners occurring in private settings (*Femicide* homicides and *Domestic* violence). Both typologies also included a type of violence among intoxicated men who did not use a weapon, motivated by some sort of fight or drunken conflict (*No Weapon–Bludgeoning* homicides and *Public No Weapon* violence type). While there was one type unique to each dataset (the *Stabbing* homicides and the *Work-related* violence type), the many similarities between the typologies suggest that the characteristics of homicide and nonlethal violence are very similar in Scotland.

When the trends over time were compared, this chapter has also concluded that subtypes in homicide and nonlethal violence follow similar trends over time. The decline evident in both homicide and nonlethal violence was driven by a decrease in the same type of violence; violence committed by young men in public places using knives or other sharp instruments. However, as these findings also have shown, this general decrease in violence obscures a hidden relative increase in both lethal and nonlethal domestic violence over time. This underlines the importance of disaggregation when exploring trends in both lethal and nonlethal violence. When the data was initially examined, the results would indicate that all homicide and nonlethal violence were decreasing

178 *Theorising homicide*

in Scotland. However, when the changing trends in homicide and nonlethal violence were disaggregated into subtypes, a different pattern emerged. Not only did these findings show that some types of lethal and nonlethal violence in fact had increased over time in relative terms, but the data also showed that similar types changed similarly over time. Overall, this chapter has therefore demonstrated that homicide and violence do follow a similar trend over time when these two crimes are broken into subtypes.

These findings have important implications for theory as well as policy and practice, which will be discussed further in the following chapter. The next chapter will also outline a novel theoretical framework in relation to lethal and nonlethal violence, building on the findings of the current and previous chapters. In this theoretical framework, lethal and nonlethal violence will be examined in relation to multiple power orders such as gender, class, ethnicity, and age in order to provide a new theory to explain the changes in homicide and violence over time, evident in this volume.

9 A theory of homicide
Towards a deeper understanding

Introduction

The previous chapters of this volume have presented some new conclusions in regards to the relationship between homicide and nonlethal violence. In order to place these conclusions in context, this chapter aims to explore these findings in relation to implications for policy as well as implications for theory, examining how the findings of this research affects these areas in the field. As this chapter will argue, it is very likely that the Scottish policy response emerging in the mid-2000s, framing violence as a public health problem, has contributed to the evident decline in homicide and violence committed in public places. However, as will be discussed, only certain types of violence appear to have been affected by this framing shift, while other types of violence appear to have received relatively little or insufficient attention. The findings outlined in the current volume will also be discussed in relation to different theories. Among the different possible theoretical frameworks theorising violence, this chapter will explore the current findings using Crime Drop theories, the privatisation of violence and the connection between violence and masculinities. The last section of this chapter will then go on to formulate a new theoretical perspective drawing on intersectional gender theory, situating violence in a structural context of power and inequality. Drawing on the frameworks of 'doing' gender (Butler, 2006; Connell, 2009) and 'doing' risk (Giritli Nygren et al., 2017), a performative framework of violence is proposed, where violence may be 'done', 'undone', and 'redone' as people position themselves in relation to structures of power and inequality.

The first section of this chapter will, however, begin by exploring the policy implications of the current findings.

Policy implications

While it was not within the scope of this research to provide an evaluation of Scottish violence policies, it is possible to explore connections between key changes in legislation and policy aimed at reducing violence, implemented in Scotland over the period that this study covers, and the key findings of this

DOI: 10.4324/9781003105282-12

180 *Theorising homicide*

volume. For instance, the fact that public acts of homicide and nonlethal violence involving knives demonstrated a marked decrease around the same time as multiple interventions aimed to reduce this particular form of violence is unlikely to be coincidental. Similarly, the 'crackdown', tough-on-crime approach dominating in Scotland during the 1990s seemed to coincide with an increase in violent crime, indicating perhaps that this 'gloves-off' approach (Orr, 1998: 106) seemed unsuccessful in decreasing violence in Scotland. Conversely, the interventions and strategies implemented by the Scottish Government in the early 2000s, including initiatives by the Violence Reduction Unit (VRU, 2016), coincided with a decrease in homicide and violence. Utilising a radically different approach to crime prevention in comparison to the 'crackdown' policies of the 1990s, the Violence Reduction Unit framed violence as a public health problem. This meant early prevention strategies aimed not only to reduce crime but also to improve social conditions for these individuals (VRU, 2016; 2017). To achieve this, multi-agency collaborations were pursued as the Violence Reduction Unit teamed up with agencies in fields of health, social work, and education, tackling violence as part of a bigger problem relating to deprivation, unemployment and homelessness. As such, these policies and interventions constituted a 'bigger picture' response to violence, where violence was considered to be part of larger issues relating to social deprivation (VRU, 2016; 2017).

The findings of the research in this volume has shown that the overall decrease in homicide and violence has been driven by a decline in public violence among young men involving sharp instruments. As mentioned, this is exactly the type of violence the strategies implemented by the Scottish Government and the Violence Reduction Unit in the early 2000s aimed to prevent. While this does not prove the success of these interventions, the overlap and timing of the policies and subsequent decline in violence suggests there is some sort of relationship between the two. The *Rivalry* homicide type and the *Public Weapon* violence type had both demonstrated significant declines and were both the least common type of homicide and violence in the final year of examination. Since Scotland has maintained record low levels of homicide since the implementation of these policies, this would suggest that the current holistic, multi-agency approach to reducing violence, where violence is framed as a public health problem, has been beneficial in reducing and preventing violence. This appears to be particularly evident in relation to public violence involving the use of knives.

However, as the research in the current volume has showed, there is more to the story. While public acts of homicide and nonlethal violence have decreased markedly over time, acts of domestic homicide and violence have in fact demonstrated relative increases over time, despite numerous implemented interventions and policies to reduce this type of violence. Even though the *Femicide* homicides and the *Domestic* violence types had decreased in absolute terms, this evident relative increase is a troubling development. As the research results have demonstrated that lethal as well as nonlethal domestic

A theory of homicide   181

violence have become more common over time compared to other types of homicide and violence, this suggest a limited effect of the implemented interventions in this area. As described in Chapter 3, the main prevention strategy aimed to reduce domestic violence in Scotland implemented during the time of the study is called the Equally Safe strategy (Scottish Government, 2016a). The Equally Safe strategy takes a holistic approach, aiming to prevent and reduce all forms of violence against women, including domestic, sexual, and honour-based violence, framing violence against women and girls as related to deep-rooted issues of inequality. The strategy prioritises preventative strategies in combination with multi-agency and multi-sector responses in order to tackle this type of violence.

Despite these interventions, which in some ways are very similar to the prevention strategies aimed to reduce knife-related violence, domestic violence has not decreased nearly as much. However, preventing violence occurring in private settings of any type is notoriously difficult since it involves state intervention in private life. As most of the lethal and nonlethal domestic violence occurs inside the home, practical, preventative measures to reduce violence is much more limited in comparison to public acts of violence. Instead, interventions and policies have to direct their resources towards changing attitudes and mindsets of people committing domestic violence which, as the Equally Safe strategy points out (Scottish Government, 2016a), therefore becomes very important. This is, however, not always an easy task as these attitudes are deeply linked to cultural and societal understandings of gender, class, and power. We will turn to these issues later in the last section of this chapter.

Overall, it is important to keep a holistic approach when aiming to prevent and reduce lethal and nonlethal domestic violence. Although specific strategies such as the creation of Multi-Agency Tasking and Co-ordinating Groups (MATAC) by Police Scotland, targeting serious and serial domestic offenders, might help to reduce and prevent domestic violence, it is unlikely that any one intervention strategy will help turn the relatively increasing trend. Instead, it is important to implement a collaborative, multi-agency approach in order to reduce domestic homicide and violence, similar to the policy strategies implemented to tackle public violence. As an example, collaborations with organisations in health is an important part of identifying cases of domestic violence; due to the hidden nature of this type of violence, health professionals may sometimes be the first responders to encounter domestic violence that does not come to the attention of the police (Carnochan, 2015). As the victims of domestic violence might not always report the crime, training medical staff to identify these victims, including dentists and even veterinaries,[1] will increase the chances of the crime being reported as well as prevent

---

1 Research has shown that perpetrators of domestic violence sometimes injure the pets of the victims in order to hurt the victims themselves (VRU, 2017).

182   *Theorising homicide*

such violence in the future. While the policy interventions aimed at reducing domestic violence in Scotland already highlight the importance of collaborative efforts, including the implementation of the MATAC groups and the establishment of the Violence against Women and Girls Joint Strategic board (Scottish Government, 2016a), perhaps this is not sufficient in order to decrease this type of violence. Policy development and the process of implementation have previously been criticised in Scotland as scholars have argued that these processes reinforce gendered as well as social hierarchies (Hearn & McKie, 2010). As Hearn and McKie (2010) argued, failing to actively gender the representation of domestic violence and reinforcing the divide between public and private violence risks relegating gendered violence to the sphere of the individual and a-gendered, framing the problem, and the associated responses to this problem, as one of 'atypical men' (Hearn & McKie, 2010: 149). As the research in the current volume also found that approximately two fifths of the domestic violence victims were men, this highlight another facet of the problem of domestic violence. Violence between intimate partners is not limited to violence against women, and neither should the policy interventions of this violence. As such, it is important that all interventions and prevention strategies are inclusive, not excluding same-sex couples or men as victims. Adhering to the Equally Safe strategy, framing the issue of lethal and nonlethal violence as a problem related to deep-rooted inequality, efforts to change such issues will take time as well as resources. As the findings of this volume have highlighted however, attempting to prevent and reduce this form of violence is very important if all types of violence, and not just the most visible types of violence, are to be reduced equally.

As explained in Chapter 3, the policies aimed to reduce violence in Scotland currently includes both lethal and nonlethal acts of violence. As such, there is no specific policy aimed at reducing homicide. While the findings of the current research have identified some types of homicides unique for lethal violence (such as the *Stabbing* homicides) and some types of violence unique to nonlethal violence (such as the *Work-related* violence type), there are strong similarities between most types of lethal and nonlethal violence. As an example, the *Rivalry* homicide type were very similar to the *Public Weapon* violence type and the *Femicide* homicides and the *Domestic* violence type were almost identical. The *No Weapon–Bludgeoning* homicides furthermore shared many similarities with the violent acts in the *Public No Weapon* violence type. Taking these results together, this would suggest that homicide indeed can be considered the extreme end of a violence spectrum, much in line with previous research (Brookman & Maguire, 2003; Fajnzylber, Lederman, & Loayza, 2002; Harries, 1989; Harris et al., 2002; Sampson, Raudenbusch, & Earls, 1997; Van Wilsem, 2004; Zimring, 1968). This would also imply that no policy aimed to reduce homicide specifically would be necessary in Scotland. Instead, perhaps it would be beneficial to introduce specific interventions in regards to violence lethality. As demonstrated by previous studies, and indeed in the current research, certain factors when present in a case of violence tend to increase the risk of a lethal outcome (Berg, 2019; Dobash, Dobash, Cavanagh, & Medina-Ariza, 2007; Ganpat, Van Der Leun, & Nieuwbeerta, 2013; Lauritzen & Lentz, 2019). For instance, the use of a weapon, whether the violent act took place in a private setting and whether or not the offender and victim knew each other are all variables that increase the risk of lethality. Interestingly, all three of these factors coincide in the *Stabbing* homicide type. This would indicate that this particular type of homicide might be exceedingly difficult to prevent; not only did this type of homicide occur in a private setting where policing is generally very difficult, but the act of violence was also often improvised and related to the consumption of alcohol. This means this type of homicide most likely occurs in the spur of the moment, making this type of lethal violence very difficult to predict. As such, it would be useful to explore the issue of violence lethality further, using these insights to develop policy strategies in order to deescalate violence and to prevent these types of homicide in the future.

Another type of violence that might require specific policy interventions in Scotland is the *Work-related* nonlethal violence type. The Scottish Government has currently no specific official policy strategy to reduce this type of violence. Instead, violence occurring in the workplace is included within the broader framework of preventing violence in general, which is mainly focused on public violence and knife crime. Due to the unique characteristics of the *Work-related* type of violence, it might, however, be relevant to introduce a prevention strategy aimed at tackling violence occurring in the context of the victim's employment. This might include the implementation of more rigorous safety structures around certain employment groups at risk, such as people working at bars or public houses, in law enforcement or night-time transportation services. Strategies might also include increased support for victims reporting violence perpetrated by colleagues or co-workers. Although work-place victimisation might not constitute the majority of violent incidents reported in Scotland, the *Work-related* type of violence identified in this research has demonstrated a significant increase over time. As such, it is important that this type of violence is recognised as well prevented.

As discussed in the previous chapter, one of the main policy implications of lethal and nonlethal violence following a similar pattern over time is that homicide trends may be used as a barometer for trends in wider violence. As homicide trends in general are regarded as more reliable indicators of violence in society compared to other measures of violence (Polk, 1994; UNODC, 2013; Van Dijk, et al., 2007), this is beneficial for a number of reasons. Not only can the changing profile of violence in Scotland be monitored using more robust homicide data, but this also allows for a more efficient planning of resources and violence prevention strategies. As demonstrated by the current research, trends in similar types of lethal and nonlethal violence follow a similar pattern over time, leading to important implications for Police Scotland as well as other organisations aiming to prevent crime. First, the similarity in trends means that the change in different types of homicide can

184   *Theorising homicide*

be observed to provide an estimation of the changes in corresponding types of violence. As reported homicides include a lower dark figure compared to other measurements of violence (UNODC, 2013; Polk, 1994; Van Dijk, et al., 2007), this means that trends in nonlethal violence can be estimated using a more reliable measure. This is perhaps most relevant in the case of lethal and nonlethal domestic violence which otherwise could be very hard to estimate and monitor due to the large dark figure of this crime. Second, interventions aimed to reduce a certain type of lethal violence can also be assumed to prevent similar types of nonlethal violence since homicide can be considered the extreme end of the same violence spectrum. This can also be seen demonstrated by the prevention strategies implemented to reduce public violence involving sharp instruments, which have reduced both lethal and nonlethal types of violence. Third, due to the increased reliability of homicide measurements, evaluations of interventions aimed to reduce a specific type of homicide could be done with greater accuracy. Since the change in lethal and nonlethal violence appears to be related, this evaluation could subsequently be extrapolated to be applicable to the same type of violence, leading to a more reliable and accurate evaluation process overall.

While generalising from lethal to nonlethal violence may not be appropriate for all types of violence, as the current study has also shown, most types of lethal and nonlethal violence follow a similar pattern over time. As such, the results of this research could therefore be beneficial for Police Scotland when directing their resources as efficiently and accurately as possible. These findings are also beneficial for targeting policy interventions to where they are needed most, and may also provide a more accurate framework for prevention strategy evaluations. The following section will discuss the theoretical implications of the findings of this research.

Theoretical implications

This section will explore the theoretical implications of the research described in this study, examining the consequences of the findings on Crime Drop Theories, the privatisation of violence and masculinities and violence.

Crime Drop Theories

As explored in the previous chapter, a number of theories make contradicting assumptions about the relationship between trends in lethal and nonlethal violence when attempting to explain the homicide decline. This, despite the fact that the nature of this relationship had previously not been proven empirically. The general crime drop theories such as the Security Hypothesis and Debut Crime Hypothesis (Farrell et al., 2010; 2014), for example, assume that all forms of crime, including homicide, have been decreasing in tandem. Other theories, such as the Medical Care Hypothesis (Blumstein, 2000; Harris et al.,

2002), conversely hypothesise that improved medical services has caused homicide to decrease while other violence crime is increasing. As we discussed in Chapter 8, this constitutes a gap within the research on crime trends, which the research in the current volume has attempted to remedy. The findings of this research has demonstrated that trends in lethal and nonlethal violence do follow a similar pattern overall. While the overall decrease in homicide and violence appears to be driven by a decline in lethal and nonlethal acts of public violence involving young people using sharp instruments, there has been a relative increase in lethal and nonlethal domestic violence over time in Scotland. As such, theories building on the assumption that homicide and violence are changing differently over time, such as the Medical Care Hypothesis, cannot explain the changes in lethal and nonlethal violence in Scotland. If the evident homicide decline could have been explained by improvements in medical care, then corresponding types of nonlethal violence would have demonstrating opposing trends. However, as the findings demonstrate, this is not the case here. The Medical Care Hypothesis furthermore assumes an equal decrease in all types of homicide. This is also challenged by the findings in the current study, since the results show that some types of homicides, namely the *Femicide* type, in fact have become more common over time.

As such, it would appear that the theories postulating similar trends in homicide and violence over time, including the general crime drop theories, have more merit when explaining these violence trends in Scotland. Both the Security Hypothesis and Debut Crime Hypothesis (Farrell et al., 2010; 2014) assume that lethal as well as nonlethal violence are decreasing due to increased securitisation in combination with decreased availability to offend. The decrease in 'debut crimes' (Farrell et al., 2011; 2014) such as burglary and car theft, evident due to increases in securitisation, has led to fewer criminal careers, which tend to begin with these minor offences. This in turn leads to fewer instances of serious crimes such as violence and homicide, leading to declines in these crimes as well. While this provides a theoretical explanation for why public violence and homicide have decreased in Scotland, this theory does not offer an explanation for changes in lethal and nonlethal domestic violence. Increased securitisation and decreased availability of debut crimes does not affect violence occurring between intimate partners in the privacy of their home. As the previous chapters of this volume have demonstrated, while homicide and nonlethal violence follow a similar pattern over time, this pattern is more complicated than a straightforward increase of decrease, highlighting further the need to disaggregate trends in lethal and nonlethal violence if these crimes are to be fully understood. No theory to date, however, has taken different types of homicide and violence into account when attempting to explain the changes in these trends. As such, the following sections of this chapter will draw on different theoretical perspectives in order to provide an explanation for the changing trends in homicide and violence in Scotland, ending with a new theoretical framework to explain these changes over time.

186   *Theorising homicide*

The privatisation of violence

When attempting to identify sound theoretical explanations for the change in homicide and violence in Scotland, it is important that we ask ourselves relevant questions relating to our findings. Why has lethal and nonlethal domestic violence increased in relative terms while both the relative and absolute trends in public violence and homicide involving sharp instruments have decreased? While this decline in knife violence among predominantly young men in public places is a very positive development, the relative increase in lethal and nonlethal domestic violence, despite numerous interventions and prevention strategies, is a source for great concern.

This change in the pattern of both lethal and nonlethal violence on the societal level might be related to an overall shift in the way we live our lives. While some scholars argue that crimes may change over time due to a displacement effect, where crime changes from one context to another due to the implementation of crime interventions (Clarke, 1983; Clark, 1995) a shift in the way we live, or in our routine activities (Cohen & Felson, 1979; Felson & Cohen, 1980) is more universal. The way people choose to spend their time, both leisurely and otherwise, has changed dramatically over the past decades. For instance, researchers have found that increasingly more time overall is spent in private settings compared to public places, such as on the street or in pubs (Aebi & Linde, 2010). While this shift might be related to socioeconomic status, where particularly young people belonging to more advantaged social classes are able to afford more expensive and alluring indoor activities such as video games and entertainment systems (Aebi & Linde, 2010), there has been an overall shift towards interactions in indoor, private settings. When the way we live our everyday lives changes, this leads to changes in how violent crime is perpetrated as well. As we discussed in Chapter 4, Cooney (2003) argues that a privatisation of violence can be discerned, which means that violence has become more private and less public in nature. As people spend more time indoors, increasingly more violent crime occur indoors too, and less violence is perpetrated outside in public locations. Interventions such as the implementation of the Smoking Ban in 2006, prohibiting smoking in public places such as nightclubs and pubs (Scottish Parliament, 2005), and the reduction of the drink-drive limit (Smoking, Health and Social Care (Scotland) Act, 2005) might also have contributed to a privatisation of time as well as violence (J. Carnochan, personal communication, 14 August 2017). As such, these changes in the way people live their lives is not only related to crime displacement; rather, this signals a general shift of societal behavioural patterns, where not only violence but our general lifestyles have become privatised. As the findings of the current research have demonstrated, the vast majority of homicides in Scotland occurred in private settings. The findings also showed that both lethal and nonlethal violence occurring in public locations have decreased while domestic homicide and violence have increased in relative terms. Homicides occurring indoors by others than intimate partners, such

A theory of homicide   187

as the *Stabbing* and *No Weapon-Bludgeoning* homicides, have remained stable over time, not demonstrating a decrease. Perhaps these findings could be explained by a general privatisation of both time and violence occurring in Scotland over time.

Masculinities and violence

However, although Cooney's (2003) theory of the privatisation of violence provides an explanation for the changing pattern of violence, this theory does not explain the possible mechanisms behind the increases in lethal and nonlethal domestic violence. This furthermore does not explain why some types of violence occurring indoors, such as the *Stabbing* and the *No Weapon–Bludgeoning* homicides, have remained stable over time while other types, such as the *Femicide* homicides and the *Domestic* violence type, have demonstrated relative increases. If a privatisation of violence has occurred, then all types of violence perpetrated indoors should be increasing while public acts of violence should demonstrate relative decreases. As such, perhaps a privatisation of violence is only part of the story. Perhaps the explanations for the differences in trends is also related to the characteristics of the people most commonly involved in these violence acts. As the current research has demonstrated, the vast majority of offenders and victims of violence in Scotland were male. Homicide and violence can therefore be described as overwhelmingly masculine activities. As explored in Chapter 4, previous research has demonstrated and theorised about the connection between the performance of masculinity and violence (see, for instance, Hatty, 2000; Messerschmidt, 1999; Polk, 1994; Ray, 2011), even describing violence as 'integral to masculinity' (Hatty, 2000: 120). Previous research has also found an intrinsic relationship between violence, masculinity and marginalisation, where marginalised men who are cut off from conventional routes of success or conflict resolution tend to use violence as an expression of their masculinity (Polk; 1994; 1999). This appears to be particularly prominent among young men (Polk, 1999), such as the individuals involved in the *Public Weapon* violence and *Rivalry* homicides. Studies have also found that marginalised, young men more commonly commit public violence compared to young people of higher socioeconomic status (Aebi & Linde, 2010). In these instances, violence is not only seen as a *possible* route of action to resolve conflict, but the *expected* cause of action, becoming a pathway for expressing masculinity. Research in Scotland has furthermore shown that there has been a great decline in criminal convictions for young men over time, including violent convictions (Matthews, 2016). This overall change in the pattern of violence might indicate a shift in the way masculinity is perceived or constructed in Scotland.

As described by Polk (1994;1999), the relationship between violence and masculinity is not only evident for public homicides involving young offenders; confrontational homicides, such as the *Stabbing* homicides and the *No Weapon-Bludgeoning* homicides, as well as lethal and nonlethal domestic

188 *Theorising homicide*

violence, are also related to the expression and affirmation of masculinity. Violence is in these instances used either as a way to resolve conflict, or as a response to jealousy or possessiveness of an intimate partner. As such, all forms of homicide and violence may therefore be said to be intrinsically related to masculinity and marginalisation (Messerschmidt, 1999; Connell & Messerschmidt, 2005; Polk, 1993; 1999; West & Zimmermann, 1987). Violence may thus be considered a way to 'do' or perform masculinity but also as a way to confirm structural and cultural norms of gender and masculinity (Butler, 2004; Hatty, 2000; Messerschmidt, 1999; Polk, 1994). 'Doing' violence also means to 'do' masculinity and vice versa.

Gender is, however, not the only power order affecting the performance and perpetration of violence. Research has demonstrated that other hierarchical structures of power such as class, ethnicity, age, and sexuality also shape the structure of violence, affecting whether people commit violence or not (Messerschmidt, 1999; Polk, 1994, 1999; Skott, 2019a, 2021; Tomsen & Mason, 2001). As these various power structures work together to affect the performance and perpetration of violence, studies have demonstrated the importance of conducting intersectional research, taking all of these power orders into account (Meyer, 2012; Sokoloff, 2008). In order to provide an explanation for the changing pattern of violence in Scotland evident in the current research, the following section will describe a new theoretical framework of *Doing Violence*. Building on an intersectional understanding of violence, this theory aims to provide an alternative interpretation of the findings in order to get a deeper understanding of how homicide and other types of violence change in relation to changing societal structures.

Towards a new theoretical framework: *Doing Violence*

As we discussed in Chapter 4, the notion that gender is a performance, something we 'do' rather than is, has been dominant in the gender literature for some time. As Butler (2004) argues, gender is not only a social category but a process – an endless, improvised performance on a stage limited by structural power orders, norms, and perceptions which are constantly in flux. 'Doing' gender thus entails various strategies to cope with these power structures, or *gender regimes*, as they construct certain types of gender identities as visible, legitimate, and recognised, while other identities are constructed as invisible, illegitimate, and unrecognised. The term 'regime' has been used previously in theoretical explanations relating to, for instance, gender (Connell, 2009) and risk (Laurendeau, 2008), and can be defined as a structured set of power orders affecting our understanding of different social constructions, such as gender, on both the individual and societal level. These regimes are ingrained in societal and institutional structures, affecting, for instance, the division of labour, work recruitment, and the formation and reproduction of social roles. Regimes have also been used as a theoretical concept to provide an explanation for different relational structures, which can both shape and disrupt individual practices, and define what actions are considered possible for individuals, as well as the consequences of such actions. While these regimes might sometimes correspond to wider societal power orders, the regimes may also be in conflict with societal norms, leading to the possibility for change. As such, while there might be a dominant gender order affecting the performance of gender on a structural level, gender regimes might exist on the subcultural level which disrupts or subverts the dominant gender order. Connell (2009) and Butler (2004) both utilise a theoretical understanding of regimes in relation to gender. These gender regimes construct certain individuals as (un)viable and (un)grievable, creating insufferable living conditions for individuals who are denied recognition by these orders of power. Some individuals therefore proceed to 'redo' or 'undo' gender, which renegotiate or disturb the conditions that dictate their behaviour (Butler, 2004; Giritli-Nygren et al., 2017). Such acts of resistance could, for instance, be expressed by the performance of alternative types of femininities or masculinities conflicting with the dominant gender norms, working instead to subvert these gender regimes rather than reproducing them.

Laurendeau (2008) utilises this theoretical understanding of regimes in a similar way in relation to risk. He describes risk regimes as subcultural patterns of risk arrangements, where individual choices are shaped as well as impeded by a dominant understanding of risk. This dominant, structural construction of risk furthermore shapes risk practices, which can be regarded as the performance of risk. Laurendeau (2008) furthermore connects regimes of risk to regimes of gender, arguing that 'doing' gender also relates to the performance of risk. The performance of risk as an intersectional process has also been explored by Giritli-Nygren et al. (2017), who similarly to Butler (2004) argues that risk is not a static category but a process that is done, undone, and redone in relation to the structural norms shaping individual choices and actions. To 'do' risk is therefore to act in accordance with existing structural norms surrounding risk, which may also reproduce the power orders underpinning regimes of risk. The performance of risk is thus an embodied, self-regulated process where 'doing' risk also involves the performance of gender, age, class, ethnicity, and other power orders (Giritli-Nygren et al., 2017).

Building on these previous theories in relation to risk and gender, this section will develop a new theoretical framework by arguing that this also applies to violence; that violence is something we 'do', and that institutions, organisations, and communities are permeated and shaped by *Violence Regimes* (Skott, 2020). As argued in the previous section, violence is shaped by many different power orders, including gender, ethnicity, age, and class, which affects how violence is perceived, constructed, and perpetrated. The theory of *Doing Violence* proposes a new way of understanding violence and the change in violence, where all of these different power orders are taken into account in the idea of violence regimes. The theory suggests that we not only need to consider how violence is affected by these power orders but also how these structures of power work together to construct certain types of violence

190 *Theorising homicide*

as visible, legitimised, and recognised while other types of violence are made invisible, illegitimate, and unrecognised. As such, violence regimes are sets of multiple power orders, working together to form a specific hierarchy of violence. Such a hierarchy, or violence regime, may exist on the state level, community level, or even on the individual level, working in concert or in conflict with dominant power orders and affect how violence is performed. Building on Schinkel's (2013) definition of the concept, this theoretical framework also interweaves ideas of violence regimes with intersectional perspectives of gender.

Schinkel (2013) defined violence regimes as a regulating system that identifies and defines different types of violence as well as the relationship between these types. As such, it is the violence regime that determines what types of violence are recognised, legitimised, ignored, or hidden. Schinkel (2013) furthermore argues that hegemonic and heteronormative power structures, including orders of gender and ethnicity, shape the current violence regimes evident in various states. While regimes of violence may not exclusively be defined by the state, Schinkel (2013) argues that the construction of violence regimes is closely related to state power. As legitimate forms of violence are most commonly defined by the state, and since violence regimes mediates the relationship between state and subject, regimes of violence are often permeated by state power. The state is not only defined as well as created by violence (Weber, 1978), but also possesses the power to construct the meaning and attribution of violence by selectively defining, recognising, and denying certain acts as violence (Schinkel, 2013). This also means that violence regimes may instigate symbolic violence (Bourdieu & Wacquant, 1992), which legitimises and confirms structures of inequality. As argued by Bourdieu (2000: 204; Schinkel, 2013), symbolic violence is violence not recognised as such, meaning that it 'takes place with the silent approval of those on whom it befalls' (Schinkel, 2013: 316). Symbolic violence can be traced to structures of dominant classifications and (self)classifying practices, which, as Schinkel (2013) argues, not only emanates from the state.

In this current theoretical framework, the ideas of Schinkel (2013) are developed by defining violence regimes as structured sets of power orders, creating specific violence hierarchies, which renders certain forms of violence visible, legitimate and recognised and others invisible, illegitimate, and unrecognised. Violence regimes may exist on the micro, macro, or meso level, and can either uphold or disrupt dominant power orders. This may be expressed through criminalisation and public recognition of certain types of violence and not others, but violence regimes may also be expressed through the construction of violence, where certain types of violence are recognised and others obscured. The definition and recognition of violence is therefore not just regulated by the relationship between subject and state but by the various power orders permeating society on all levels. Unlike Schinkel (2013), I would therefore argue that there isn't just one violence regime prevalent in society but several, depending on context; what types of violence that are considered

A theory of homicide   191

legitimate and recognised differ between different social groups and different environments. As such, the current violence regimes, permeating both local and global contexts, are shaped by current hegemonic and heteronormative power orders (such as gender, ethnicity, and class) and are also related to structures of inequality. These violence regimes consequently needs to be identified, highlighted, and explored if violence and the change in violence is to be fully understood. At the same time, it is important to separate the social construction of violence (which is arguably shaped by violence regimes) from the actual perpetration of violence. Just as the social construction of risk is separated from whatever occurrence actually constituting the risk (for instance, illnesses, wars, or disasters) (Giritli-Nygren et al., 2017), violence is here defined as the *social construction* of violent actions, perpetrators, and victims, where some people and actions are constructed as violent while others are not. As such, this theory does not presume that changes in violence regimes, such as, for instance, a shift in how society regards domestic violence, directly result in increases or decreases of perpetrated acts of domestic violence. Rather, the theory proposes that a change in violence regimes, for instance leading to a decreased tolerance for domestic violence, leads to changes in how domestic violence is constructed. While the way violence is socially constructed may in turn affect the actual perpetration of violence, the theory of *Doing Violence* is concerned with the social construction of violence rather than actual instances of violent acts.

Similarly to gender regimes (Butler, 2004; Connell, 2009) and risk regimes (Giritli Nygren et al., 2017; Laurendeau, 2000), the current theoretical framework of *Doing Violence* presumes that individuals adopt and invent strategies to renegotiate as well as to cope with the power structures shaping the violence regimes. Just as when risk is performed, the performance of violence involves actions and embodiments conducted in relation to the dominant norms of violence dictated by the violence regime. To 'do' violence is therefore also to 'do' gender, ethnicity, class, and other power orders, performed through strategies and everyday practices. To illustrate, let us explore a few examples of the performance of violence based on the dominant violence regime on the structural level. For instance, a young, white man engaging in physical violence as a way to resolve a conflict with another young man arguably does violence through his performance of gender, ethnicity, and age. His violent response is anticipated, if not expected, in the context of hegemonic masculinity and current dominant power orders. As such, the violence perpetrated by this young man would reinforce the dominant violence regime, as well as orders of gender and age; he has 'done' violence. By contrast, if an elderly woman engages in violence as a way to resolve a conflict, her performance of violence would undermine the dominant violence regime as it violates the dominant gender orders as well as the dominant age orders. Her performance of violence might even be considered a subversion of the current violence regimes, as a strategy to cope with the hegemonic ideas of femininity and age permeating society. As such, she has 'redone' violence, contesting the

192 *Theorising homicide*

established discourses of violence and reshaping the conditions dictating her life. However, her performance of violence is more likely to be constructed as self-defence or even nonviolence due to her position in relation to the dominant violence regimes. Although she might have acted just as violently as the man in our other example, her violence might be diminished or even made invisible in narratives following the violence.

Acts of nonviolence can also be part of the performance of violence. For instance, a white, heterosexual, middle-class woman might 'do' violence by being nonviolent, as the dominant violence regimes positions her outside of the frame of who is constructed as 'violent'. As the dominant power orders of gender, age, sexuality, and ethnicity underpinning the violence regime are more likely to construct her as a victim of violence than an offender, her performance of violence through nonviolence reinforces the dominant violence regime. Contrastingly, a young, black man from a marginalised area may refrain from violence as a strategy to subvert and renegotiate the terms of the violence regime. As he might be expected to engage in violence, his nonviolent performance of violence may be understood as an act of resistance against the power orders shaping his life; he has 'undone' violence. As such, performing violence is to position oneself in relation to the prevalent violence regimes currently permeating society. This could entail violent as well as nonviolent acts, evidenced through everyday practices, which may reinforce, disturb, renegotiate, challenge, or undermine current violence regimes. The examples above are illustrating instances where this could happen, but since we 'do' violence simultaneously as we 'do' gender, age, class, ethnicity, and other power orders, *Doing Violence* is a continuous process that is always in flux.

If violence is understood in relation to violence regimes, violence in itself can be regarded as a strategy to do, redo, and undo these various power orders in order to survive the (un)bearable conditions of life created by the regimes of violence. As such, violence becomes a mechanism used to cope with structures of power and inequality, sometimes reinforcing the existing violence regimes and in other instances subverting them, underlining its limits and taboos. Violence, then, can be utilised both in order to reproduce the current violence regimes but also in order to undermine them.

The changing regimes of violence in Scotland

All of the power orders we have mentioned and discussed, including orders of gender, ethnicity, age, and class, change over time, resulting in similar changes in how people perform these power orders. Scotland is not different. Over time, old ideals relating to gender and class have transformed and shifted in time with greater ontological shifts of late modernity (Young, 2007). Previously dominant hegemonic masculinities, evident through the archetypes of 'the hardman' or 'the fighting man' (Fraser, 2015: 68), are no longer upheld as Scottish ideals. As the gender regimes of society change (Connell, 2009), so do the strategies used to cope with these regimes. Similarly, the theoretical framework of *Doing Violence* assumes that violence regimes shift over time as they are underpinned by sets of changing power orders. As such, violence that was considered legitimate 20 years ago may not necessarily be considered legitimate today.

As discussed in Chapter 3, violence, particularly knife-related violence among young people, has been a traditional problem in Scotland (Carnochan, 2015; Damer, 1989; Fraser, 2015). Constituting one of the most serious problems for public health, leading to the unenviable moniker of 'the most violent country in the developed world' (BBC News, 2005; The Guardian, 2005), the deep-rooted problem of violence in Scotland was also tied in with social issues such as increases in drug abuse and widespread unemployment. During the peak of violence in the mid-1990s, violence in Scotland seemed both normalised as well as inevitable (Carnochan, 2015).

However, as this volume has demonstrated, the pattern of both lethal and nonlethal violence in Scotland has changed dramatically. While public violence among young men committed with knives or sharp instruments have decreased, lethal and nonlethal domestic violence have demonstrated relative increases over time. The theory of *Doing Violence* may be used in order to understand this changing pattern of homicide and violence. The fact that violence among young men in Scotland has decreased might suggest that young men no longer use public violence as a strategy when navigating the structures dictated by different power orders. This could indicate that due to changes in the power orders relating to gender, age, and ethnicity, violence is no longer seen as a legitimate or preferred response to conflict. The tendency of non-violence can also be regarded as a strategy to 'undo' the structures of the violence regime, subverting or disturbing current power orders. As described in the examples above, not using violence then becomes a way for these young men to position themselves in relation to societal structures shaping their identities and living conditions. As violence is almost expected for these young men, not engaging in violence becomes a conscious or subconscious act of resistance against the demands and expectations placed upon them by hegemonic ideals of gender, age, and ethnicity. In both of these scenarios, the decrease in public violence between young men in Scotland can be understood as an effect of changing power orders, which in turn generates changes in the current violence regimes, shifting what type of violence is considered legitimate and recognised. How young men are doing gender, class, and age has changed, leading to a changed performance of violence. The violence itself then can be understood as an expression of the violence regime, as well as a demarcation of its boundaries.

Another example of how the theory of *Doing Violence* can be used to provide a theoretical understanding of the changing pattern of violence in Scotland relates to the increase of violence occurring inside the home by primarily adult men, committed against other male friends, family members, or intimate partners (see Chapter 8). While the decrease in public violence between young men can be understood in the context of changing violence regimes on the micro

194 *Theorising homicide*

level, the increase in the violence occurring in private may be understood in the context of changing violence regimes on the macro level. As demonstrated in Chapter 3, the violence policies in Scotland have changed dramatically over the past 15 years. During this shift, moving away from a 'crack-down on crime' to constructing violence a public health problem, the main focus of these prevention policies has been public violence among young men, primarily involving knives. Although the violence policies in Scotland also has been focused on combatting domestic violence, public violence among young men has been constructed as the primary problem (NKBL, 2014; VRU, 2016). This has given rise to a violence regime on the macro level where public, male violence is prioritised and highlighted, obscuring other types of violence, such as violence occurring in private residences or at the work place, which are not given the same focus, time, or interventions. Violence committed by female offenders and violence against male intimate partners are other examples of violence which have been rendered invisible. These types of violence are not mentioned in policies or prevention strategies and are thus not constructed as a 'problem', rendering these acts of violence unrecognised in the current violence regime. In these instances, these acts of violence might not even be considered violence at all, and are often relegated to the individual rather than the structural level. This further illustrates the importance of identifying and exploring violence regimes in relation to different types of violence, as the violence regimes not only dictates how violence is constructed but also how it is prevented.

The increased privatisation of violence evident in Scotland, resulting in more and more acts of violence occurring inside in private settings between individuals who know each other, can therefore be understood as a repro-duction of the current violence regimes, which prioritise public violence, neglecting private violence, rendering certain types of violence invisible. Perpetrators of private violence may in these circumstances understand this violence as normal facets of interpersonal conflicts, becoming part of the per-formance of gender, class, age, and other power orders. The increase of vio-lence in private settings can therefore be understood as a performance of the current violence regime. If violence is understood in this way, the changing pattern of lethal and nonlethal violence in Scotland is related to changes in structural power orders both on the micro and macro levels, where violence both reinforces and undermines the violence regimes shaped by these power orders.

Overall, the theoretical framework of *Doing Violence* illustrates the import-ance of using an intersectional perspective when exploring violence. In order to fully understand violence and how patterns of violence change within a society, it is important to explore how violence is affected by multiple factors, such as gender, age, class, and ethnicity, simultaneously. This provides a more nuanced understanding of violence, as the performance of violence is a con-current performance of multiple power orders. The theory of *Doing Violence* also underlines the importance of power and inequality in relation to the social construction of violence. As Schinkel (2013) argues, violence regimes can also be used for governing and the reproduction of power as regimes of violence, similarly to gender regimes, constructs certain lives as meaningful, viable, and grievable (Butler, 2006), while others are not constructed as such. For instance, state actions against individuals who are constructed as less meaningful and grievable, such as refugees or transgender individuals, may not be recognised as violent acts according to dominant violence regimes, even if these state actions reduce the living space and freedom of these individuals. This also relates to colonial violence, where some bodies are constructed as threatening, violent, and dangerous (Gökariksel, Neubert, & Smith, 2019). In a time where violence is justified by the reversal of aggressor and potential victim (Gökariksel et al., 2019), it is important to critically examine violence regimes and state definitions of violence. Violence regimes can similarly also give rise to symbolic violence (Bourdieu, 2000; Bourdieu & Wacquant, 1992), legitimising and consolidating structures of inequality, as well as benevolent violence (Barker, 2017). Benevolent violence has been defined as coercive actions and practices enacted by the state in order to uphold state goals, which may also have violent effects (Barker, 2017). Such violence may also be read as an expression of current violence regimes enacted on the macro level. As such, critical examinations of current violence regimes is very important in order not to risk an uncritical reproduction of state definitions of violence.

The reason why the theoretical framework of *Doing Violence* is important is that it creates a space to theoretically explore how violence is shaped and permeated by power relations and inequality and how violence is performed, embodied, and negotiated on a daily basis to deal with these structures. By theorising violence as a performance, related to regimes of violence existing on all levels of society, the structures of inequality and power become visible, as the everyday practices of violence are dictated by these normative structures, affecting not only how people live their daily lives but who is constructed as violent or dangerous and who is not. While the way people position themselves in relation to current violence regimes is always changing, the way people negotiate their positions is also highly dependent on structures of power and inequality. Individuals who are privileged or who in other ways possess greater money or power may employ strategies to negotiate their position in relation to the violence regimes in ways that are inaccessible to people with less privilege, power, or money. Consequently, the proposed theoretical framework of *Doing Violence* outlined here is not only useful when attempting to understand violence and the change in violence over time but also creates a space to theoretically engage with the inequality and power dynamics of violence. Violence against others, violence against oneself, state violence, symbolic violence, and nonviolence all relates to structures of power and inequality dictated by violence regimes. By theorising violence in this way, we situate violence in a wider societal context and can therefore move towards a deeper, more critical understanding of both violence and homicide.

196 *Theorising homicide*

Conclusions

This chapter has explored the implications of the research outlined in this volume, both for policy and for theory. While the evaluation of the effects of various policy interventions was beyond the scope of the current research, the findings show that the type of violence demonstrating the most dramatic decrease over time, namely lethal and nonlethal public violence committed by young men using knives, was matched by corresponding policy interventions and prevention strategies. The reframing of the violence problem as a public health issue appears to have had an effect in decreasing some types of lethal and nonlethal violence in Scotland over time. However, similar interventions against lethal and nonlethal domestic violence do not appear to have had the same effect, underlining a challenge moving forward in relation to violence prevention in Scotland. As demonstrated by this volume, it is of outmost importance to prevent all types of violence, and not only the ones most visible.

This chapter has also explored the theoretical implications of the findings of the current research. As demonstrated, the research of the current volume has had an effect on Crime Drop Theories, ideas of the privatisation of violence and masculinities and violence, further highlighting the need to theoretically explore different types of lethal and nonlethal violence. As different types of violence demonstrate different trends and patterns over time, theoretical perspectives exploring the change of violence over time need to take these differences into account. As such, disaggregation of violence and homicide is not only important for empirical purposes, but is also relevant in order to achieve a theoretical understanding of these crimes as well.

Finally, this chapter has also presented a new theoretical framework of *Doing Violence* in order to theorise violence in relation to structures of power and inequality. The theory proposes that violence is performed; done, undone, and redone by people's everyday practices as strategies to position themselves in relation to structures of power and inequality. As such, violence is constructed, defined, and performed in terms of violence regimes; a structured set of power orders rendering some types of violence visible, legitimised, and recognised, while other forms of violence are rendered invisible, illegitimate, and unrecognised. Violence regimes exist on micro, meso, and macro levels of society and are permeated by multiple power orders, including gender, class, ethnicity, age, risk, and sexuality. By theorising the changing pattern of violence in Scotland using the *Doing Violence* framework, this chapter illustrates that violence can be read not only as an expression of dominant power orders shaping the violence regimes but also as a demarcation of their boundaries and taboos. The theory of *Doing Violence* thus creates a space where violence can be theoretically explored from an intersectional perspective, making visible the structures of power and inequality that shape the violence regimes dictating the performance of violence. Theorising violence in this way not only provides a deeper understanding for violence and the changing patterns

A theory of homicide   197

of violence, but also increases our understanding of the orders and regimes of power that permeates people's everyday lives.

The next chapter of this volume is also the last chapter and will provide an overview of everything we have covered so far, pulling together the findings in order to summarise the main conclusions of the book. The next chapter will also discuss some of the limitations of the current research, as well as outlining directions for future research regarding homicide.

10 Overview and conclusions

Introduction

Over the course of this book, we have explored various facets of homicide, starting with what homicide actually is (and is not) in the first place. While this may seem like an obvious question, the answer is less than clear, as we have discovered. We have also explored the legal definitions of this crime and how this may differ depending on jurisdiction, particularly emphasising the differences between Scotland and England and Wales. As the research described in this volume is centred in Scotland, we have also delved into the contextual history of violence in this country and how various policy changes may have affected the changing trends of lethal violence. This book has furthermore provided an overview of the most prominent theories attempting to explain homicide using various different perspectives, including biological, psychological, and sociological theories of homicide. This also involved the examination of the relationship between gender and homicide. While homicide can occur between any types of people in any type of context, research has shown us that the vast majority of both victims and offenders of homicide are male. It is therefore important to explore this relationship further in order to understand what it is about being a man that seems conducive of serious violence.

This volume has also explored relatively new critical theories relating to the medial impact of homicide, including Gothic and popular criminology. These perspectives explore the reciprocal relationship between academic and aesthetic constructions of homicide and how our understanding of this crime is reflected in modern day media. To illustrate this, we have explored serial killings using a Gothic lens, examining how this extreme type of homicide is constructed in popular culture. This not only provides a better understanding of what discourses that shape the public imaginary of homicide but also how these discourses affect criminal justice policies and our understanding of this crime. All of these aspects are important in order to gain a full understanding of homicide and its place in society.

The second part of this book has provided an empirical overview of different types of homicide in Scotland, starting with homicide disaggregated

DOI: 10.4324/9781003105282-13

Overview and conclusions 199

by gender and age. Problematising this way of dividing homicide into different types, we have also explored a data-driven, inductive method for disaggregating homicide subtypes, which led to the identification of four main homicide types in Scotland; *Stabbing, No Weapon–Bludgeoning, Rivalry*, and *Femicides*. When the change in these four types were examined over time, the findings showed that even though there has been an absolute decrease in homicide, some homicide subtypes have declined more than others. While there was a marked decrease in public lethal violence occurring between young people using knives, domestic violence between intimate partners had demonstrated a relative increase over time. The research covered in this volume has therefore demonstrated that not all homicide types change similarly over time.

We have also delved into an in-depth exploration of a very rare form of homicide, namely sexual homicide. Moving beyond what sexual homicide is and is not, we have explored different types of sexual homicide, including sexual homicides committed by male offenders against female victims, sexual homicide committed by female offenders, and sexual homicide committed against child victims. We have also examined different subtypes of sexual homicides in Scotland and Canada, using the same explorative, inductive approach covered in earlier chapters. This volume has demonstrated that while there are some differences between different forms of sexual homicide, sexual homicide is a very distinct type of homicide that should be explored separately from other types of homicide. The findings of this book have also showed that sexual homicide appears to demonstrate similar underlying patterns, universal across jurisdictions, which suggests a limited number of behavioural patterns for sexual homicide offenders internationally.

In the third and final part of this volume, we theorised homicide by synthesising the previous findings of this research with innovative theories on violence. This first involved the examination of the relationship between homicide and violence, attempting to amend a long-lasting gap in previous research. While different subtypes of homicide and violence change differently, the findings of these studies have shown that similar subtypes change similarly over time, supporting the idea of a continuum of violence. We have explored the implications of these findings for policy as well as theory, and this book has also presented a new theoretical framework aimed to explain lethal and nonlethal violence called *Doing Violence*. By regarding violence as a performance, related and governed by multiple power orders including gender, age and class, the theory of *Doing Violence* creates a space where violence can be theoretically explored from an intersectional perspective, making visible the structures of power and inequality which shape this performance.

In this final chapter, we will revisit the main argument laid forward in the first chapter, drawing together the main conclusions of this volume. We will then review the original aspects of this research, clearly stating what you as a reader can take away from this book. Limitations and directions for future research will subsequently be considered, before the book will end with some concluding remarks.

200 *Theorising homicide*

The overall argument

Over the course of this volume, this book has argued a series of key points. First, this book has argued that there is a lacking knowledge in regards to the relationship between homicide and nonlethal violence, which is problematic for a number of reasons. Not only does this gap in the literature mean that we do not have a full understanding of homicide as a crime, but, as this book has demonstrated, not knowing whether lethal and nonlethal violence follow a similar pattern over time may lead to misinformed theories and erroneous implications for crime prevention. There has furthermore been a lack of research regarding homicide and violence in Scotland, despite the violent legacy of this country and the dramatic changes in crime trends evident over the past decades, which has prompted this research.

Second, this volume has argued that two key elements of the relationship between homicide and violence needed to be explored in order to get a deeper understanding of this relationship – the characteristics of homicide and violence in terms of variables relating to the victims, offenders, and incidents, and the changing patterns in both homicide and violence over time. By exploring both these facets of the relationship between lethal and nonlethal violence, this research has demonstrated that homicide and violence are more similar than different, and may be regarded along a violence continuum. While this may seem like an obvious conclusion to some, certain theories are built on the assumption that trends in homicide and violence change differently, which the research in the current volume has refuted.

Third, it has been argued that in order to examine these two key elements, it was necessary to disaggregate homicide and violence into subtypes. As previous research has demonstrated, homicide and violence are heterogeneous crimes (Blumstein, 2000; Lehti, 2014; Messner & Savolainen, 2001; Roberts & Willits, 2015; Thompson, 2015). This suggests that the examination of aggregate trends in these crimes may lead to inaccurate results. As such, this volume has argued that subtypes of homicide and violence should be identified before being compared over time in order to get a comprehensive understanding of the relationship between homicide and violence.

Fourth, this volume has argued that homicide is related to nonlethal violence since similar types of lethal and nonlethal violence have been identified. These types have furthermore changed similarly over time, giving further support to the idea of a continuum of violence. Fifth, this research has demonstrated that although all types of homicide and violence have decreased in absolute terms, some types have demonstrated relative increases over time. This is true for lethal as well as nonlethal domestic violence, which has increased in relative terms over time in Scotland. This further highlights the fact that the examination of aggregate trends in homicide and violence does not tell the full story but can in fact obscure certain trends.

This research has also made a few arguments in regards to the policy implications for the current findings. It has been argued that many of the

Overview and conclusions 201

policy interventions framing violence as a public health problem, implemented during the mid-2000s, were likely to have contributed to the decline in public lethal and nonlethal violence perpetrated among young men. However, due to the relative increase in domestic homicide and violence demonstrated in the current study, occurring in spite of numerous policy interventions aimed at reducing this type of violence, this research has argued that future interventions should focus on tackling the cultural and social issues related to violence. This is important in order to keep preventing and reducing all types of lethal and nonlethal violence, not only the types most visible.

Finally, this volume has also made a few theoretical arguments. As aggregate trends may indeed obscure hidden trends in the data, this research has argued for the importance for any theoretical perspective attempting to explain homicide and violence to disaggregate these crimes in order to ensure accurate theoretical explanations. In line with Cooney (2003), this research has also argued that both lethal and nonlethal violence have become more privatised over time, with more violent acts occurring in private rather than public settings. This volume has also argued for a new theoretical perspective of *Doing Violence*, where violence is regarded from an intersectional, performative perspective that enables the exploration of the structures of power and inequality that shape violence.

What have we learned?

Over the course of this book, we have touched upon a range of different aspects of homicide with the aim to provide a deeper understanding of this crime. In this section, we will briefly try to summarise the most important points to take away from this research. First, by examining the similarities and differences of the characteristics of lethal and nonlethal violence, this study has contributed to the research field of violence by exploring whether homicide and violence measure similar underlying behaviour, only differentiated by outcome. The findings of this volume have demonstrated the similarities between certain types of lethal and nonlethal violence, suggesting that homicide indeed can be regarded as the extreme end of spectrum of violence.

Second, while trends in homicide and violence have been examined previously, this is the first study to compare disaggregated trends of lethal and nonlethal violence over time. As this volume has demonstrated, there was no consensus in the previous research literature regarding the relationship between the trends in homicide and violence. One of the reasons for this disagreement may be that lethal and nonlethal violence simply are so heterogeneous in nature that aggregate trends fail to capture the full story. As such, this volume has taken the first steps towards determining the relationship between these two crimes by comparing disaggregated trends of homicide and violence, rather than exploring aggregate changes in these crimes.

Third, this volume has made two contributions to typology research in violence. By using an inductive, explorative approach when identifying

202 *Theorising homicide*

subtypes of lethal and nonlethal violence, this research has provided a more nuanced, data-sensitive typology of both homicide and violence. As previous typology methodologies usually have employed the *a priori* method, which limits the possibility of identifying new subtypes, this study provides a multifaceted alternative, allowing not only for new subtypes to be identified but also for context-specific subtypes to be identified. Moreover, this research has contributed to typology research by using multilevel LCA as a statistical technique when identifying subtypes. No previous study has used this technique to identify subtypes of lethal and nonlethal violence, and no previous study has explored how these subtypes have changed over time. As multilevel LCA allows complex data to be modelled on more than one level, the use of this particular statistical technique has provided unique insights into subtypes of lethal and nonlethal violence. This further highlights the value and potential of using advanced statistical methods in order to fully acknowledge the complex and often messy structures of data. While this study could have utilised less complex methods, such methods would not have represented the data as well and could consequently have led to interpretation error, diminishing the validity of the results. It is therefore also encouraged that this method should be used in the future in order to take such data complexities into account.

Fourth, this volume has made some original theoretical contributions by presenting the new theoretical framework of *Doing Violence*. The theory of *Doing Violence* considers violence from an intersectional, performative perspective, where violence (both lethal and nonlethal) is considered to be performed – done, undone, and redone by people's everyday practices. These everyday practices can be regarded as strategies that help people to position themselves in relation to structures of power and inequality. According to the theory of *Doing Violence*, violence is constructed, defined, and performed in terms of *Violence Regimes* – a structured set of power orders rendering some types of violence visible, legitimised, and recognised, while other forms of violence are rendered invisible, illegitimate. and unrecognised. Such violence regimes exist on all levels of society and are in turn shaped by multiple power orders, including gender, class, ethnicity, age, risk, and sexuality. Theorising violence in this way, making visible the structures of power and inequality that shape the violence regimes, not only provides a deeper understanding for violence and the changing patterns of violence but also increases our understanding of the orders of power that permeates people's everyday lives.

Finally, this research has been the first in-depth examination of homicide and violence in Scotland. While other studies have explored different aspects of violence in this country, no previous study has explored the changing trends or characteristics of lethal and nonlethal violence in this way. Considering the problematic history of violence in Scotland, this study therefore provides important findings relating to both lethal and nonlethal violence in this country, taking the first steps towards filling the gap in knowledge about these two crimes.

Limitations and directions for future research

While the research presented in this volume has provided new, important insights regarding homicide, no study is without limitations. Perhaps the most obvious limitation of the current research is the differences between the two datasets. While the homicide dataset included data from 2000 to 2015, the violence data only spanned from 2008–2009 to 2014–2015. The datasets also consisted of different types of data; while the homicide dataset was based on police recorded data, the violence dataset was based on data from victim surveys. This meant that certain variables, such as motive, differed substantially between the datasets as one was recorded as part of a police investigation and one was estimated by the victim. The information of the offenders was furthermore less reliable in the violence dataset as this also was estimated by the victim and not verified by any official records. This means that some aspects of the data remained incomparable across the datasets. However, since no previous study had compared homicide and violence in this way before, the comparison between the two typologies was still relevant, despite these shortcomings. As such, while the data remained imperfect, the findings and conclusions drawn from this research would still be valuable. Extensive measures were furthermore taken in order to ensure the highest possible comparability and similarity between the datasets. This included careful recoding and matching of the variables, as well as careful attention to the data structures when conducting the data modelling. An attempt to add more sweeps to the violence dataset was also undertaken; however, this had to be abandoned due to insurmountable differences between the earlier and later SCJS sweeps. As such, future research exploring the trends in homicide and violence in Scotland should attempt to explore this for a longer time period, examining whether the typologies identified in the current study have changed over a longer time period. Another limitation of the violence dataset was that it did not include any victims under the age of 16, while victims of the homicide dataset could be of any age.

Despite these differences between the homicide and violence datasets, it was still considered more favourable to use victimisation data rather than police recorded data to measure violence. As argued in Chapter 8, victimisation data is usually considered superior to police recorded crime data for two main reasons. First, police-recorded crime data has been found to be more sensitive to changes in reporting and recording compared to victimisation data (Tonry, 2014; Van Dijk, Van Kesteren, & Smit, 2007). Second, the dark figure of crime has been estimated to be lower for victimisation data compared to police recorded data, particularly regarding domestic abuse (Scottish Government, 2016d; Brookman, 2005). Despite the issues of the violence dataset evident in this study, it was therefore decided to be most appropriate to use victimisation data. It would, however, be valuable for future studies to identify subtypes of police recorded violence in order to compare these to the types found in the victimisation data in the current study. Similar identified

204 *Theorising homicide*

types would further validate these types as well as improve the reliability of police recorded measures of violence.

Another limitation to the current research was the high level of missing data in the homicide dataset. This missingness still remained even after several measures were taken to reduce it, such as the recoding of certain variables, conducting an in-depth examination of case files and excluding the first ten years of the dataset (1990–1999). As such, this research also has important implications for the management of police-recorded data. It might be necessary to impose stricter rules about coding, such as the introduction of a codebook, in order to improve the quality of police-recorded data. Such rules should also include the rigorous implementation of entering negative categories rather than just leaving the box blank; if the answer is 'no', then 'no' should be entered. If the box instead is left blank, this is interpreted as missing data. While this is partly a resource problem as police offers are often pressed for time when introducing these variables in the database, improving the data quality is important for future work on homicide, as well as for the understanding of this crime.

It is furthermore important to note that while this research has identified different types of homicide and violence, no causal inferences should be drawn from this analysis. The type of analysis conducted here does not 'explain' the causal mechanisms behind the relationship between homicide and violence. To illustrate, while this study has demonstrated that lethal as well as nonlethal domestic violence has increased in relative terms over time, the analysis does not provide an explanation of *why* this type of violence has increased. Such causal inferences would require specific experimental analysis exploring the effects of various policy interventions and the personal narratives of individuals committing these crimes. While this has been theorised in Chapter 9, future research will have to answer the question of causality.

While this study was the first of its kind to explore subtypes of homicide and violence in this way, future studies are encouraged to repeat this analysis in different contexts. As the methodology used here was exploratory and data-driven, sensitive to the context in which the study was made, different types would probably be identified in different countries or cultural contexts. While this is not necessarily a limitation of the current study, it does restrict the generalisability of the findings. It would therefore be of great interest to see this type of study conducted in other contexts, which would also enable comparative analysis of the results. As different types of homicide and violence have demonstrated different patterns over time, future studies should take the heterogeneity of violence into account when examining trends in homicide and violence.

Concluding remarks

Violence has irrupted into the everyday. We are confronted by it. We are forced to watch. We are forced to respond.

(Fiddler, 2013: 295)

Overview and conclusions 205

Despite the limitations mentioned above, this volume has aimed to provide a deeper, more critical understanding of homicide. Within this volume, homicide has been explored as a crime but also as a social construction, detailing not only the characteristics of this crime and how this crime has changed over time but how we can understand homicide, culturally as well as theoretically. As outlined in the first chapter of this book, the knowledge of homicide was lacking. While we knew that homicide had decreased in Scotland as well as in most of the Western world, we did not know the extent or details of this decrease. We did not know if all types of homicide were decreasing or if there were in fact hidden countertrends in the aggregated data. We did not know the relationship between homicide and nonlethal violence, and we did not know whether homicide could be regarded as the extreme end of a violence spectrum.

This book has provided answers to these questions and has thus begun to fill the gap in the homicide literature. We have seen that homicide and nonlethal violence in fact are following a similar pattern over time, and although homicide and violence are decreasing overall, some types of homicide and violence are increasing in relative terms. While public acts of lethal and nonlethal violence have decreased, lethal and nonlethal domestic violence has demonstrated a relative increase over time, and should therefore be a prioritised focus for preventative policies. We have concluded that the findings of this research support the idea of homicide and nonlethal violence separable only by outcome, not process, meaning that lethal and nonlethal violence should be regarded to reflect the same underlying behaviour. Finally, we have also critically examined homicide and nonlethal violence using the new theory of *Doing Violence*, which intersectionally analyses homicide the a performance, shaped by structures of power and inequality. As this theory proposes, violence, lethal as well as nonlethal, is not just insidious acts aiming to hurt or injure but can also be viewed as a strategy for people to navigate and renegotiate the power structures permeating their everyday lives. As other critical perspectives on violence have argued, emanating from cultural, Gothic and the emerging Ghost criminology (Fiddler, Kindynis, & Linneman, 2022), violence may also have a tendency to linger in our everyday lives, affecting not only our everyday imaginations but the public imaginary of crime and violence. As Linneman (2015: 520, 530) states, '[as] the ghostly presence of past violence haunt[s] contemporary social relations. [...] we must confront these ghosts of past violence and reckon the force of haunting as a social phenomenon'. As such, future studies of homicide should also look to explore the 'haunting' effects of violence, shaping the understanding of this crime. This would include studies examining texts and spaces where violence and violent imagery seem to linger; haunted by its past in order to inform our future (cf. Derrida, 1994). Such texts and spaces, 'stained by time' (Fisher, 2012: 19) may affect not only our construction of homicide and violence but political discourses surrounding this crime as well. Such research is therefore important if we are to achieve a critical, comprehensive understanding of homicide and the effect of this crime on people and our society.

206 *Theorising homicide*

Overall, this volume has taken the first steps to bridging the knowledge gap in the homicide literature and to provide a deeper understanding of lethal violence. As the quote by Fiddler at the beginning of this section would indicate, 'violence has irrupted into the everyday' (Fiddler, 2013: 295). As such, violence is ubiquitous; not only insidious acts by a few, deranged individuals but a pervasive, performative part of our everyday lives. I would, however, like to amend this statement slightly. While the manner in which we have considered violence may have resulted in a feeling of irruption in the everyday, it would seem that violence, in fact, was *always and already present* within our everyday lives. What has changed is our perspective, our way of seeing. As this perspective shifts, as we move beyond the 'readily visible to the in-visible and un-seen' (Giritli-Nygren, Nyhlén, & Skott, 2022), we are not only able to see violence in a different light but the meaning of violence as well. It is not until we are confronted by this ever-present everyday violence, 'forced to respond' (Fiddler, 2013: 295) to the practices and power structures which shape our understanding of this crime, that we are finally able to gain a deeper understanding of homicide.

References

Abbott, S. (2018). Not just another serial killer show: *Hannibal*, complexity, and the televisual palimpsest. *Quarterly Review of Film and Video*, *35* (6), 552–567.

Abusive Behaviour and Sexual Harm (Scotland) Act. (2016). Accessed 16 April 2021. Retrieved from: www.legislation.gov.uk/asp/2016/22/contents

Addington, L. A., & Perumean-Chaney, S. E. (2014). Fatal and non-fatal intimate partner violence: What separates the men from the women for victimisations reported to the police? *Homicide Studies*, *18* (2), 196–220.

Aebi, M. F., & Linde, A. (2010). Is there a crime drop in Western Europe? *European Journal of Policy and Research*, *16*, 251–277.

Aebi, M. F., & Linde, A. (2012). Regional variation in Europe between homicide and other forms of external death and criminal offences. In M. C. A. Liem, & W. A. Pridemore (Eds), *Handbook of European homicide research patterns, explanations and country studies* (pp. 71–94). New York: Springer.

Akers, R. L. (1998). *Social learning and social structure: A general theory of crime and deviance*. Boston, MA: Northeastern University Press.

Alder, A., & Polk, K. (2001). *Child victims of homicide*. Cambridge, UK: Cambridge University Press.

American Psychiatric Association. (2013). *Diagnostic and statistical manual of mental disorders, fifth edition (DSM-V)*. Arlington, VA: American Psychiatric Association.

Archer, J. (1991). The influence of testosterone on human aggression. *British Journal of Psychology*, *82*, 1–28.

Arsenault, L., Moffitt, T. E., Caspi, A., Taylor, P. J., & Silva, P. A. (2000). Mental disorders and violence in a total birth cohort. *Archives of General Psychology*, *57* (10), 979–986.

Azores-Gococo, N. M., Brook, M., Teralandur, S. P., & Hanlon, R. E. (2017). Killing a child: Neuropsychological profiles of murderers of children. *Criminal Justice and Behavior*, *44* (7), 946–962.

Baker, L. A., Tuvblad, C., & Raine, A. (2010). Genetics and crime. In E. McLaughlin & T. Newburn (Eds), *The SAGE handbook of criminological theory* (pp. 21–39). Thousand Oaks, CA: SAGE

Bandura, A. (1973). *Aggression: A social learning analysis*. Englewood Cliffs, NJ: Prentice-Hall.

Bannister, J., Pickering, J., Batchelor, S., Burman, M., Kintrea, K., & McVie, S. (2010). *Troublesome youth groups, gangs and knife carrying in Scotland*. Edinburgh: Scottish Government.

208 References

Barker, V. (2017). Nordic vagabonds: The Roma and the logic of benevolent violence in the Swedish welfare state. *European Journal of Criminology*, *14* (1), 120–139.

BBC News. (2005). *Scotland worst for violence – UN*. Published 18 September 2005. Accessed 9 February 2015. Retrieved from: http://news.bbc.co.uk/1/hi/scotland/4257966.stm

Beauregard, E., & Proulx, J. (2002). Profiles in the offending process of nonserial sexual murderers. *International Journal of Offender Therapy and Comparative Criminology*, *46* (4), 386–399.

Beauregard, E., & Proulx, J. (2007). A classification of sexual homicide against men. *International Journal of Offender Therapy and Comparative Criminology*, *51* (4), 420–432.

Beauregard, E., Proulx, J., Rossmo, K., Leclerc, B., & Allaire, J. F. (2007). Script analysis of the hunting process of serial sex offenders. *Criminal Justice and Behavior*, *34* (8), 1069–1084.

Beauregard, E., Stone, M. R., Proulx, J., & Muchaud, P. (2008). Sexual murderers of children: Developmental, precrime, crime, and postcrime factors. *International Journal of Offender Therapy and Comparative Criminology*, *52* (3), 253–269.

Beccaria, C. (1767/1995). *On crimes and punishments and other writings*, edited by Richard Bellamy, Cambridge: Cambridge University Press.

Beck, U. (1992). *Risk society: Towards the new modernity*. London: Sage.

Becker, S., & McCorkel, J. A. (2011). The gender of criminal opportunity: The impact of male co-offenders on women's crime. *Feminist Criminology*, *6* (2), 79–110.

Berg, M. T. (2019). Trends in the lethality of American violence. *Homicide Studies*, *23* (3), 262–284.

Bijleveld, C., & Smit, P. (2006). Homicide in the Netherlands on the structuring of homicide typologies. *Homicide Studies*, *10* (3), 195–219.

Bleetman, A., Perry, C. H., Crawford, R., & Swann, I. J. (1997). Effect of Strathclyde police initiative 'Operation Blade' on accident and emergency tendencies due to assault. *Journal of Accident and Emergency Medicine*, *14* (3), 153–156.

Block, C., & Block, R. (1995). *Trends, risks and interventions in lethal violence: Proceedings of the third annual spring symposium of the Homicide Research Working Group*. Atlanta: National Institute of Justice.

Blumstein, A. (2000). Disaggregating the violence trends. In A, Blumstein, & J, Wallman (Eds), *The crime drop in America* (pp. 13–42). Cambridge: Cambridge University Press.

Bossarte, R. M., Simon, T. R., & Barker. L. (2006). Characteristics of homicide followed by suicide incidents in multiple states, 2003–2004. *Injury Prevention*, *12*, 33–38.

Bourdieu, P. (2000). *Pascalian meditations*. Oxford: Polity Press.

Bourdieau, P., & Wacquant, L. (1992). *An invitation to reflexive sociology*. Chicago: University Chicago Press

Boudreaux, M., C., Lord, W. D., & Dutra, R. L. (1999). Child abduction: Ages-based analyses of offender, victim and offense characterises in 550 cases of alleged child disappearances. *Journal of Forensic Sciences*, *44* (3), 539–553.

Boudreaux, M. C., Lord, W. D., & Jarvis, J. P. (2001). Behavioral perspectives on child homicide: The role of access, vulnerability, and routine activities theory. *Trauma, Violence, & Abuse*, *2*, 56–78.

Bourget, D., & Gagné, P. (2002). Maternal filicide in Québec. *The Journal of the American Academy of Psychiatry and the Law*, *30*, 345–351.

References 209

Breetzke, G. D. (2017). The importance of space and time in aggravated assault victimisation. *Journal of Interpersonal Violence, 0*, 1–22.

Brookman, F. (2005). *Understanding homicide*. London: Sage.

Brookman, F., & Maguire, M. (2003). *Reducing homicide: A review of the possibilities*. London: Crown Office.

BSC, (2016). *Building safer communities programme*. Accessed 25 October 2016. Retrieved from: www.bsc.scot/

Butler, J. (2004). *Undoing gender*. London: Routledge.

Butler, J. (2006). *Precarious life*. London: Verso.

Bye, E. K. (2008). Alcohol and homicide in Eastern Europe. *Homicide Studies, 12* (1), 7–27.

Calvo, F., Watts, B., Panadero, S., Giralt, C., Rived-Ocaña, M., & Carbonell, X. (2021). The prevalence and nature of violence against women experiencing homelessness: A quantitative study. *Violence Against Women*, advanced online publication, https://doi.org/10.1177/10778012211022780

Campbell, J. C., Webster, D., Koziol-McLain, J., Block, C., Campbell, D., Curry, M. A., … Laughon, K. (2003). Risk factors for femicide in abusive relationships: Results from a multisite case control study. *American Journal of Public Health, 93*, 1089–1097.

Carnochan, J. (2015). *Conviction: Violence, culture and a shared public service agenda*. Glasgow: Argyll Publishing.

Carroll, A. (2015). 'We're just alike': Will Graham, Hannibal Lecter, and the monstrous-human. *Studies in Popular Culture, 38* (1), 41–63.

Carter, A. J., Barnett, G. D., Stefanska-Hodge, E., & Higgs, T. (2014). Offense pathways of extrafamilial child molesters: A UK study. In J. Proulx, E. Beauregard, P. Lussier, & B. Leclerc (Eds), *Pathways to sexual aggression* (pp. 316–334). New York, NY: Routledge.

Caspi, A., McClay. J., Moffitt, T., Mill, J., Martin, J., Craig, I., Taylor, A., & Pulton, R. (2002). The role of genotype in the cycle of violence in maltreated children. *Science, 297*, 851–854.

Cavanagh, K., Dobash, R. E., & Dobash, R. P. (2005). Men who murder children inside and outside the family. *British Journal of Social Work, 35*, 667–688.

Chan, H. C. O. (2015). *Understanding sexual homicide offenders: An integrated approach*. Basingstoke, UK: Palgrave McMillan.

Chan, H. C. O. (2017). Sexual homicide: A review of recent empirical evidence (2008 to 2015), In F. Brookman, E. R. Maguire & M. Maguire (Eds), *The handbook of homicide* (pp. 105–130). Hoboken, NJ: John Wiley & Sons.

Chan, H. C. O. (2018). Sexual homicide: A review of the main theoretical models. In J. Proulx, E. Beauregard, A. J. Carter, A. Mokros, R. Darjee, & J, James (Eds), *Routledge international handbook of sexual homicide studies* (pp. 15–36). New York, NY: Routledge.

Chan, H.-C., & Heide, K. M. (2008). Weapons used by juveniles and adult offenders in sexual homicides: An empirical analysis of 29 years of US data. *Journal of Investigative Psychology and Offender Profiling, 5*, 189–208.

Chan, H-C., & Heide, K. M. (2009). Sexual homicide: A synthesis of the literature. *Trauma, Violence and Abuse, 10* (1), 31–54.

Chan, H.-C., & Heide, K. M. (2016). Sexual homicide offenders distinguished from non-homicidal sexual offenders: A review of the literature. *Aggression and Violent Behavior, 31*, 147–156.

210   References

Chan, H. C. O., Heide, K. M., & Beauregard, E. (2011). What propels sexual murderers: A proposed integrated theory of social learning and routine activities theories. *International Journal of Offender Therapy and Comparative Criminology*, 55 (2), 228–250.

Chan, H. C. O., Heide, K. M., & Beauregard, E. (2019). Male and female single-victim sexual homicide offenders: Distinguishing the types of weapons used in killing their victims. *Sexual Abuse*, 31 (2), 137–150.

Chan, H. C. O., & Frei, A. (2013). Female sexual homicide offenders: An examination of an underresearched offender population. *Homicide Studies*, 17 (1), 96–118.

Chilton, R., & Chambliss, J. (2015). Urban homicide in the United States, 1980–2010: The importance of disaggregated trends. *Homicide Studies*, 19, 257–272.

Chopin, J., & Beauregard, E. (2019). Sexual homicide in France and Canada: An international comparison. *Journal of Interpersonal Violence*, 1–24. doi:10.1177/0886260519875547

Clarke, R. V. (1983). Situational crime prevention: Its theoretical basis and practical scope. *Crime and Justice*, 4, 225–256.

Clark, R. V. (1995). Situational crime prevention. *Crime and Justice*, 19, 91–150.

Cohen, J. W. (1988). *Statistical Analysis for the behavioral sciences (2nd ed.)*. Hillsdale, NJ: Lawrence Erlbaum Associates.

Cohen, L. C., & Felson, M. (1979). Social change and crime rate trends: A routine activity approach. *American Sociological Review*, 44, 588–608.

Collins, R. (2008). *Violence: A micro-sociological theory*. Princeton, NJ: Princeton University Press.

Connell, R. W. (2009). *Om gGenus*. Göteborg: Daidalos.

Connell, R. W., & Messerschmidt, J. W. (2005). Hegemonic masculinity: Rethinking the concept. *Gender and Society*, 19, 829–859.

Cooney, M. (2003). The privatization of violence. *Criminology*, 41 (4), 1377–1406.

Cornell, D. G., Warren, J., Hawk, G., Stafford, E., Oram, G., & Pine, D. (1996). Psychopathy in instrumental and reactive violent offenders. *Journal of Consulting and Clinical Psychology*, 64 (4), 783–790.

Cornish, R. (2007). *Cluster analysis*. Mathematics Learning Support Centre. Accessed 26 July. Retrieved from: www.statstutor.ac.uk/resources/uploaded/clusteranalysis.pdf

Corporate Manslaughter and Corporate Homicide Act (2007). c. 1. Accessed 4 February 2021. Retrieved from: www.legislation.gov.uk/ukpga/2007/19/pdfs/ukpga_20070019_en.pdf ().

Cortoni, F., Babchishin, K. M., & Rat, C. (2017). The proportion of sexual offenders who are female is higher than thought: A meta-analysis. *Criminal Justice and Behavior*, 44 (2), 145–162.

COSLA. (2017). *About COSLA*. Accessed 7 August 2017. Retrieved from: www.cosla.gov.uk/about-cosla

Crawford, J. (2014). *The twilight of the Gothic? Vampire fiction and the rise of the paranormal romance, 1991–2012*. Cardiff: University of Wales Press.

Criminal Justice and Licensing (Scotland) Act. (2010). Accessed 14 March 2021. Retrieved from: www.legislation.gov.uk/asp/2010/13/contents

Crown Office, (2017a). *About us*. Accessed July 2021. Retrieved from: www.crownoffice.gov.uk/about-us/about-us.

Daly, K., & Bouhours, D. (2010). Rape and attrition in the legal process: A comparative analysis of five countries. *The University of Chicago*, (565–650).

Daly, M., & Wilson, M. (1988). *Homicide*. New York: De Gruyter.

References   211

Damer, S. (1989). *From Moorepark to 'Wine Alley'*. Edinburgh University Press: Edinburgh

Davies, A. (2007). Glasgow's 'Reign of Terror': Street gangs, racketeering and intimidation in the 1920s and 1930s. *Contemporary British History, 21* (4), 405–427.

Denov, M. (2003). To a safer place? Victims of sexual abuse by females and their disclosure to professionals. *Child Abuse and Neglect, 27* (1), 47–61.

Denov, M. (2004). *Perspectives on female sex offending: A culture of denial*. Burlington, VT: Ashgate.

Derrida, J. (1994). *Specters of Marx*. London: Routledge.

DiCristina, B. (2004). Durkheim's theory of homicide and the confusion of the empirical literature. *Theoretical Criminology, 8* (1), 57–91.

Dietz, P. E., Hazelwood, R. R., & Warren, J. (1990). The sexually sadistic criminal and his offenses. *Journal of the American Academy of Psychiatry and the Law Online, 18* (2), 163–178.

Dobash, R. E., & Dobash, R. P. (2011). What were they thinking? Men who murder an intimate partner. *Violence Against Women, 17* (1), 111–134.

Dobash, R. E., & Dobash, R. P., Cavanagh, K., & Medina-Ariza, J. (2007). Lethal and non-lethal violence against an intimate female partner. *Violence Against Women, 13* (4), 329–353.

Domestic Abuse (Scotland) Act. (2018). Accessed 16 April 2021. Retrieved from: www.legislation.gov.uk/asp/2018/5/contents

Drescher, J. (2015). Out of DSM: Depathologising homosexuality. *Behavioral Sciences, 5* (4), 565–575.

Drury vs Her Majesty's Advocate. (2001). S.C.C.R, 583.

Durkheim, Emile (1951 [1897]). *Suicide: A study in sociology*. Trans. J. A. Spaulding and G. Simpson. New York: The Free Press.

Durkheim, Emile (1957 [1900]). *Professional ethics and civic morals*. Trans. C. Brookfield. New York: Routledge.

Eck, J. E., & Maguire, E. R. (2000). Have changes in policing reduced violent crime? In A. Blumstein and J. Wallman (Eds), *The crime drop in America* (pp. 207–265). New York: Cambridge University Press.

Edens, J. F., Desforges, D. M., Fernandez, K., & Palac, C. A. (2004). Effects of psychopathy and violence risk testimony on mock juror perceptions of dangerousness in a capital murder trial. *Psychology, Crime & Law, 10* (4), 393–412.

Edens, J. F., & Petrila, J. (2006). Legal and ethical issues in the assessment and treatment of psychopathy. In C. J. Patrick (Ed.), *Handbook of psychopathy* (pp. 573–588). New York: Guilford Publications.

Elias, N. (1939). *Civilizing process, vol. 1: The development of manners*. New York, NY: Urizen Books.

Evans, B., & Giroux, H. A. (2015). *Disposable futures: The seduction of violence in the age of spectacle*. San Francisco, CA: Open Lights Books.

Eurostat. (2017). Intentional homicide and sexual offences by legal status and sex of the person involved – Number and rate for the relevant sex group. Accessed 21 April 2021. Retrieved from: http://data.europa.eu/euodp/data/dataset/xG6uYkcAiQYrdkVbIHfg

Fajnzylber, P., Lederman, D., & Loayza, N. (2002). Inequality and violence crime. *Journal of Law and Economics, 45*, 1–40.

Farrell, G., & Brantingham, P. J. (2013). The crime drop and general social survey. *Canadian Public Policy, 39* (4), 559–580.

212   *References*

Farrell, G., Tilley, N., Tseloni, A., & Mailley, J. (2010). Explaining and sustaining the crime drop: Clarifying the role of opportunity-related theories. *Crime Prevention and Community Safety, 12*, 24–41.

Farrell, G., Tilley, N., & Tseloni, A. (2014). *Why the crime drop?* Chicago: University of Chicago.

Farrington, D. (1989). Early predictors of adolescent aggression and adult violence. *Violence and Victims, 4* (2), 79–100.

Farrington, D. P., Loeber, R., & Berg, M. T., (2012). Young men who kill: A prospective longitudinal examination from childhood. *Homicide Studies, 16* (2), 99–128.

Fawcett, C., & Kohm, S. (2019). Carceral violence at the intersection of madness and crime in batman: Arkham asylum and batman: Arkham city. *Crime Media Culture*, Advanced Online Publication, *16* (2), 1–21. https://doi.org/10.1177/1741659019865298

Federal Bureau of Investigation [FBI]. (2004). *Child abduction response plan: An investigative guide*. Quantico, VA: Critical Incident Response Group.

Federal Bureau of Investigation [FBI]. (2015). *Uniform crime reports*. Accessed 6 August 2015. Retrieved from: www.fbi.gov/about-us/cjis/ucr/ucr

Federman, C., Holms, D., & Jacob, J. D. (2009). Deconstructing the psychopath: A critical discursive analysis. *Cultural Critique, 72*, 36–65.

Felson, M., & Cohen, L. E. (1980). Human ecology and crime: A routine activity approach. *Human Ecology, 8* (4), 389–406.

Felson, R. B., & Messner, S. F. (1996). To kill or not to kill? Lethal outcomes in injurious attacks. *Criminology, 34* (4), 519–545.

Ferrell, J. (1997). Youth, crime and social space. *Social Justice, 24* (4), 21–38.

Fiddler, M. (2013). Playing funny games in the last house on the left: The uncanny and the 'home invasion' genre. *Crime, Media, Culture: An International Journal*, 9(3), 281–299. https://doi.org/10.1177/1741659013511833.

Fiddler, M., Kindynis, T., & Linnemann, T. (Eds). (2022). *Ghost criminology*. New York, NY: New York University Press

Firestone, P., Bradford, J. M., Greenberg, D. M., Larose, M. R., & Curry, S. (1998). Homicidal and nonhomicidal child molesters: Psychological, phallometric, and criminal features. *Sexual Abuse: A Journal of Research and Treatment, 10*, 305–323.

Fisher M (2012). What is hauntology? *Film Quarterly, 66* (1), 16–24.

Foucault, M. (1978). About the concept of the 'Dangerous Individual' in 19th-century legal psychiatry. *International Journal of Law and Psychiatry, 1* (1), 1–18.

Fox, B., & DeLisi, M. (2019). Psychopathic killers: A meta-analytic review of the psychopathy-homicide nexus. *Aggression and Violent Behavior, 44*, 67–79.

Fox, J. A., & Fridel, E. E. (2017). Gender differences in patterns and trends in US homicide, 1976–2015. *Violence and Gender, 4* (2), 37–43.

Francis, B., & Soothill, K. (2010). Does sex offending lead to homicide? *The Journal of Forensic Psychiatry, 11* (1), 49–61.

Fraser, A. (2013). Street habitus: Gangs territorialism and social change in Glasgow. *Journal of Youth Studies, 16* (8), 970–985.

Fraser, A. (2015). *Urban legends: Gang identity in the post-industrial city*. Oxford: Oxford University Press.

Fraser, A., Burman, M., Batchelor, S., & McVie, S. (2010). *Youth violence in Scotland: Literature review*. Edinburgh: Scottish Government.

References 213

Fredriksson, T. (2019). Abject (m)othering: A narratological study of the prison as an abject and uncanny institution. *Critical Criminology*, *27* (2), 261–274. https://doi.org/10.1007/s10612-.

Gacono, C. B., Meloy, J. R., & Kennedy, L. (1994). A Rorschach investigation of sexual homicide. *Journal of Personality Assessment*, *62* (1), 58–67.

Ganpat, S. M., Van Der Leun, J., & Nieuwbeerta, P. (2013). The influence of event characteristics and actors' behaviour on the outcome of violent events: Comparing lethal with non-lethal events. *British Journal of Criminology*, *53* (4), 685–704.

Garland, D. (2001). *The culture of control: Crime and social order in contemporary society*. Oxford: Oxford University Press.

Giddens, A. (1991). *Modernity and self-identity self and society in the late modern age*. Stanford: Stanford Universtiy Press.

Giritli-Nygren, K., Nyhlén, S., & Skott, S. (2022). Haunting the margins: Excavating vulnerable EU citizens as the 'social ghosts' of our time. Manuscript submitted for publication.

Giritli-Nygren, K., Öhman, S., & Olofsson, A. (2017). Doing and undoing risk: The mutual constitution of risk and heteronormativity in contemporary society. *Journal of Risk Research*, *20* (3), 418–438.

Giroux, H. A. (2013, May). Violence USA: The warfare state and the hardening of everyday life. *Monthly Review*, *65* (1). Accessed 3 March 2021. Retrieved from: https://monthlyreview.org/2013/05/01/violence-usa/

Goffman, E. (1967). *Interaction ritual: Essays on face-to-face behavior*. Garden City, NY: Doubleday.

Gonzalez, R. A., Kallis, C., & Coid, J. W. (2013). Adult attention deficit hyperactivity disorder and violence in the population of England: Does comorbidity matter? *PLoS ONE*, *8* (9), 1–10.

Gottfredson, M. R., & Hirschi, T. (1990). *A general theory of crime*. Stanford, CA: Stanford University Press.

Granath, S. (2011). *Det dödliga våldets utveckling: Fullbordat och försök till dödligt våld i Sverige på 1990 och 00-talet*. [Change in lethal violence: Homicide and attempted murder in Sweden in the 1990s and 00s]. Brå-rapport 2011:5. Stockholm: Brottsförebyggande rådet.

Granath, S., Hagstedt, J., Kivivuori, J., Lehti, M., Ganpat, S. M., Liem, M., & Nieuwbeerta, P. (2011). *Homicide in Finland, the Netherlands and Sweden: A first study on the European homicide monitor data*. Stockholm: The Swedish National Council for Crime Prevention.

Grann, M., & Wedin, I. (2002). Risk factors for recidivism among spousal assault and spousal homicide offenders. *Psychology, Crime and Law*, *8* (1), 5–23.

Guerette, R. T., & Bowers, K. J. (2009). Assessing the extent of crime displacement and diffusion of benefits: A review of situational crime prevention evaluations. *Criminology*, *47* (4), 1331–1368.

Gökariksel, B., Neubert, C., & Smith, S. (2019). Demographic fever dreams: Fragile masculinity and population politics in the rise of the global right. *Journal of Women in Culture and Society*, *44* (3), 561–587.

Haen Marshall, I., & Summers, D. L. (2012). Contemporary differences in rates and trends of homicide among european nations. In M. C. A. Liem, & W. A. Pridemore (Eds), *Handbook of European homicide research patterns, explanations and country studies* (pp. 39–70). New York: Springer.

214 *References*

Hagenaars, J. A., & McCutcheon, A. L. (2002). *Applied latent class analysis*. Cambridge: Cambridge University Press.

Hale, C. (1998). Crime and business cycle in post-war Britain revisited. *British Journal of Criminology, 38* (4), 681–698.

Hare, R. D. (1980). A research scale for the assessment of psychopathy in criminal populations. *Personality and Individual Differences, 1*, 111–119.

Hare, R. D. (1996). Psychopathy: A clinical construct whose time has come. *Criminal Justice and Behavior, 23* (1), 25–54.

Hare, R. D., & Neumann, C. S. (2006). The PCL-R assessment of psychopathy development, structural properties, and new directions. In I. C. J. Patrick (Ed.), *Handbook of Psychopathy* (pp. 58–88). New York: Guilford Publications.

Harries, K. D. (1989). Homicide and assault: A comparative analysis of attributes in Dallas neighbourhoods 1981–1985. *The Professional Geographer, 41* (1), 29–38.

Harris, A. R., Thomas, S. H., Fisher, G. A., & Hirsch, D. J. (2002). Murder and medicine the lethality of criminal assault 1960–1999. *Homicide Studies, 6* (2), 128–166.

Harper Wood, D., & Voigt, L. (2007). Homicide followed by suicide an integrated theoretical perspective. *Homicide Studies, 11* (4), 295–318.

Hart, S. D., Cox, D. N., & Hare, R. D. (1995). *Hare PCL:SV* (H. Belfrage övers.) Toronto: Multi-Health Systems.

Hatty, S. E. (2000). *Masculinities, violence and culture*. London: Sage Publishing.

Harvey, M. J., Williams, D. J., & Donnelly, P. D. (2012). Testing a method to develop preliminary cost estimates of homicide in Glasgow: A research note. *Criminal Justice Policy Review, 24* (4), 510–523.

Haw, C., Hawton, K., Sutton, L., Sinclair, J., & Deeks, J. (2005). Schizophrenia and deliberate self-harm: A systematic review of risk factors. *Suicide and Life-Threatening Behavior, 35* (1), 50–62.

Hazelwood, R. R., & Douglas, J. E. (1980). The lust murderer. *FBI Law Enforcement Bulletin, 49*, 18–22.

Hazelwood, R. R., & Warren, J. (2000). The sexually violent offender: Impulsive or Ritualistic? *Aggression and Violent Behavior, 5* (3), 267–279.

Hearn, J., & McKie, L. (2010). Gendered and social hierarchies in problem representation and policy processes: 'Domestic violence' in Finland and Scotland. *Violence Against Women, 16* (2), 136–158.

Heide, K. M. (2003). Youth homicide: A review of the literature and a blueprint for action. *International Journal of Offender Therapy and Comparative Criminology, 47* (1), 6–36.

Heide, K. M., Roe-Sepowitz, D., Solomon, E. P., & Chan, H. C. (2012). Male and female juveniles arrested for murder: A comprehensive analysis of US data by offender gender. *International Journal of Offender Therapy and Comparative Criminology, 56* (3), 356–384.

Heide, K. M., Solomon, E. P., Sellers, B. G., & Chan, H. C. (2011). Male and female juvenile homicide offenders: An empirical analysis of US arrests by offender age. *Feminist Criminology, 6* (1), 3–31.

Henderson, J. P., Morgan, S. E., Patel, F., & Tiplady, M. E. (2005). Patterns of nonfirearms homicide. *Journal of Clinical Forensic Medicine, 12* (3), 128–132.

Henry, K. L., & Muthén, B. (2010). Multilevel latent class analysis: An application of adolescent smoking typologies with individual and contextual predictors. *Structural Equation Modeling, 17*, 193–215.

References 215

Higgs, T., Carter, A. J., Stefanska, E. B., & Glorney, E. (2017). Toward identification of the sexual killer: A comparison of sexual killers engaging in post-mortem sexual interference and non-homicide sexual aggressors. *Sexual Abuse: A Journal of Research and Treatment, 29* (5), 479–499

Higgs, T., Carter, A. K., Tully, R. J., & Browne, K. D. (2017). Sexual murder typologies: A systematic review. *Aggression and Violent Behavior, 35*, 1–12.

Hohl, B. C., Wiley, S., Wiebe, D. J., Culyba, A. J., Drake, R., & Branas, C. C. (2017). Association of drug and alcohol use with adolescent firearm homicide at individual, family and neighbourhood levels. *JAMA Internal Medicine, 177* (3), 317–324.

Holmes2. (2017). *What is Holmes2?* Accessed 17 January 2017. Retrieved from: www.holmes2.com/holmes2/whatish2/

Holtzworth-Munroe, A. (2000). A typology of men who are violent toward their female partners: Making sense of the heterogeneity in husband violence. *Current Directions in Psychological Science, 9* (4), 140–143.

Hox, J. (2002). *Multilevel analysis: Techniques and applications*. London: Lawrence Erlbaum Associates.

HMICS [HM Inspectorate of Constabulary of Scotland]. (2008). *Crime audit* 2014. Edinburgh: HMICS.

Humphreys, L., Francis, B., & McVie, S. (2014). *Understanding the crime drop in Scotland. Research Briefing 1*. Edinburgh: AQMeN.

Hääkänen-Nyholm. H., Putkonen, H., Lindberg, N., Holi, M., Rovamo, T., & Weizmann-Henelius, G. (2009). Gender differences in Finnish homicide offence statistics. *Forensic Science International, 186* (1–3), 75–80.

Häkkänen-Nyholm, H., Repo-Tiihonen, E., Lindberg, N., Salenius, S., & Weizmann-Henelius, G. (2009). Finnish sexual homicides: Offence and offender characteristics. *Forensic Science International, 188*, 125–130. doi:10.1016/j.forsciint.2009.03.03

Jacobs, D., & Richardson, A. M. (2008). Economic inequality and homicide in the developed nations from 1975 to 1995. *Homicide Studies, 12* (1), 28–45.

James, J., & Proulx, J. (2014). A psychological and developmental profile of sexual murderers: A systematic review. *Aggression and Violent Behavior*, 19, 592–607.

James, J., Proulx, J., Vuidard, E., Renard, A., La Maout, S., & Brunel-Dupin, M-L. (2018). Sexual homicide in France. *International Journal of Offender Therapy and Comparative Criminology, 63* (9), 1575–1596.

Johansson-Love, J., & Fremouw, W. (2006). A critique of the female sexual perpetrator research. *Aggression and Violent Behaviour, 11* (1), 12–26.

Jolliffe, D., & Farrington, D. P. (2010). Individual differences and offending. In E. McLaughlin & T. Newburn (Eds), *The SAGE handbook of criminological theory*(pp. 40–55). Thousand Oaks, CA: SAGE.

Katz, J. (1988). *The seductions of crime: The moral and sensual attractions of doing evil*. New York: Basic Books.

Kelling G. and Wilson, J. (1982). Broken windows. *The Atlantic Monthly, 38*, 29–36.

Ketchen, D. J., & Shook, C. L. (1998). The application of cluster analysis in strategic management research: An analysis and critique. *Strategic Management Journal, 17*, 441–458.

Kouichi, Y. (2016). Substance-related and addictive disorders as a risk factor of suicide and homicide among patients with ADHD: A mini review. *Current Drug Abuse Review, 9* (2), 80–86.

Kreiger, T. C., & Dumka, L. E. (2006). The relationships between hypergender, gender, and psychological adjustment. *Sex Roles, 54*, 777–785.

216   *References*

Kubrin, C. E. (2003). Structural covariates of homicide rates: Does type of homicide matter? *Journal of Research in Crime and Delinquency, 40* (2), 139–170.

Kubrin, C. E., & Wadsworth, T. (2003). Identifying the structural correlates of African American killings what can we learn from data disaggregation? *Homicide Studies, 7* (1), 3–35.

Kushel, M. B., Evans, J. L., Perry, S., Robertson, M. J., & Moss, A. R. (2003). No door to lock: Victimisation among homeless and marginally housed persons. *Archives of Internal Medicine. 163* (20), 2492–2499.

LaFree, G., Curtis, K., & McDowall, D. (2015). How effective are your 'better angels?' Assessing country-level declines in homicide since 1950. *European Journal of Criminology, 12* (4), 482–504.

Land, K. C., McCall, P. L., & Cohen, L. E. (1990). Structural covariates of homicide rates: Are there any invariances across time and social space? *American Journal of Sociology, 95* (4), 922–963.

Langevin, R., Ben-Aron, M., Wright, P., Marchese, V., & Handy, L. (1988). The sex killer. *Annals of Sex Research, 1*, 263–301. doi:10.1177/107906328800100206

Lanza, S. T., Tan, X., & Bray, B. C. (2013). Latent class analysis with distal outcomes: A flexible model-based approach. *Structural Equational Modeling, 20* (1), 1–26.

Laurell, J., Belfrage, H., & Hellström, Å. (2010). Facets on the psychopathy checklist screening version and instrumental violence in forensic psychiatric patients. *Criminal Behaviour and Mental Health, 20*, 285–294.

Laurendeau, J. (2008). 'Gendered risk regimes': A theoretical consideration of edgework and gender. *Sociology of Sport Journal, 25* (3), 293–309.

Lauritzen, J. L., & Lentz, T. S. (2019). National and local trends in serious violence, firearm victimisation and homicide. *Homicide Studies, 23* (3), 243–261.

Lauritzen, J. L., Rezey, M. L., Heimer, K. (2016). When choice of data matters: Analyses of US crime trends, 1973–2012. *Journal of Quantitative Criminology, 32* (3), 335–355.

Law Library of Congress. (2015). Firearms-control legislation and policy: Great Britain. Retrieved from: www.loc.gov/law/help/firearms-control/greatbritain.php

Lehti, M. (2014). Homicide drop in Finland, 1996–2012. *Journal of Scandinavian Studies in Criminology and Crime Prevention, 15* (2), 182–199.

Leyland, A. H. (2006). Homicides involving knives and other sharp objects in Scotland, 1981–2003. *Journal of Public Health, 28* (2), 145–147.

Lester, D. (1995). The association between alcohol consumption and suicide and homicide rates: A study of 13 nations. *Alcohol and Alcoholism, 30* (4), 465–468.

Levitt, S. D. (2004). Understanding why crime fell in the 1990s: Four factors that explain the decline and six that do not. *The Journal of Economic Perspectives, 18* (1), 163–190.

Liem, M., Barber, C., Markwalder, N., Killias, M., & Nieuwbeerta, P. (2011). Homicide-suicide and other violent deaths: An international comparison. *Forensic Science International, 207* (1–3), 70–76.

Liem, M., & Ganpat, S., Granath, S., Hagstedt, J., Kivivuori, J., Lehti, M., & Nieuwbeerta, P. (2013). Homicide in Finland, The Netherlands, and Sweden: First findings from the European Homicide Monitor. *Homicide Studies, 17* (1), 75–95.

Liem, M., & Nieuwbeerta, P. (2010). Homicide followed by suicide: A comparison with homicide and suicide. *Suicide and Life-Threatening Behaviour, 40* (2), 133–145.

Liem, M., & Reichelmann, A. (2014). Patterns of multiple family homicide. *Homicide Studies, 18* (1), 44–58.

References 217

Liem, M., Suonpää, K., Lehti, M., Kivivouri, J., Granath, S., Walser, S., & Killias, M. (2016). Homicide clearance in Western Europe. *European Journal of Criminology, 16* (1), 81–101.

Lindley, D. V., & Novick, M. R. (1981). The role of exchangeability in inference. *The Annals of Statistics, 9* (1), 45–58

Linnemann, T. (2015). Capote's ghosts: Violence, media and the spectre of suspicion. *British Journal of Criminology, 55* (3), 514–533.

Linneman, T., Wall, T., & Green, E. (2014). The walking dead and killing state: Zombification and the normalization of police violence. *Theoretical Criminology, 18* (4), 506–527.

Lombroso, C., Ferrero, G. (1893/2004). The female born criminal. In *Criminal woman, the prostitute and the normal woman* (pp. 182–192). Durham, NC: Duke University Press.

Luckenbill, D. F. (1977). Criminal homicide as a situated transaction. *Social Problems, 25,* 176–186.

Lyng, S. (1990). Edgework: A social psychological analysis of voluntary risk taking. *American Journal of Sociology, 95* (4), 851–886.

MacAskil, K. (2011). *Parliamentary statement on police and fire reform.* 8 September 2011. Edinburgh: Scottish Parliament.

Magidson, J., & Vermunt, J. (2004). Latent class models. In D. Kaplan (Ed.), *Handbook of quantitative methodology for the social sciences* (pp. 175–198). Newbury Park, CA: Sage.

Maguire, M. (2012). Criminal statistics and the construction of crime. In M. Maguire, R. Morgan, & R. Reiner (Eds), *The Oxford handbook of criminology (fifth edition)* (pp. 206–244). Oxford: Oxford University Press.

Mares, D. (2010). Social disorganization and gang homicides in Chicago: A neighborhood comparison of disaggregated homicides. *Youth Violence and Juvenile Justice, 8* (1), 38–57.

Markwalder, N., & Killias, M. (2013). Homicide in Switzerland. In M. C. A. Liem, & W. A. Pridemore (Eds), *Handbook of European homicide research: Patterns, explanations and country patterns* (pp. 343–354). London: Springer.

Matthews, B. (2016). *Criminal careers and the crime drop in Scotland, 1989–2011: An exploration of conviction trends across age and sex* (doctoral thesis). University of Edinburgh, Edinburgh.

McAra, L. (2010). Scottish youth justice: Convergent pressures and cultural singularities. In Bailleau, F, & Cartuyvels, Y. (Eds), *The Criminalisation of youth: Juvenile justice in Europe, Turkey and Canada.* Brussels: Vubpress.

McAra, L., &. McVie, S. (2012). Critical debates in developmental and lifecourse criminology. In M. Maguire, R. Morgan, & R. Reiner (Eds), *The Oxford Handbook of Criminology (fifth edition)* (pp. 531–562). Oxford: Oxford University Press.

McClintock, F. H., & Wikström, P. O. H. (1990). Violent crime in Scotland and Sweden. *British Journal of Criminology, 30* (2), 207–228.

McClintock, F. H., & Wikström, P. O. H. (1992). The comparative study of urban violence criminal violence in Edinburgh and Stockholm. *British Journal of Criminology, 32* (4), 505–520.

McCutcheon, A. L. (2002). Basic concepts and procedures in single- and multiple-group latent class analysis. In J. A. Hagenaars, & A. L. McCutcheon (Eds), *Applied latent class analysis* (pp. 56–88). Cambridge: Cambridge University Press.

218   *References*

McDiarmid, C. (2018). *Culpable homicide*. Presented at the Seminar on the Structure of Homicide and the Mental Element, the Scottish Law Commission, 5 October 2018.

McKenzie, C. (1995). A study of serial murder. *International Journal of Offender Therapy and Comparative Criminology, 39* (1), 3–10.

McVie, S. (2010). *Gang membership and knife carrying: Findings from the Edinburgh Study of Youth Transitions and Crime*. Edinburgh: Scottish Government.

McVie, S., Norris, P., & Pillinger, R. (2020). Increasing inequality in experience of victimisation during the crime drop: Analysing patterns of victimisation in Scotland from 1993 to 2014–15. *British Journal of Criminology, 60* (3), 782–802.

Meier, R. F., Kennedy, L. W., & Sacco, V. F. (2001). Crime and the criminal event perspective. In R. F. Meier, L. W. Kennedy, & V. F. Sacco (Eds), *The process and structure of crime: Criminal events and crime analysis* (pp. 1–27). New Brunswick, NJ: Transaction Publishers.

Meier, R. F., Miethe, T. D. (1993). Understanding theories of criminal victimization. *Crime and Justice, 17*, 459–499.

Messerschmidt, J. M. (1999). Making bodies matter: Adolescent masculinities, the body, and varieties of violence. *Theoretical Criminology, 3* (2), 197–220.

Messner, S. F., & Savolainen, J. (2001). Gender and the victim-offender relationship in homicide: A comparison of Finland and the United States. *International Criminal Justice Review, 11*, 34–57.

Meyer, D. (2012). An intersectional analysis of lesbian, gay, bisexual, and transgender (LGBT) people's evaluations of anti-queer violence. *Gender and Society, 26* (6), 849–873.

Miles, C., & Buehler, E. (2020). The homicide drop in England and Wales 2004–2014. *Criminology and Criminal Justice, 22* (1), 3–23.

Mjanes, K., Beauregard, E., & Martineau, M. (2018). Revisiting the organized/disorganized model of sexual homicide. *Criminal Justice & Behavior, 44* (12), 1604–1619.

Mokros, A. (2018). Sexual sadism and sexual homicide. In J. Proulx, E. Beauregard, A. Carter, A. Mokros, R. Darjee, & J. James (Eds), *Routledge international handbook of sexual homicide studies* (pp. 253–268). Abingdon: Routledge

Moore, M. D., Heirigs, M. H., & Barnes, A. K. (2021). A state-level analysis of gender inequality on male and female homicide. *Crime and Delinquency, 67* (12), 1879–1902.

Morton, E., Runyan, C. W., Moracco, K. E., & Butts, J. (1998). Partner homicide-suicide involving female homicide victims: A population-based study in North Carolina, 1988–1992. *Violence and Victims, 13* (2), 91–106.

Murray, K. (2015). *Landscape review on stop and search in Scotland*. Dundee: Scottish Institute for Policing Research.

Murray, K., & Harkin, D. (2016). Policing in cool and hot climates: Legitimacy, power and the rise and fall of mass stop and search in Scotland. *British Journal of Criminology, 57* (4), 885–905.

Muthén, L. K., & Muthén, B. O. (1998–2012). *Mplus User's Guide*. Seventh Edition. Los Angeles, CA: Muthén & Muthén

Mutz, R., Bornmann, L., & Daniel, H-D. (2013). Types of research output profiles: A multilevel latent class analysis of the Austrian Science Fund's final project report data. *Research Evaluation, 22*, 118–133.

References 219

Myers, W. C., & Monaco, L. (2000). Anger experience, styles of anger expression, sadistic personality disorder, and psychopathy in juvenile sexual homicide offenders. *Journal of Forensic Sciences, 45* (1), 698–701.

Nagin, D. S., & Tremblay, R. E. (2005). Developmental trajectory groups: Fact or a useful statistical fiction? *Criminology, 43* (4), 973–904.

Nakagawa, S. (2004). A farewell to Bonferroni: The problems of low statistical power and publication bias. *Behavioral Ecology, 15* (6), 1044–1045.

Neuilly, M.-A., & Zgoba, K. (2006). Assessing the possibility of a pedophilia panic and contagion effect between France and the United States. *Victims & Offenders, 1*, 225–254.

NKBL. (2014). *No Knives Better Lives about us.* Accessed 17 December 2014. Retrieved from: http://noknivesbetterlives.com/info/about-us/

Nolan-Hoeksema, S. (2011). *Abnormal psychology (5th ed.).* New York, NY: McGraw-Hill.

Norris, P., Pillinger, R., & McVie, S. (2014). *Changing patterns of victimisation in Scotland, 1993–2011. Research briefing 2.* Edinburgh: AQMeN.

NRS (2017). Mid-*year population esti*mates, Scotland *m*id-2016. Accessed 22 October 2022. Retrieved from: https://webarchive.nrscotland.gov.uk/20210313160705/ https://www.nrscotland.gov.uk/statistics-and-data/statistics/statistics-by-theme/population/population-estimates/mid-year-population-estimates/archive/mid-2016

Nylund, K., Asparouhov, T., & Muthén, B. O. (2007). Deciding on the number of classes in Latent Class Analysis and Growth Mixture Modeling: A Monte Carlo simulation study. *Structural Equation Modeling, 14* (4), 535–569.

Oleson, J. C. (2005). King of killers: The criminological theories of Hannibal Lecter, Part One. *Journal of Criminal Justice and Popular Culture, 12* (3), 186–210.

Ormston, R., Mullholland, C., & Setterfield, L. (2016). *Caledonian system evaluation: Analysis of a programme for tackling domestic abuse in Scotland.* Edinburgh: The Scottish Government.

Orr, J. (1998). Strathclyde's Spotlight Initiative. In N. Dennis (Ed.), *Zero tolerance: Policing in a free society (2nd ed.)* (pp. 105–125). London: Hartington Fine Arts

Pallant, J. (2010). *SPSS survival manual.* Berkshire: Open University Press.

Perkins, D. D., & Taylor, R. B. (1996). Ecological assessment of community disorder: Their relationship to fear of crime and theoretical implications. *American Journal of Community Psychology, 24* (1), 63–107.

Perneger, T. V. (1998). What's wrong with Bonferroni adjustments. *British Medical Journal, 316*, 1236–1238.

Perkins, D. D., & Taylor, R. B. (1996). Ecological assessment of community disorder: Their relationship to fear of crime and theoretical implications. *American Journal of Community Psychology, 24* (1), 63–107.

Picart, C. J. (2006). Crime and the Gothic: Sexualising serial killers. *Journal of Criminal Justice and Popular Culture, 13* (1), 1–18.

Picart, J. K. S. (2016). Media myths regarding serial killers: A Gothic criminology. In M H Jacobsen (Ed.), *The Poetics of Crime: Understanding and researching crime and deviance through creative sources* (pp. 173–183). London: Routledge.

Picart, C. J., & Greek, C. (2003). The compulsion of real/reel serial killers and vampires: Toward a Gothic criminology. *Journal of Criminal Justice and Popular Culture, 10* (1), 39–68.

220 *References*

Picart, C. J. K., & Greek, C. (2007). Introduction: Toward a Gothic criminology. In C. J. K. Picart, & C. Greek (Eds), *Monsters in and among us: Toward a Gothic criminology* (pp. 11–44). Madison: Fairleigh Dickinson University Press.

Pinker, S. (2011). *The better angels of our nature: A history of violence and humanity*. London: Penguin.

Pizarro, J. M. (2008). Reassessing the situational covariates of homicides: Is there a need to disaggregate? *Homicide Studies, 12* (4), 323–349.

Pizarro, J. M., Zgoba, K. M., & Jennings, W. G. (2011). Assessing the interaction between offender and victim criminal lifestyles and homicide type. *Journal of Criminal Justice, 39* (367–377).

Polk, K. (1994). *When men kill: Scenarios of masculine violence*. Cambridge: Cambridge University Press.

Polk, K. (1999). Males and honor contest violence. *Homicide Studies, 3* (1), 6–29.

Police and Fire Reform Act. (2012). Accessed 4 January 2022. Retrieved from: www. legislation.gov.uk/asp/2012/8/contents

Police Scotland. (2017). *Policing 2026: Our 10 year strategy for policing in Scotland*. Edinburgh: Police Scotland.

Porter, S., & Rose, K. (2018). The sexual psychopath. In J. Proulx, E. Beauregard, A. J. Carter, A. Mokros, R. Darjee & J. James (Eds), *Routledge international handbook of sexual homicide studies* (pp. 37–48). New York, NY: Routledge.

Pridemore, W. A., & Eckhardt, K. (2008). A comparison of victim, offender, and event characteristics of alcohol- and non-alcohol-related homicides. *Journal of Research in Crime and Delinquency, 45* (3), 227–255.

Pritchard, C., Davey, J., & Williams, R. (2013). Who kills children? Re-examining the evidence. *British Journal of Social Work, 43* (7), 1403–1438.

Proulx, J., Blais, E., & Beauregard, E. (2007). Sadistic sexual offenders. In J. Proulx, E.Beauregard, M. Cusson, & A. Nicole (Eds), *Sexual murderers: A comparative analysisand new perspectives* (pp. 107–122). Chichester, UK: John Wiley.

Proulx, J., Cusson, M., & Beauregard, E. (2007). Sexual murder: Definitions, epidemiology and theories. In J Proulx, E Beauregard, M Cusson, & A Nicole (Eds), *Sexual Murderers: A Comparative Analysis and New Perspectives* (pp. 9–28). Chichester: John Wiley & Sons Ltd.

Proulx, J., McKibben, A., & Lusignan, R. (1996). Relationship between affective components and sexual behaviors in sexual aggressors. *Sexual Abuse: A Journal of Research and Treatment, 8*, 279–289.

Proulx, J., & Sauvêtre, N. (2007). Sexual murderers and sexual aggressors: Psychopathological considerations. In J Proulx, E Beauregard, M Cusson, & A Nicole (Eds), *Sexual murderers: A comparative analysis and new perspectives* (pp. 9–28). Chichester: John Wiley & Sons Ltd.

Quetelet, A. (1842). *A treatise on man*. Edinburgh: William and Robert Chambers.

Quinet, K. (2011). Prostitutes as victims of serial homicide: Trends and case characteristics,1970–2009. *Homicide Studies, 15*, 74–100.

Rafter, N. (2007). Crime, film and criminology. *Theoretical Criminology, 11* (3), 403–420. https://doi.org/10.1177/1362480607079584.

Raine, A., Buchsbaum, M., & LaCasse, L. (1997). Brain abnormalities in murderers indicated by positron emission tomography. *Biological Psychiatry, 42* (6), 495–508.

Raine, A., Lencz, T., Bihrle, S., LaCasse, L., & Colletti, P. (2000). Reduced prefrontal grey matter volume and reduced autonomic activity in antisocial personality disorder. *Archives of General Psychology, 57* (2), 119–127.

References 221

Ray, L. (2011). *Violence and society*. London: Sage Publishing.

Ray, L. (2018). *Violence and society (2nd ed.)*. London: Sage Publishing.

Rape Crisis Scotland [RCS], (2016). *Annual report 2015–16*. Glasgow: Rape Crisis Scotland.

Ressler, R. K., Burgess, A. W., & Douglas, J. E. (1988). *Sexual homicide: Patterns and motives*. New York, NY: Lexington Books.

Richardson, E. G., & Hemenway, D. (2011). Homicide, suicide and unintentional firearm fatality: Comparing the United States with other high-income countries, 2003. *The Journal of Trauma, Injury Infection and Critical Care, 70* (1), 238–243.

Ritter, K., &., Stompe, T. (2013). Unemployment, suicide- and homicide-rates in the EU countries. *Neuropsychiatry, 27* (3), 111–118.

Road Traffic Act. (1991). Accessed 29 November 2021. Retrieved from: www.legislation.gov.uk/ukpga/1991/40/contents

Roach, J., & Pease, K. (2013). Evolutionary perspectives on crime prevention. In G. Bruinsma & D. Weisburg (Eds), *Encyclopaedia of criminology and criminal justice* (pp. 1447–1456). London: Springer.

Roberts, J. V., & Grossman, M. G. (1993). Sexual homicide in Canada: A descriptive analysis. *Annals of Sex Research, 6*, 5–25.

Roberts, A., & Willits, D. (2015). Income inequality and homicide in the United States: Consistency across different income inequality measures and disaggregated homicide types. *Homicide Studies, 19* (1), 28–57.

Rokach, L., & Maimon, O. (2010). Clustering methods. In O. Maimon & L. Rokach, (Eds), *Data mining and knowledge discovery handbook* (pp. 321–352). New York: Springer.

Romesburg, C. (1984). *Cluster analysis for researchers*. North Carolina: Lulu Press.

Salfati, C. G. (2000). The nature of expressiveness and instrumentality in homicide implications for offender profiling. *Homicide Studies, 4* (3), 265–293.

Salfati, C. G. (2003). Offender interaction with victims in homicide: A multidimensional analysis of frequencies in crime scene behaviors. *Journal of Interpersonal Violence, 18* (5), 490–512.

Salfati, C. G., & Canter, D. V. (1999). Differentiating stranger murders: Profiling offender characteristics from behavioral styles. *Behavioral Science and the Law, 17*, 391–406.

Salfati, C. G., James, A. L., & Ferguson, L. (2008). Prostitute homicides: A descriptive study. *Journal of Interpersonal Violence, 23*, 505–543.

Sampson, R. J., & Laub, J. H. (2005). Seductions of method: Rejoinder to Nagin and Tremblay's 'Developmental trajectory groups, fact or fiction?'. *Criminology, 43* (4), 905–913.

Sampson, R. J., Raudenbusch, S. W., & Earls, F. (1997). Neighborhoods and violent crime: A multilevel study of collective efficacy. *Science, 277*, 918–924.

Schinkel, W. (2013). Regimes of violence and the trias violantae. *European Journal of Social Theory, 16* (3), 310–325.

Schmidt, P., & Madea, B. (1999). Rape homicide involving children. *Journal of Clinical Forensic Medicine, 6*, 90–94.

Scotland's Census. (2011). *Ethnicity, identity, language and religion*. Accessed 17 February 2021. Retrieved from: www.scotlandscensus.gov.uk/ethnicity-identity-language-and-religion

Scottish Government. (2009). *Safer lives, changed lives: A shared approach to tackling violence against women in Scotland*. Edinburgh: Scottish Government.

222   References

Scottish Government. (2012). *The strategy for justice in Scotland.* Edinburgh: Scottish Government.

Scottish Government. (2013). *Recorded crime in Scotland, 2012–13.* Statistical Bulletin. Edinburgh: Scottish Government.

Scottish Government. (2014a). *Equally Safe Scotland's strategy for preventing and eradicating violence against women and girls.* Edinburgh: Scottish Government.

Scottish Government. (2014b). *Recorded crime: Non-sexual crimes of violence. Ad hoc query.* Edinburgh: Scottish Government.

Scottish government. (2015). *Domestic abuse statistics published.* Accessed 13 July 2017. Retrieved from: https://news.gov.scot/news/domestic-abuse-statistics-published

Scottish Government. (2016a). *Equally Safe.* Accessed 8 June 2017. Retrieved from: www.gov.scot/Publications/2016/03/7926

Scottish Government. (2016b). *Homicide in Scotland, 2015–16.* Statistical bulletin. Edinburgh: Scottish Government.

Scottish Government. (2016c). *Recorded crime in Scotland, 2015–16.* Statistical bulletin. Edinburgh: Scottish Government.

Scottish Government. (2016d). *Scottish crime and justice survey 2014–15: Main findings.* Edinburgh: Scottish Government.

Scottish Government. (2017a). *Action to tackle violence against women.* Accessed 30 April 2015. Retrieved from: www.gov.scot/Topics/Justice/policies/reducing-crime/violence-against-women

Scottish Government. (2017b). *Justice programme: Building safer communities.* Accessed 8 June 2017. Retrieved from: www.gov.scot/Topics/Justice/justicestrategy/programmes/building-safer-communities

Scottish Government. (2017c). *Reducing crime, particularly violent and serious organized crime.* Accessed 24 April 2017. Retrieved from: www.gov.scot/Topics/Justice/policies/reducing-crime

Scottish Government. (2017d). *Strengthening the law.* Accessed 18 July 2017. Retrieved from: https://beta.gov.scot/policies/violence-against-women-and-girls/strengthening-the-law/

Scottish Government. (2017e). *The Caledonian system.* Accessed 8 June 2017. Retrieved from: www.gov.scot/Topics/People/Equality/violence-women/CaledonianSystem

Scottish Government. (2017f). What works to reduce crime?: A summary of the evidence. Accessed 17 April 2017. Retrieved from: www.gov.scot/Publications/2014/10/2518/6

Scottish Government. (2020). *Homicide in Scotland, 2019–20.* Statistical bulletin. Edinburgh: Scottish Government.

Scottish Government. (2021). *Crime prevention.* Accessed 15 October 2021. Retrieved from: www.gov.scot/policies/crime-prevention-and-reduction/

Scottish Parliament. (2017). *Justice Committee endorses proposed reduction to drink driving limits.* Published 12 November 2014. Accessed 31 October 2017. Retrieved from: www.parliament.scot/newsandmediacentre/83619.aspx

Scottish Law Commission. (2021). *Discussion paper (172) on the mental element in homicide.* Edinburgh: Scotland.

Scottish Sentencing Council. (2021). *Prison sentences.* Accessed 29 November 2021. Retrieved from: www.scottishsentencingcouncil.org.uk/about-sentencing/prison-sentences/

References 223

Sea, J., Beauregard, E., & Martineau, M. M. (2019). A cross-cultural comparison of Canadian and Korean sexual homicide. *International Journal of Offender Therapy and Comparative Criminology, 63,* 1538–1556.

Sea, J., Youngs, D., & Tkazky, S. (2019). Sex difference in homicide: Comparing male and female violent crimes in Korea. *International Journal of Offender Therapy and Comparative Criminology, 62* (11), 3408–3435.

Selmini, R., & McElrath, S. (2014). Violent female victimisation trends across Europe, Canada and the United States [Abstract]. *Crime and Justice, 43* (1), 367–319.

Serban, N., & Jiang, H. (2012). Multilevel functional cluster analysis. *Biometrics, 68,* 805–814.

Sexual Offences (Scotland) Act. (2009). Accessed 20 February 2021. Retrieved from: www.legislation.gov.uk/asp/2009/9/contents

Shaw, J., Hunt, I. M., Flynn, S., Meehan, J., Robinson, J., Bickley, H., Parsons, R., McCann, K., Burns, J., Amos, T., Kapur, N., & Appleby, L. (2006). Rates of mental disorder in people convicted of homicide. *British Journal of Psychiatry, 188* (2), 143–147.

Skardhamar, T. (2009). *Reconsidering the theory on adolescent-limited and life-course persistent antisocial behaviour.* Discussion Papers No. 857, May 2009. Kongsvinger: Statistics Norway.

Skott, S. (2019a). Disaggregating homicide: Changing trends in subtypes over time. *Criminal Justice and Behavior, 46* (11), 1650–1668.

Skott, S. (2019b). Sexual homicide targeting children: Exploring offender, victim, and modus operandi factors. *International Journal of Offender Therapy and Comparative Criminology, 63* (9), 1663–1680.

Skott, S. (2020). Maskulinitet och våld i förändring: Våldsregimer och privatisering av våld i Skottland [Masculinities and changing violence: Violence regimes and the privitisation of violence in Scotland]. In K. Gillander Gådin (Ed.), *Genusrelaterat våld, trakasserier och diskriminering – ett globalt problem i lokal kontext [Gender-based violence, harassment and discrimination – a global problem in a local context]* (pp. 45–54). Sundsvall: Mittuniversitetet.

Skott, S. (2021). Disaggregating violence: Understanding the decline. *Journal of Interpersonal Violence, 36* (15–16), 7670–769.

Skott, S., Beauregard, E., & Darjee, R. (2019). Female sexual homicide offenders: A descriptive and comparative study. *Journal of Forensic Sciences, 64* (1), 154–162.

Skott, S., Beauregard, E., & Darjee, R. (2021). Sexual and nonsexual homicide in Scotland: Is there a difference? *Journal of Interpersonal Violence, 36* (7–8), 3209–3230.

Skott, S., Beauregard, E., Darjee, R., & Martineau, M. (2021). The consistency of sexual homicide characteristics and typologies across countries: A comparison of Canadian and Scottish sexual homicides. *Journal of Sexual Aggression, 27* (1), 18–34.

Skott, S., Nyhlén, S., & Giritli Nygren, K. (2021). In the shadow of the monster: Gothic narratives of violence prevention. *Critical Criminology, 29* (2), 385–400.

Skott, S., & Skott Bengtson, K. (2021). 'You've met with a terrible fate, haven't you?': A hauntological analysis of carceral violence in Majora's mask. *Games and Culture,* Advanced online publication. https://doi.org/10.1177/15554120211049575

Smit, P. R., Bijleveld, C. C. J. H., & Van Der Zee, S. (2001). Homicide in the Netherlands: An exploratory study of the 1998 cases. *Homicide Studies, 5* (4), 293–310.

224 *References*

Smit, P. R., de Jong, R. R., & Bijleveld, C. C. J. H. (2012). Homicide data in Europe: Definitions, sources and statistics. In M. C. A. Liem, & W. A. Pridemore (Eds), *Handbook of European homicide research patterns, explanations and country studies* (pp. 5–24). New York: Springer.

Smith, D. J. (2005). Crime and punishment in Scotland, 1980–1999. *Crime and Justice*, *33*, 83–121.

Smoking, Health and Social Care (Scotland) Act. (2005). Accessed 15 February 2021. Retrieved from: www.legislation.gov.uk/asp/2005/13/contents

Sokoloff, N. J. (2008). Expanding the intersectional paradigm to better understand domestic violence in immigrant communities. *Critical Criminology*, *16*, 229–255.

Somander, L.K.H., & Rammer, L. M. (1991). Intra- and extrafamilial child homicide in Sweden, 1971–1980. Child Abuse and Neglect, *15* (1–2), 45–55.

Sommers, I., & Baskin, D. R. (1993). The situational context of violent female offending. *Journal of Research on Crime and Delinquency*, *30* (2), 136–62.

Soothill, K., Francis, B., Ackerley, E., & Collett, S. (1999). *Homicide in Britain: A comparative study of rates in Scotland and England and Wales*. Edinburgh: Scottish Executive Central Research Unit. Accessed 4 December 2014. Retrieved from: www. scotland.gov.uk/Publications/2000/03/2ff917ae-270d-47d9-acd0-f89c30688868

Soothill, K., Francis, B., Ackerley, E., & Humphreys, L. (2008). Changing patterns of offending behaviour among young adults. *British Journal of Criminology*, *48*, 75–95.

Sothcott, K. (2016). Late modern ambiguity and gothic narratives of justice. *Critical Criminology*, *24* (3), 431–444. https://doi.org/10.1007/s10612-015-9287-2.

South, N., Smith, R., Green, G. (2006). Mental health, social order, system disorder. *Criminal Justice Matters*, *61* (1), 4–5.

Spehr, A., Hill, A., Habermann, N., Briken, P., & Berner, W. (2010). Sexual murderers with adult or child victims: Are they different? *Sexual Abuse: A Journal of Research and Treatment*, *22*, 290–314.

Stefanska, W. B., Higgs, T., Carter, A. J., & Beech, A. R. (2017). When is a murder a sexual murder? Understanding the sexual element in the classification of sexual killings. *Journal of Criminal Justice*, *50*, 53–61.

Steinmetz, K. F. (2018). Carceral horror: Punishment and control in silent hill. *Crime, Media, Culture: An International Journal*, *14* (2), 265–287. https://doi.org/10.1177/1741659017699045.

Stroud, J., & Pritchard, C. (2001). Child homicide, psychiatric disorder and dangerousness: A review and an empirical approach. *British Journal of Social Work*, *31*, 249–269.

Tabachnick, B. G., & Fidell, L. S. (2013). *Using Multivariate Statistics (6th ed.)*. New Jersey: Pearson Education Inc.

Tapscott, J. L., Hancock, M., & Hoaken, P. N. S. (2012). Severity and frequency of reactive and instrumental offending divergent validity of subtypes of violence in an adult forensic sample. *Criminal Justice and Behaviour*, *39* (2), 202–219.

Templer D. I., Connelly, H. J., Lester, D., Arikawa, H., & Mancuso, L. (2007). Relationship of IQ to suicide and homicide rate: An international perspective. *Psychological Reports*, *100* (1), 108–112.

The Guardian, (2005). *Scotland has second highest murder rate in Europe*. Published: 26 September 2005. Accessed 19 March 2015. Retrieved from: www.theguardian.com/uk/2005/sep/26/ukcrime.scotland

Thompson, S. K. (2015). The spatial distribution and social ecology of 'public' and 'private' homicide types in Toronto: A case for data disaggregation. *Homicide Studies*, *19* (2), 149–174.

References 225

Tomsen, S., & Mason, G. (2001). Engendering homophobia: Violence, sexuality and gender conformity. *Journal of Sociology, 37* (3), 257–273.

Tonry, M. (2014). Why crime rates are falling throughout the Western world. *Legal Studies Research Paper Series, 14* (41), 1–63.

Tonry, M., & Farrington, D. P. (2005). Punishment and crime across space and time. *Crime and Justice, 33*, 1–39.

Trägårdh, K., Nilsson, T., Granath, S., & Sturup, J. (2016). A time trend study of Swedish male and female homicide offenders from 1990 to 2010. *International Journal of Forensic Mental Health, 15* (2), 125–135.

UNODC. (2013). *Global study on homicide 2013*. Vienna: United Nations Office on Drugs and Crime.

UNODC. (2015). *International Classification of Crime for Statistical Purposes (ICCS)*. Vienna: United Nations Office of Drugs and Crime.

UNODC. (2021). *DataUNODC*. Accessed 3 March 2021. Retrieved from: https://dataunodc.un.org/

Van Dijk, J., Van Kesteren, J., & Smit. P (2007). *Criminal victimisation in international perspective key findings from the 2004–2005 ICVS and EU ICS*. Hague: UNODC

Van Wilsem, J. (2004). Criminal victimization in cross-national perspective. *European Journal of Criminology, 1* (1), 89–109.

Vermunt, J. K. (2003). Multilevel latent class models. *Sociological Methodology, 33*, 213–239.

Vermunt, J. K., & Magidson, J. (2002). Latent class cluster analysis. In J. Hagenaars, & A. McCutcheon (Eds), *Applied latent class analysis* (pp. 89–106). Cambridge: Cambridge University Press.

VRU. (2016). *The Violence Reduction Unit*. Accessed 25 October 2016. Retrieved from: www.actiononviolence.org.uk/about-us

VRU. (2017). *Scottish Violence Reduction Unit, 10 year strategic plan*. Glasgow: VRU Scotland.

VRU. (2021). *Navigator*. Accessed 1 January 2022. Retrieved from: www.svru.co.uk/navigator/

Walsh, E., Gilvarry, C., Samele, C., Harvey, K., Manley, C., Tattan, T., Tyrer, P., Creed, F., Murray, R., & Fahy, T. (2004). Predicting violence in Schizophrenia: A prospective study. *Schizophrenia Research, 64* (2–3), 247–252.

Warr, M. (2000). Fear of crime in the United States: Avenues for research and policy. *Criminal Justice, 4*, 451–489.

Waters, H. R., A. A. Hyder, Y. Rajkotia, S. Basu, & A. Butchart. 2005. The costs of interpersonal violence – An international review. *Health Policy, 73* (3), 303–315.

Waters, H. R., A. A. Hyder, Y. Rajkotia, S. Basu, & A. Butchart. 2005. The costs of interpersonal violence – An international review. *Health Policy, 73* (3), 303–315.

Weber, M. (1978). *Economy and society: An outline of interpretive sociology*. Berkeley; University of California Press.

Weiss, D. B., Santos, M. R., Testa, A., & Kumar, S. (2016). The 1990s homicide decline: A Western world or international phenomenon? A research note. *Homicide Studies, 20* (4), 321–334.

West, C., & Zimmerman, D. H. (1987). Doing gender. *Gender and Society, 1* (2), 125–151.

Wikström, P-O. (2019). Situational action theory: A general, dynamic, and mechanism-based theory of crime and its causes. In M. D. Krohn, N. Hendrix, G. Penly Hall, & A. J. Lizotte (Eds), *Handbook on crime and deviance (2nd ed.)* (pp. 259–281). Cham: Springer.

226   References

Williamson, S., Hare, R. D., & Wong, S. (1987). Violence: Criminal psychopaths and their victims. *Canadian Journal of Behavioural Science, 19* (4), 454–462.

Wilson, J. O., & Hernstein, R. J. (1985). *Crime and human nature*. New York: Simon and Schuster.

Wolfgang, M. E. (1958). *Patterns in criminal homicide*. Philadelphia: University of Philadelphia.

Wood Harper, D., & Voigt, L. (2007). Homicide followed by suicide an integrated theoretical perspective. *Homicide Studies, 11* (4), 295–318.

Wood, T., & Johnston, D. *The World's End murders: A thirty-year quest for justice*. Brilinn: Edinburgh.

Woodworth, M., & Porter, S. (2002). In cold blood: Characteristics of criminal homicides as a function of psychopathy. *Journal of Abnormal Psychology, 111* (3), 436–445.

Yang, Y., & Raine, A. (2009). Prefrontal structural and functional brain imaging findings in antisocial, violence and psychopathic individuals: A meta-analysis. *Psychiatry Research: Neuroimaging, 174* (2), 81–88.

Yarvis, R. M. (1990). Axis I and Axis II diagnostic parameters of homicide. *Bulletin of the American Academy of Psychiatry and Law, 18*, 249–269.

Yarvis, R. M. (1994). Patterns of substance abuse and intoxication among murderers. *Bull Am Acad Psychiatry Law, 22* (1), 133–144.

Yarvis, R. M. (1995). Diagnostic patterns among three violent offender types. *The Bulletin of the American Academy of Psychiatry and the Law, 23*, 411–419.

Young, J. (2003). Merton with energy, Katz with structure: The sociology of vindictiveness and the criminology of transgression. *Theoretical Criminology, 7* (3), 389–414.

Young, J. (2007). *The vertigo of late modernity*. London: Sage Publishing.

Young, J., & Hayward, K. (2012). Cultural criminology. In M. Maguire, R. Morgan, & R. Reiner (Eds), *The Oxford handbook of criminology (5th ed.)* (pp. 113–137). Oxford: Oxford University Press.

Yu, H.-T., & Park, J. (2014). Simultaneous decision on the number of latent clusters and classes for multilevel latent class models. *Multivariate Behavioral Research, 49*, 232–244.

Zimring, F. (1968). Is gun control likely to reduce violent killings? *The University of Chicago Law Review, 35* (4), 721–737.

Index

Note: Page numbers in *italics* indicate figures and in **bold** indicate tables on the corresponding pages.

Abusive Behaviour and Sexual Harm Act 2017 39
Ackerley, E. 27
Addington, L. A. 154
ADHD (Attention Deficit Hyperactivity Disorder) 44
Adjusted Bayesian Information Criteria (ABIC) 100, 161
Aebi, M. F. 53–54
Akaike Information Criteria (AIC) 100, 161
Akers, R. L. 50
American Psychiatry Association 48
antisocial personality disorder 48
Ask, Document, Validate, Refer (ADVR) intervention 38

Bandura, A. 50
Batman: Arkham Asylum 60
Batman: Arkham City 60
Bayesian Information Criteria (BIC) 100, 138, **138**, 161
Beauregard, E. 137, 149
Beccaria, C. 43
between (incident and victim) subtypes of homicide 101–108, **102**, *103–107*
Bijleveld, C. C. J. H. 92, 93
biological theories of homicide 43–46
Bleetman, A. 36
Blumstein, A. 68, 155–156, 159
both drinking typology 91, 112
Broken Window theory 37
Brookman, F. 45, 47, 87
Building Safer Communities Program (BSC) 38
Bundy, T. 62

Burgess, A. W. 121
Butler, J. 188, 189
Butts, J. 90

Canada, sexual homicide in Scotland versus 137–147, **138**, **140**, *142–145*
Carroll, A. 62
Chan, H. C. O. 149
children: homicides committed against **78–80**, 78–81; homicides committed by 81–85, **82–83**; sexual homicides committed against 132–137, **133–135**
Chopin, J. 137
Cohen, L. C. 53
Collett, S. 27
Collins, R. 50
Community Initiative to Reduce Violence (CIRV) 38
conflict resolution homicides 113
confrontational homicides 113
Connell, R. W. 189
Cooney, M. 54, 186, 187, 201
Criminal Justice and Licencing Act 2010 39
culpable homicide 10–13; included in Scottish Homicide Database 15–16
cultural theories of homicide 54–56
Culture of Violence 56

Daly, M. 46–47
Debut Crime Hypothesis 52, 158, 184–185
DeLisi, M. 49
disaggregation of homicide 89–119, 201; change over time 115–118, *116–117*, **118**; conclusions on 118–119;

228   Index

exploratory approach to **93**, 93–96, **99**; introduction to 89; previous typologies of homicide in research and 89–93, **91**; subtypes of homicide 101–115, **102**; typologies based on offender, incident, and victim variables 90–93, **91**; using multilevel latent class analysis (MCLA) 96–100, **99**, **101**
Doing Violence theoretical framework 188–195, 199, 205; changing regimes of violence in Scotland and 192–195
Domestic Abuse Act 2018 39–40
domestic homicide subtype 115
domestic violence 38–40; evolutionary psychology and 47
Douglas, J. E. 89, 121
downward trends in crime 25–26, 51–54, 155–157, 184–185
drug homicide 92
Durkheim, E. 54–55

Eckhardt, K. 91–94, 112–113
Ed Gein 62
Elias, N. 51–52
employed offender class *109–110*, 111–112
employed offender femicides 115
Equally Safe 39, 182
European Homicide Monitor (EHM) 14
Evans, B. 55–56
evolutionary psychology 46–47
extended parricide subtype 115

Family Annihilation-Suicides 90
Farrell, G. 52
Farrington, D. P. 44
Fawcett, C. 60
Federal Bureau of Investigation (FBI) 121, 155
Federman, C. 49
Felson, M. 53
female offenders: as serial killers 62; sexual homicides committed by 126–132, **128–129**, **131**; types of homicides committed by **74–76**, 74–78
Femicide subtype **102**, *103–107*, 108, 112, 113–114; absolute change over time 116, *116*; relative change over time *117*, 117–118, **118**
Ferrell, J. 51
Fiddler, M. 204, 206
Fox, B. 49

Francis, B. 27, 28
Freud, S. 46

Ganpat, S. M. 58
Gein, E. 62
gender and homicide 56–59, 188
gender identities 57
General Theory of Crime, A 44
genetic predispositions to crime 45–46
Giritli-Nygren, K. 189
Giroux, H. A. 55–56
Goffman, E. 58
goodness of fit 100
Gothic criminology 42; serial homicide and 59–63
Gottfredson, M. R. 44
Greek, C. 61

Hääkänen-Nyholm, H. 73
Harries, K. D. 153–154
Harris, A. R. 155–156, 159
Hatty, S. E. 57, 58–59
Hazelwood, R. R. 89
Hearn, J. 39, 182
Heimer, K. 156–157
Hernstein, R. J. 44
Hirschi, T. 44
homicide: defined in research 13–14; disaggregating (*see* disaggregation of homicide); downward trends in 25–26, 51–54, 155–157, 184–185; gaps in knowledge about 2, 198–199, 200; gender and 56–59; international rates of 33–36, *34–35*; legal definitions of 9–13, *11*; limitations and directions for future research on 203–204; objectives in studying 3–5, 205–206; relationship between violence and 153–178; serial, in popular culture 59–63; sexual (*see* sexual homicide); subtypes of 101–115, **102**; typologies in research 89–93, **91**, 201–202; why study 1–3
homicide in Scotland: changing regimes of violence and 192–195; common characteristics of 24; policy implications of deeper understanding of theory of 179–184; privatisation of violence and 186–187; reputation as murder capital of the world 26–29; sexual homicide in Canada versus 137–147, **138**, **140**, *142–145*; trends over time 29–36, *30–31*, *34–35*; types

of (*see* types of homicide); *see also*
Scottish Homicide Database
honour contests 58
House, S. 38
Humphreys, L. 28

impulsivity 44
incident, typologies based on 90–93, **91**
Independent Domestic Abuse Advisors
(IDAAs) 40
intelligence and self-control theories of
homicide 44
international context of homicide
subtypes 112–115
interpersonal dispute homicide 92, 112
Intimate or Domestic Lethal Violence-
Suicide 90
intimate-partner domestic lethal
violence-suicide 115
involuntary culpable homicide 11

James, J. 137
Jamieson, C. 37–38
Jennings, W. G. 89–90
Jung, C. 46

Katz, J. 50–51
Kohm, S. 60

latent class analysis (LCA) 95–96, 122,
138; multilevel 96–100, **99**, **101**
Laurendeau, J. 189
Lauritzen, J. L. 156–157
legal definitions of homicide 9–13,
11
Lehti, M. 68
Leyland, A. H. 36
Liem, M. 115
Linde, A. 53–54
Linnemann, T. 1, 205
Lombroso, C. 43
Luckenbill, D. F. 58
Lyng, S. 51

Majora's Mask 60
male offenders, types of homicide
committed by **69–70**, 69–74, **72**
Mann Whitney U-tests 99, 117, **118**
MAO-A gene 45
masculinity 57–59, 187–188
McClintock, F. H. 26
McKie, L. 39, 182
McVie, S. 28

Medical Care Hypothesis 52, 159,
184–185
Meier, R. F. 53
mens rea 11
mental disorders 47–49
Mercy Killing-Suicides 90
Miethe, T. D. 53
Mistaken or Accidental Homicide-
Suicide 90
mixed unemployed offender class
109–110, 110–111, 112
modus operandi 21
Monster 62
Moracco, K. E. 90
Morton, E. 90, 94, 115
Multi-Agency Tasking and Co-
ordinating Groups (MATAC) 39,
181–182
multilevel latent class analysis (MCLA)
96–100, **99**, **101**, 153
multiple correspondence analysis 92–93
murder, definition of 10–13

National Domestic Abuse Task Force 40
Neither Participant Drinking typology
91
No Knives Better Lives (NKBL)
initiative 38
Norris, P. 28
No Weapon-Bludgeoning type
homicides 102, **102**, *103–107*, 112–114;
absolute change over time 116, *116*;
relative change over time *117*,
117–118, **118**

offender drinking typology 91, 113
offenders of homicide 19–21, **20**;
typologies based on 90–93, **91**
Oleson, J. C. 61
Operation Blade 36
Operation Phoenix 15
Operation Spotlight 37
Operation Turnkey 36
Orr, J. 37
Othering violence 59

Paradigm of Violence 55, 56
paraphilia 148
Pease, K. 47
personality disorders 47–49; sexual
homicide and 148
Perumean-Chaney, S. E. 154
Picart, C. J. 61

230 *Index*

Pillinger, R. 28
Pinker, S. 51–52
Pizarro, J. M. 89–90, 92–94, 112–115
Police and Fire Reform (Scotland) Act
   2012 16–17
Police Scotland 39, 40, 98
policy implications of deeper
   understanding of homicide 179–184
Polk, K. 56, 57, 58, 113, 115, 187–188
Popular Criminology 60
popular culture, serial homicide in
   59–63
Pridemore, W. A. 91–94, 112–113
privatisation of violence 186–187
Proulx, J. 148
psychological theories of homicide
   46–51; sexual homicide and 149
psychopathy 48–49
Psychopathy Checklist 48
Public Killing Spree-Suicide 90

Rae, W. 37
Ray, L. 56
Reichelmann, A. 115
relationship between homicide and
   violence 153–178; change in lethal and
   nonlethal trends over time 176–177;
   characteristics of homicide and
   violence and 154–155, **173**, 173–175;
   conclusions on 177–178; implications
   of lack of knowledge for theory and
   policy and 157–159; introduction to
   153; lack of previous research on
   153–159; over time **173**, 173–177;
   subtypes of nonlethal violence
   and 159–173; trends over time and
   155–157
Ressler, R. K. 121
Rezey, M. L. 156–157
Rivalry type homicides **102**, *103–107*,
   107, 112, 113; absolute change over
   time 116, *116*; relative change over
   time *117*, 117–118, **118**
Roach, J. 47
robbery homicide 92
Routine Activities Theory 53, 54
Runyan, C. W. 90

Safer Lives, Changed Lives 38, 39
Schinkel, W. 190
schizophrenia 47–48
Scottish Crime and Justice Survey
   (SCJS) 159–173; change in violence

types over time 170–173, *171*, **172**;
   classifying variables of the violence
   dataset **160**; class selection statistics
   of two-level LCA violence model **162**;
   domestic subtype 162, **163**, *163–167*,
   164; female victim class *169*, 170; male
   victim class 168–169, *169*; public no
   weapon subtype **163**, *163–167*, 164,
   166; public weapon subtype **163**,
   163–167, 168; violence typology
   162–170, **163**; work-related subtypes
   163, *163–167*, 168
Scottish Crime Recording Standard
   (SCRS) 29
Scottish Homicide Database 9; cases
   included in 15–18; comparison of
   sexual and nonsexual homicide using
   122–126, **123–124**, **126**; creation of
   14–15; cross-tabulation of number of
   victims and offenders **18**; distribution
   of homicide cases in each legacy
   police force **17**; homicide dataset
   16–23; homicide incidents included in
   21–23, **23**; number of offenders and
   victims in homicide case **17**; offenders
   of homicide in 19–21, **20**; victims of
   homicide in 18–19, **19**
Security Hypothesis 52, 158, 184–185
Seductions of Crime, The 50
sexual homicide 28, 120–149; biological
   explanations of 45; committed against
   children 132–137, **133–135**; committed
   by female offenders 126–132, **128–129**,
   131; compared to nonsexual
   homicides 122–126, **123–124**, **126**;
   conclusions on 149; defined 121;
   introduction to 120–122; rarity of 120;
   in Scotland versus Canada 137–147,
   138, **140**, *142–145*; studies of 121;
   theories of 147–149
Sexual Offences Act 2009 39
Sharpe, L. 36
Silence of the Lambs, The 61
Silent Hill 60
Simpson's Paradox 68
Situational Crime Prevention 53
Skott, S. 60
Skott Bengtson, K. F. 60
Smit, P. R. 92, 93
Smith, D. J. 26–27
social construction of violence 191
social learning theory 50–51
sociological theories of homicide 51–56

Index 231

Soothill, K. 27
Stabbing homicides 101–102, **102**,
  103–107, 112–114; absolute change
  over time 116, *116*; relative change
  over time *117*, 117–118, **118**
Steinmetz, K. F. 60
subtypes of homicide 101–115, **102**;
  between (incident and victim)
  101–108, *103–107*; change over
  time 115–118, *116–117*, **118**; within
  (offender) classes 108–112, *109–110*;
  in international context 112–115;
  sexual homicide 137–147, **138**, **140**,
  142–145
subtypes of nonlethal violence 159–173,
  200–201; change in violence types over
  time 170–173, *171*, **172**; classifying
  variables of the violence dataset
  160; classifying variables of violence
  dataset **160**; class selection statistics
  of two-level LCA violence model **162**;
  domestic subtype 162, **163**, *163–167*,
  164; female victim class *169*, 170; male
  victim class 168–169, *169*; public no
  weapon subtype **163**, *163–167*, 164,
  166; public weapon subtype **163**,
  163–167, 168; violence typology
  162–170, **163**; work-related subtypes
  163, *163–167*, 168
symbolic violence 190, 195

theories of homicide: biological
  43–46; conclusions on 63–64; crime
  drop theories and 184–185; deeper
  understanding in 179–197; Doing
  Violence 188–195, 199, 205; dominant
  43–56; introduction to 42–43;
  masculinities and violence and
  187–188; policy implications of
  179–184; privatisation of violence
  and 186–187; psychological 46–51;
  relationship between homicide and
  violence and 153–178; serial homicide
  in popular culture and 59–63;
  sexual homicide 147–149;
  sociological 51–56; theoretical
  implications of deeper
  understanding of 184–188
Tonry, M. 32
trauma in offender's childhood and
  sexual homicide 148
type I errors 99–100
type II errors 100

types of homicide 67–88; changes
  over time 85–86, *85–86*; committed
  against children **78–80**, 78–81;
  committed by children 81–85, **82–83**;
  committed by men **69–70**, 69–74, **72**;
  committed by women **74–76**, 74–78;
  conclusions on 86–88; introduction
  to 67–68

Uniform Crime Reports (UCR)
  155–156
United Nations Office of Drugs and
  Crime (UNODC) 33
United States, homicide subtypes
  in 92

Van Der Zee, S. 92
Vertigo of Late Modernity 55
victim drinking typology 91, 112
victims of homicide 18–19, **19**; between
  (incident and victim) subtypes of
  homicide 101–108, **102**, *103–107*;
  typologies based on 90–93, **91**
video games 60
violence: changing regimes of, in
  Scotland 192–195; committed by
  young people 37–38; culture of 56;
  domestic 38–40; masculinities and
  57–59, 187–188; Othering 59; overall
  decrease in Scotland 28; paradigm
  of 55, 56; policies and interventions
  in Scotland 36–40; privatisation of
  186–187; rates in England and Wales
  versus Scotland 27; relationship
  between homicide and 153–178; social
  construction of 191; subtypes of
  nonlethal 159–173, 200–201;
  symbolic 190, 195; trends over time
  155–157
Violence Against Women and Girls Joint
  Strategic Board 39, 182
Violence Reduction Unit 37–38,
  180
violence regimes 188–190
Voigt, L. 90–91, 94, 115
voluntary culpable homicide 11

Wikström, P.-O. 44
Wikström, P. O. H. 26
Wilson, J. O. 44
Wilson, M. 46–47
within (offender) classes 108–112,
  109–110

232 *Index*

Wolfgang, M. E. 89
women *see* female offenders
Wood Harper, D. 90–91, 94, 115
World's End Murders 14
Wuornos, A. 62

Young, J. 55
young male syndrome 58
young unemployed offender class 108–110, *109–110*, 112

Zgoba, K. M. 89–90

Printed in the United States
by Baker & Taylor Publisher Services